P9-DDX-939

WOLSEY

BOOKS BY HILAIRE BELLOC

Historical:
RICHELIEU
JOAN OF ARC
JAMES II
DANTON
MARIE ANTOINETTE
ROBESPIERRE
HISTORY OF ENGLAND
MINIATURES OF FRENCH HISTORY
ETC.

Essays:
CONVERSATION WITH AN ANGEL
SHORT TALKS WITH THE DEAD
HILLS AND THE SEA
THE PATH TO ROME
ON ANYTHING
ON NOTHING
ETC.

Novels:
BELINDA
THE MISSING MASTERPIECE
SHADOWED
THE HAUNTED HOUSE
THE EMERALD
THE GIRONDIN
THE GREEN OVERCOAT
ETC.

General:
THE CRUISE OF THE NONA
AVRIL
THE FOUR MEN
THE CONTRAST
ESTA PERPETUA
ETC.

Poetry:
VERSES 1910
SONNETS AND VERSES 1923

Children's Books:
BAD CHILD'S BOOK OF BEASTS
MORE BEASTS FOR WORSE CHI
A MORAL ALPHABET
CAUTIONARY TALES
ETC.

Religious:
HOW THE REFORMATION HAP
SURVIVALS AND NEW ARRIVAI
EUROPE AND THE FAITH
ETC.

WOLSEY: FROM THE MINIATURE BY HOLBEIN
Belonging to the Duke of Buccleuch
From the Victoria and Albert Museum, London

CONTENTS

FIRST PART

THE SETTING OF THE TRAGEDY

SECOND PART

THE ACTION

ILLUSTRATIONS

FIRST PART

THE SETTING OF THE TRAGEDY

I
THE STAGE

THE tragedy on which we enter is this:—
A man of powers exceptional, in their day unique, was given for his field of action a time in which all Christendom was in the delirium of a new, most powerful wine. Knowledge had come pouring in a double stream from two torrential sources. There had arrived a sudden expansion of the world, the discovery of whole distant continents, of the very globe; then had also arrived the discovery of antiquity; of Greece and Rome as they were; of the noble Pagan despair; the less noble but conquering Pagan appetite, the Pagan stability of beauty.

These two new banquets of the soul combined, created a new spirit: intense and exuberant. It is called the spirit of the "Renewal", the "New Birth", *The Renaissance,* We of the restricted west, pinned in for centuries by the barbarism of the Steppes and of the Eastern plains, the hostile Mohammedan world, learnt of an unexpected universe. All oceans were traversed. The Americas appeared, the mysterious Indies were opened. We of Europe had returned to our origins, we had begun to breathe the air of our beginnings and were thereby exhilarated to a sort of resurrection. We of Christendom, were invaded by the host of new life, out of which was born conflict, adventure, and such a spout of creation as no other age had known. Painting grew glorious, scholarship at once profound and wide, sculpture took on flesh, music changed and began to grow—perhaps to its hurt.

All this vital flood, throbbing and mounting upwards, drummed in the framework of an ancient society, whose

3

forms had grown stiff through centuries of usage, had set and hardened with age.

Therefore was there a growing menace of disruption and ruin. The loosing of such wild forces against containing barriers so fixed, so deadened and so decayed, boded immediate anarchy, and, after anarchy, after the dust of the explosion should have settled down, the complete disunion of Christian men, the ruin of that by which we had lived and achieved, the loss of a society wherein all could repose.

That great civilisation of which all were members from the frontiers of the dark north-east, beyond Poland, to the Atlantic seas, from the isles of the Mediterranean to the snows of Scotland and Norway, was rocking.

The mind of Europe had been formed under the hand of the Christian Church, its spirit had been drawn from that one source. The impulse of these new fires might indeed have cast it all into a new mould, enlarging the past, and producing a glorious heritage of a novel kind out of the sufficiently glorious middle ages. Had there been a sufficient control over the driving energies at work, had there been sufficient management of that cauldron as it seethed, some society still happier than that of the Middle Ages and still more permanently possessed of enduring beauty might have arisen. The men of our race might have been free at last and the Christian message fulfilled. But against that vision and that hope, which the burning vitality of the time could promise, there was corresponding peril. Lacking sufficient control, the spirits let loose in the great change and uprising might in their clash breed chaos, and our great but aged civilisation might perish in the ordeal. Christendom was in peril of shipwreck and of dissolution.

In the midst of such things did Wolsey live his days. The printing press showed its first social powers in his boyhood. The Cape of Good Hope was doubled when he was in his fourteenth year. Columbus sighted the new world in his twentieth. He was in his vigorous forties when Magellan's crew returned, the first of the human race to circumnavigate the world. He was of an age with Copernicus. He was in the height of his power when Luther's name was first heard.

With Wolsey did it lie more than with any other man whether the good or the evil fate should prevail. More than any other man in that time of conquerors, discoverers and insane ambitions, flaming protests against evil, and evil unchained, this man had it in his power, had he but known his chances, to save our world; because he alone stood for so many years at the helm of a united nation free from foreign menace and with all its resources at his command. There was no other such complete opportunity in Europe.

He failed. The tragedy is the tragedy of his failure. It is a tragedy general and particular; European and domestic. Christendom made shipwreck. His domestic achievements were taken from him, his private desires sank down pitifully into nothing. He saw the beginning of the Church's ruin. His own glories ended in humiliations, and he lived to see the end of all that he had been.

He failed from two defects, one of the intelligence, the other of the will. He failed from a defect of his high intelligence in this:—that he had no vision. The thing of the moment absorbed him; he was concerned solely with the events of day to day, in which the statesmen who follow foreign affairs are easily absorbed.

This defect of intelligence was serious; but the defect of will was fatal. It was the defect of ambition.

Ambition is the putting of oneself before one's chief task, just as avarice is the putting of money before that task, and sensuality the putting of immediate physical pleasure before that task. In so far as a man gives something else the preference to a task he must accomplish, that task will be neglected and his achievement in it will fail.

Wolsey attained to full power over England, a complete direction of main civil affairs, and a complete direction of ecclesiastical affairs, at a time when these equally shared society. England, by an accident, became in those critical years determinant. Had the weight of the English crown and wealth (though England was then among the lesser powers of Europe) been thrown into the scale of tradition, had the England of Wolsey ended by supporting unity, Christendom would be Christendom today.

The divorce of Henry, King of England, was the test. Wolsey saw it not. Then, when he began to see, he, through ambition, wavered. England by his fault fell to the other side of the barricade, joined the foreign forces of disunion, and that principle whereby Europe had been one was dissolved and was lost. We were all torn asunder.

Every wise man has desired the reunion of our civilisation and has desired it in spite of increasing despair, for now 400 years. Wise men are rare, but the most foolish can see today that the reunion of our civilisation is vital to its mere survival. For our disunion has reached a pitch in which we are capable of destroying ourselves in mutual combat to no purpose, nation against nation, each killing itself in the struggle; after that, class against class.

Well, at the origin of this disaster stands Wolsey. With
a soul more inspired he might have saved the ship of
Europe and steered it through that dreadful passage. He
did not. And in failing to do it he looked, at the end, not
only on the ruin of Christendom (which ruin he but
dimly apprehended) but also upon the broken fragments of his own majestic career. He lived to see that
he himself had failed in his own personal field. He lived,
to see a whole nation which had been his instrument
change its course. And he dimly perceived in his last
agony of degradation that not only had he failed, but
that the salvation of Europe was failing too.

.   .   .   .

Such was the tragedy. Upon what stage was it acted?
What was that late 15th century in which he grew to
early manhood (1473-1500), that early 16th century
(1500-1530) in which he rose first to recognition, then
to great influence, then to unrivalled power—at the end
of which he fell down altogether?

In that world to which Wolsey belonged there were
four elements making it widely different from our time.
These four were, its arrangement of wealth; its dual control by Church and State; its devotion to Princes; its
international structure: that is, the form in which the
various states of Christendom lay and their relations to
one another.

To grasp the elements of these four things is to understand the stage on which the drama of Wolsey's career
was played out.

We must then first grasp the arrangement of Christian
society as a whole in village units, cultivated by peasants
who paid to the lord of the village certain fixed dues,

which dues formed the annual "value" or "worth" of a village, reckoned as a fixed revenue to its lord.

Secondly we must perceive the all-embracing organisation of the Church, common to all Europe, interwoven with the civil organisation of each district, but distinct from it. This universal organisation of the Church or rather the Church itself, its officers (that is its priesthood and hierarchy) its routine methods had sunk during the last two generations into an increasingly diseased condition. Its rules had become mechanical; the clergy, especially in the higher ranks, were worldly and their lives often scandalous. Against this state of affairs within the Church all men had long been protesting and had by Wolsey's time begun to clamour.

Thirdly, there was that awe of local rulers of particular districts—Kings over realms (such as England), certain independent Dukes and Marquises over their territories large or small (such as Bavaria, Montferrat), aristocratic councils over their cities and districts (such as that of Venice)—which was the chief mark of political life at the time. It was the mood which possessed each realm or district, from the greatest to the least. It gave the monarch in such a kingdom as England or the State in such a republic as Venice, almost unlimited power in civil matters, especially if the area governed were small and well organised.

Lastly, there was the presence (due to this devotion to Princes which had recently grown up) of rivalries within the common body of Christendom. Christendom was still the universal State superior to all particular States within it: at least, that was the theory; but in practice this new devotion to the separate local governments, to the Princes, divided this ideal unity of the Christian peasants on the manor was not wholly consumed by those who made it; there was a surplus payable to the lord of the manor, the descendant through many generations of the old land-owning class of the Roman Empire all those centuries ago. Thus every manor had as I have said its fixed quota of profit, payable to its lord. This "value" attaching to a piece of land did not come as a rule from competitive rents, as land values do today. It still came, in Wolsey's time, for the most part, from customary payments to the lord of each village. A man or corporation, supported by those who grew the crops, was powerful and wealthy through the possession of such lordships. Of this surplus wealth the universal Church, which was common to all the west from Poland to the ocean, claimed and received a large proportion payable to individual Churchmen or Corporations as endowment for parish work, for bishop's sees, for colleges, hospitals, monasteries. The proportion of such Church Lordships to Lay Lordships differed in different countries but it was everywhere large. In England it was probably about one fifth, or a little more, of the total manorial values: that is, of the surplus wealth produced by the manors of England, and paid annually by the peasants to their respective lords. Though the towns and crafts, and gains through commerce were exceptions in the mass of agricultural life, yet, for the providing of revenue, they were organised in much the same fashion. The endowment of a bishopric or an abbey would often include dues paid from town-dwellers; the same was true of the parish clergy and the whole clerical organisation.

The clerics received their incomes in just such a fashion as the lay lords, and these varied in importance from the lords of one manor, a numerous class, to the great men

who were lords of dozens of manors scattered throughout a realm. While the ruler of a state such as England,
the King, held far more manors and towns than anyone
else and had also the profits of the lands outside the
village communities: the greater woods, heaths and
mountain pastures.

Such was, in the main, the arrangement of wealth in
that world and the form of support given to the ruling
classes. Now let me turn to that clerical organisation and
power, the presence of which in Wolsey's time marks it
off sharply from our own.

The Church formed throughout Europe one body, the
centre of whose administration was at Rome, whose
head was the Pope, the Bishop of that city, and which
had its own court of justice deciding on a mass of matters
connected with all men's daily lives. It decided disputes
on marriage and wills, it had the discipline and management of everyone in Holy Orders—a term meaning
much more than the priests and including an army of
officials legal and other. This jurisdiction of the Church
overlapped and often clashed with the civil power. It
had rights not only of deciding on marriage cases, wills
and the rest, but of punishing, (with the support of the
civil power), and of regulating morals. It issued injunctions which had to be obeyed just as the injunctions of a
civil government were obeyed; and especially did it in-
quire into and undertake to expose and repress attempts
at disruption within the general body of Christendom,
such as the promulgation of doctrines in faith or morals
opposed to those of general society around, and known
as heresies.

We cannot understand a society so different from our
own, we cannot understand a life such as Wolsey's was,

unless by an effort of imagination we call up the image of a world in which these two powers, the Church, one body spiritually governing all Europe, and the civil governments presiding each over its own district (some of these were already nations) existed side by side. This double government seemed as normal and natural to Wolsey's time as the absolute and single power of a modern government seems to its citizens today. There was friction between the two powers, and constant dispute as to the limits of each; but the presence of both in all men's activities was taken for granted.

The Church was of course very much more than this organisation of a legal authority; it was also, and had been for generation upon generation, back to the beginning of that world in the very remotest of time, the principle whereby society lived. The Church held all the hospitals, the universities and schools (in which the teachers were all clerics). It furnished most of the men of learning, many, or most, of the envoys sent by Prince to Prince, and a great number of the chief ministers in each state. All the life of Europe had been formed by the Church: its unity was the unity of Christendom. Through the universal Church with its universal religion Europe was still essentially one great state, the conception of which was superior to that of the separate states of which it was composed.

For many generations the rising independence of the separate Rulers in Europe, the development of local languages and literature side by side with the universal Latin, and therefore of subdivisions in our common culture had correspondingly separated the various provinces of the Church. Kings, in practice, nominated their subjects to Bishoprics and even to great Abbotships: the

bulk of the hierarchy in each country had become national. But the overshadowing jurisdiction of the Church
was still unquestioned. Clerics could not be tried in lay
courts. A Bishop however nominated or chosen could
not be Bishop without papal sanction. No monarch however powerful but must get dispensation from Rome if
he would marry within prohibited degrees. The Church
was still in men's minds the superior of all because it
stood for all civilisation as against any one part of it,
and because it represented the spiritual principle whereby
Christendom had come into being.

But that spiritual principle, with its external forms
and its strong complete machinery everywhere present,
was menaced at Wolsey's moment by two things, either
of which was a peril to it, both of which combined
might prove mortal. The first, the most serious, for it
went to the heart, to the principle whereby the Church
lived, was corruption. The second, everywhere increasing in strength, was the power of the civilian states over
which a common religion continued to rule.

The corruption of the Church was of that sort which
always comes to any institution when the effects of
time have accumulated uncorrected, and especially
when its members have come to feel themselves immune
and secure. Perpetually in the age-long story of the
Church and the development of its government at Rome,
reformation had succeeded reformation; and by each
such salutary resurrection the situation had been saved.
But somewhat more than a century before Wolsey's
birth there had fallen upon Christendom a blow from
which the old society of the Middle Ages, and especially its clerical organisation, had not recovered. This
blow was the great plague, or "Black Death," which had

killed off perhaps half the population within three or four years. Innumerable were the effects following upon that disaster; they did not wear out, they increased. The externals of civilisation continued. Our Europe grew more brilliant, her discoveries increased; but the confidence and simplicity of a united Christian life had gone. Efforts at recovery were made and failed. For a century the air had been full of the cry "A reform of head and members." Great general councils had been called, rival Popes had been deposed, the spiritual principle reaffirmed. But the disease had struck root and evil increased upon evil.

It was in the contrast between the ideal which the clerical organisation existed to maintain and its practice that the peril of destruction lay. Thus the great monastic orders, the whole of the hierarchy with the Pope at the head, were bound, under a common discipline of chastity confirmed by an oath, to enforced celibacy. It was a rule made with the idea that the priesthood was of an awful sanctity, sacrificed, and set apart for a mirror and model to the lay world around.

This obligation was now mocked. It was not mocked universally; most of the obscure life within the clerical body was sound, most of the great Abbeys were well and strictly conducted, many, perhaps most, of the great Prelates still observed the discipline of their calling. But the scandal of loose living had become a commonplace, and at the very heart, in the Papacy itself where scandal was of the very worst effect, it broke out continually.

This was but one aspect of the corruption, the other, of perhaps worse effect, was the presence of avarice. The economic system on which the Church depended for its vast possessions, the dues the members of the clergy claimed, the oppressive routine of collection, the treatment of benefices from the highest to the lowest as a mere source of revenue, all these lowered the spiritual force, the moral sanction, of the machine.

For one man to hold more than one piece of ecclesiastical revenue, to fill (nominally) offices the duties of which he could not be present to perform, had in all the earlier and better centuries of Church life been held in abomination. Now it had become a matter of course.

In everything, then, the clergy were bringing on themselves contempt and hatred, while their huge revenues were creating envy and were more and more regarded as the natural prey upon which the lay lords should seize when, or if, a general attack should arise.

Ever since the Black Death the anarchic and revolutionary movements which were grouped as "heresies" were not in their essential cause nor in their motive force doctrinal; rather were they anti-clerical. The discussion or denial of the mysteries (especially the Real Presence in the Mass) were not the revolt of a Pagan or sceptical mood against the Christian mood, they were rather attacks upon the priesthood which was the agent of the mysteries; and the priesthood was attacked because it was found unworthy of the task it had to perform: not unworthy as a whole, but unworthy in a sufficient number of examples to weaken the foundations of the whole.

No long succession of Popes were unworthy of their office, but there was recurrent appearance, especially in the generation before Wolsey's birth and in the time through which he lived, of Pontiffs whose whole lives were at issue with the nature of their high function. And when their lives were at issue with that function it was always from one source: it had one root, worldliness. Here would come the reign of a man cynically dissolute, later the reign of a man chaste but absorbed in the arts and the luxuries of the time. What was lacking, not in individuals but in the corporate character of the Hierarchy, was that contempt, whether for the senses or for wealth, which is an essential of holiness.

Now with holiness in its guardians insufficient, absent, or even ridiculed, an institution whose very purpose is holiness went direct to its own destruction. Ever since the end of the efforts at reform through great councils the Pope had thought of himself more and more as an Italian Prince governing certain territories, concerned with their defence or enlargement and with the enrichment of his family. Christendom still demanded a universal head; it was obtaining one who was local even at the best, concerned with provincial and personal things, not the awful head of all Christendom but an Italian prince.

The next mark of the time in which Wolsey lived was the Renaissance State with its worship of princely power.

While these things were so with the inner life of the hierarchy, with its spiritual character; while that malady of the senses and of avarice was weakening and undermining their hold, that other rival power, the power of the civil governments, was increasing. Great states were arising, each tending to complete sovereignty, some of them, as I have said, already nations.

The power of their Princes came nearer and nearer to a complete independence as against other rulers, clerical or lay, and complete mastery over their subjects. We must have some picture of this new Renaissance State in our minds to perceive what it was that Wolsey served, in what conflict of wills he found himself, and why the rapidly growing worship of Princes might destroy the commonwealth of Christian men. The Renaissance State was one in which adoration of the executive in civil matters had become the mood of men's minds.

That is the best way of putting, I think, a point very difficult to explain: for nothing is more difficult than to interpret the mood of one period to the mood of another.

A government today is more actively and physically powerful than it was then; for instance, it can tax un-limitedly and without fear of revolt. It can compel all its citizens to endure in person the horrors of a war, neither of which things a Renaissance Government could have done. But it is not worshipped. No one has the feeling of sanctity about it, it does not excite "sacred awe." On the contrary, it is a little ridiculous, is the mod-ern absolute government, in spite of its absolute powers. The governments are not worshipped today. What men worship today is the nation. What they will not tolerate is an accusation of lack of patriotism. What seems to them the highest virtue is a passionate love for one's country.

Now in this period of Wolsey's life, it was not yet the nation, it was the *Prince* that was worshipped. The wickedness which seemed to excuse any punishment was treason to the *Prince*. The Person who governed was a sort of God.

It is idle to discuss how these moods come upon men, why they last for so long or short a time as they do, and it is futile to seek their explanation in material causes alone. The new artillery could destroy the feudal castles. Feudalism,—that is the local rule of the local territorial magnate—had also decayed from mere old age. Men, in England especially, were sick of the wars between such magnates. The study of antiquity had brought back the Roman idea of central power. But all these things put together do not suffice to account for the Mood. External causes never suffice to account for such spiritual convictions. The social and political mood of a civilisation is of the mind, and varies with forces invisible more than with forces visible.

The best that history can do is to record those moods and to make it plain to the reader that however strange a past mood may seem it really *was* the passion of the time. When we understand that, we understand what the power of a man like Henry Tudor could be; why the strongest minister in Europe could only act as his Prince's servant, and fell at the orders of such a master. So also can we understand how, without an army and without police or any of the modern machinery for absolute government, government could be so strong.

Behind the Prince of the Renaissance, served by his great ministers, his captains, his ambassadors, lay somewhat vaguely the idea of the realm which he governed. Men did not serve the realm, they served the Prince. The realm was only an idea and could be left vague, as its boundaries often were. The Prince was a person, a concrete object, and the men of the time understood serving a real man much better than serving the nebulous idea of the State which he governed. Nevertheless that idea of the Realm was always present and later was developed into that conception of the Nation which is the object of our idolatry today.

That idolatry will pass in its turn and some new mood succeed to it.

There were four examples of more or less complete princely powers, more or less complete kingships, with realms attached to them, in the world which was filled with Wolsey's fame.

These four were France, Spain, England and Scotland.

France had a Kingship of longer standing than any other: one which had increased its power slowly for a long time past, gradually absorbing the half independent districts, and centring power in the throne. It had only quite recently acquired the last of such half independent districts, Brittany.

Spain was a comparatively recent coalition of various smaller princedoms. These princedoms had grown from the separate efforts of groups of Christian warriors each fighting down southwards, and conquering more and more land from the Mohammedans, until the whole of the peninsula was under their rule. The two principal ones were Aragon and Castile. The King of Aragon, Ferdinand, had married the heiress of Castile, Isabella. Between them they had conquered the last strip of Mohammedan territory in the extreme south and established a united rule; except that the district of Portugal had remained independent under its own kings. Spain even thus united was not as wealthy or as powerful as France, it had not so much fruitful land nor as many great cities, but the Spanish crown also claimed Southern Italy and Sicily by inheritance. Just in the midst of this period, in 1492, when Wolsey was a young unknown man of twenty, the discovery of America had opened a new source of wealth and power to Spain. By the time Wolsey was in full career the wealth of the New World was beginning to pour into Spain and the maritime power of Spain to develop with it.

England, though a new and virtually usurping dynasty (the Tudors) had seized power when Wolsey was already well into his teens, had certain special advantages. It had strict bounds; for everywhere save on the Scottish border its frontier was the sea. The power of local nobles had yielded to the crown more than in France. Government was therefore far more centralised in England than in France. England was of a more manageable size than its rivals, and though it was much less populous than its great continental neighbours, it was wealthy for its numbers. The King of England could generally be master of the seas round about him, and, what was very important, he had a stronghold on the mainland opposite, the port of Calais, which the English Kings had captured, garrisoned and securely held for the better part of 200 years. They could land armies at that port from which to begin an invasion.

Scotland was much the smallest of the four countries we are considering, and very much the poorest. It was the hereditary enemy of England and regularly in alliance with France.

Europe to the East of these four western kingships was in a condition curiously divided.

We have to consider there in the first place the Empire and the Emperor at its head.

There had come down from remote Roman times the idea that the unity of Europeans, expressed in a common Christian religion, should also be expressed in a common lay monarch, theoretically the head of all. In practice the application of this idea had long decayed; there was an Emperor and an Empire, but even such

THE POLITICAL DIVISIONS OF EUROPE IN WOLSEY'S DAY

actual power as the Emperor still had only extended
to a limited though large region. It took in the whole
mass of German-speaking districts (save that its power
over the German-speaking Swiss valleys had virtually
disappeared) and it came west of the Rhine covering a
considerable belt of French-speaking territory. It held
old and perpetually disputed claims to overlordship in
the Italian plains beyond the Alps, but of the various
Italian states only one had any real link with the Empire and that was the district round Milan, called the
Milanese. Those who succeeded in getting hold of
Milan confirmed their power by getting the Emperor to
admit their claim.

That great bulk of the Empire which consisted in the
big German-speaking mass (occupying much the same
region as it does today) was not one realm under one
Prince. It was a mass of separate, nearly independent,
districts and cities—something like 300 of them, varying
from wealthy merchant town states of very small area
to considerable principalities, such as Saxony and Hesse.
All of these professed to regard the Emperor as their
suzerain but he could only get from them such small
sums as they chose to give, nor could he compel them to
come and fight for him; they came if they chose. The
bulk of the Empire being made up of German-speaking
folk, a great German Prince was commonly Emperor,
and for a long time past that Prince had been a Hapsburg with a few fleeting exceptions. The Hapsburgs were
the Princes whose capital was at Vienna and who directly ruled a number of districts, most of them in a
ring-fence to the south of the Germanies, with Vienna
for their centre and capital.

The Empire was not hereditary, it was elective. An

Emperor was chosen for life by the votes of seven electors, three of them great Church Prelates, princes over their own districts, four of them powerful lay princes. On the death of each Emperor a new one had to be elected; and though it had for a very long time been a man of German birth and usually a Hapsburg, there was no necessity that it should be so. A foreigner or the head of another German family might have been chosen at any time.

Italy was in the following condition. All the south (later called the "Kingdom of the Two Sicilies" or the "Kingdom of Naples"—including the islands of Sicily and Sardinia) had after passing through many hands come into those of the King of Spain.

The middle belt with Rome for its capital was a Principality directly governed by the Pope and called the States of the Church.

The northern part was a mosaic of greater and lesser states, some quite tiny, some as large as a small French province or very large English county. There was Savoy which meant the north-western passes of the Alps and the Italian plain at their foot; there was Genoa, which meant the sea port and the narrow strip of coast on either side under the mountains; there was the Republic of Florence, holding down sundry lesser cities; and, more important than the other lesser states, there were those two on which the policies of the time turned, the district of Milan (called the Milanese) and the big district against the eastern Alps and including all the plain at their foot which was ruled in complete independence by the very wealthy and very powerful Republic of Venice.

The struggle for power among these various princes

and States, great and small, turned upon the principle of heredity and descent. There was no such thing as right of conquest among Christian men; there was no such thing in theory as going with an army into another man's land, seizing it by force and compelling him to give it up. In theory no one could rule a district save by hereditary right (if that district had a prince at its head), or by the continuity of the Republic if it was a City State like Venice or Genoa, with a Council at its head. When a Prince desired to become wealthier by ruling more territory he schemed for an alliance by marriage, or, failing that, he would make a claim to a district through some right of descent. He would say, when the Prince of the district died, that the new man to inherit, whoever he might be, had less right than himself, his right as claimant being based on descent from some former owner of the district.

This strong theory of heredity, which was not a mere fiction for obtaining power but a reality governing all men's minds, caused the politics of Europe to turn upon alliances of blood; and nearly all the international interests of the time during which Wolsey was working his diplomacy throughout western Europe turned upon marriages between the heirs and heiresses of the greater powers: marriages through which what had been separate realms coalesced and grew into larger units.

Such a marriage had made possible the usurpation of the Tudors in Wolsey's boyhood. Henry VII could never have held the throne if the heiress of the Plantagenets had not been his wife. Such a marriage had consolidated Spain, joining up Aragon and Castile; later for a brief time another such marriage was to bring Portugal under the same crown.

But the greatest example was the Burgundian marriage of Maximilian the Emperor which, just before Wolsey's career began, opened that attempt at universal dominion by the Hapsburgs of which Europe stood in dread for two centuries. The great Burgundian house, an offshoot of the House of France, sovereign over the old Duchy of Burgundy with its capital at Dijon and over the eastern part thereof, holding of the Empire, ended in an heiress. She was sovereign of the Jura mountain district called "The Free County", but—much more important—she was sovereign also of all those great towns, growing wealthier than ever at this time, which crowd the Low Countries. These commercial republics (for that is what they really were), Arras, Tournai, Brussels, Ghent, Bruges, Antwerp, as rich as—some of them richer than—their Italian rivals, stood on the flat delta of the great rivers the Meuse, the Rhine, and the Scheldt. These were the Netherlands, later divided, through the Reformation, into two opposing halves today called Holland and Belgium, but essentially one as a society, four hundred years ago.

Maximilian, the Hapsburg, who was Emperor through all Wolsey's youth, had married this woman. Thenceforward his house held in the Netherlands a source of wealth and greatness which was a key-point in northern Europe. The liberties of these towns were respected; their ancient burgess constitutions under which they had grown and flourished were a pride to their rulers; and to this day, though politically broken up, some under Holland, some under Belgium, some within the north-eastern frontiers of France, they remember the glory of the old Burgundian rule.

But there was yet another marriage following on this

which forwarded the advance of the Hapsburgs towards the mastery of Europe. The son of Ferdinand and Isabella, the heir of Spain, died: he would have been the master not only of Spain but of South Italy and the Two Sicilies and of that immense wealth which was about to pour in from the New World. His two sisters remained as heiresses, Catherine and Joan. Catherine renounced her rights in marrying into the House of England, and was that Catherine of Aragon upon whose misfortunes the fall and ending of Wolsey turned. The other sister Joan, who lost her mind later on and was known as Joan the Mad, would bring with her all the great mass of Ferdinand and Isabella's realm. Maximilian married to her his son Philip, and by that act gathered up into Hapsburg hands all the strength of Europe save the French kingdom which lay, an island in peril, between the German and the Spanish halves of this vast dominion.

Such were royal marriages in that time. They held the place which wars of conquest and alliances held until lately; they held the place which economic combinations subjecting one nation to another hold today. And in all that we are to follow we shall find this note of alliance by marriages running. A proposed marriage between the Princess heiress of England and Philip's son, the young Hapsburg heir, and then between that same heiress and the heir of France, a marriage between a Hapsburg and the niece of a Pope, a marriage between the King of England's sister and the King of France—all international politics of the time turns upon such things.

To this map of rival powers, as they stood when Wol-

ST. BONAVENTURE LIBRARY
ST. BONAVENTURE, N. Y.

sey entered upon the scene in the early years of Henry
VIII's reign in England, four points must be added.

First, the Papal States whereby the independence of
the Holy See was guaranteed, were but a comparatively
small Italian district, going from the Adriatic to the
Tyrrhenian sea. Whatever foreign power grew strong in
Italy threatened to make the Pope its servant; and therefore the Papacy, when it is not too much alarmed by the
strength of such an invader, manœuvres to expel him by
the help of a rival. It is this obvious principle which lends
unity to the perpetual changes of Papal foreign policy all
during Wolsey's career: now making a league against
France when France has won victories in Northern Italy:
now uniting against the Emperor when the Emperor has
done so.

Second, the pivot is always the Milanese. When the
French kings can hold Milan and its territory (which
they claimed by right of inheritance, but which had its
own native duke) they are masters of North Italy and,
later, when all the Empire and Spain and South Italy
were under one man, it is life and death for the French
to thrust the wedge of Northern Italy between the two
halves of this menacing power: that is, between the Germanies and the South. That is why the French cross the
Alps over and over again in this period.

The foreign affairs with which Wolsey had to do are
simplified by the fact that they all turn upon Northern
Italy.

The rest of Europe, its alliances, counter-alliances, betrayals, secret negotiations and the rest, all revolve round
the Duchy of Milan: because it had the strongest citadel
in North Italy, and because it was the very centre of the
rich Lombard plain, because it commanded the middle

passes of the Alps, the shortest roads from the wealthier part of Germany to the mass of Italy and to Rome, because it was a large well-organised town, and most of all because it was geographically balanced between the Empire and Austria on the north-east, the Swiss Cantons on the north-west, Savoy on the west, the entry from the sea at Genoa on the south-west, Medicean Florence and the Papal States beyond, to the south, the road through the Romanian plain along the Apennines to the southeast, and the solid, permanent, serene mass of Venetian power controlling the Brenner Pass and the sea to the east.

The chief governments of Europe, subtly struggling among themselves, met in many another field: the House of Burgundy—now Hapsburg—marched with France all the way from the Alps to the North Sea, Spain marched with France along the Pyrennees, and challenged France at the Atlantic end of the mountains over the disputed kingdom of Navarre. There was discussion and war upon the kingdom of Naples. But the true centre to which all returns is the Milanese.

What we have to watch in every one of Wolsey's diplomatic movements is the support England gives through his agency to one or other claimants for, or occupiers of, the Duchy of Milan. What we have to notice in all he does is his constant adhesion to the Papal policy, for and against the alternate holders of Milan.

Third, although Northern Italy was such a "Mosaic of States" small and large, the Papal State independent in the midst, the Southern part with Naples held by Spain, yet a vague but strong Italian feeling, opposed to all invaders, had arisen. That is why you get Italians, and especially the Milanese, generally supporting the rivals of the last victor, of the last successful invader. If the French seize Milan they wish well to the Germans and their Emperor and his Spanish allies; if the Imperialists seize Milan they wish well to the French, for the moment. Only Venice stands out quite separate in the midst of all this: an orderly and prosperous aristocratic state acting alone: independent of Empire; willing to encroach on the Papal States. It often allied with France.

Fourth, the armies of the day were mercenary and very expensive. Their hire was expensive, their maintenance and, above all, their artillery. That is what explains two main facts of the time: the power of England to interfere on the continent and the value of the independent Swiss. England, with its small but compact and wealthy population, when it was entirely in the hands of the despotic government under Wolsey, could raise (and send abroad to hire soldiers for an ally) armies which made all the difference. As to the Swiss, they could not be prevented by any lord from hiring themselves out as they chose. They had gained their independence. They were trained to be the best soldiers in Europe and they sold their skill indifferently in the highest market. We shall find them perpetually, even after Marignano, turning the scale of war.

II

THE PROGRAMME

SOME four centuries and a half ago was born an Englishman, Thomas Wolsey, destined to the height of power and to fall from it in most significant disaster.

I propose to present his character and story with this object: to cite him as the great example of those who do mightily yet cannot see what they are doing and who stand on the edge of doom with no vision of its approach.

The great religious revolution which was at last to destroy the unity of our civilisation, arose at his side. Under his very eyes, during his most active years. It grew clamorous while he was directing all in his own country and much of Europe as well. It was fully armed while he was still in the forefront of affairs. Its ultimate success was apparent before he died. It was to destroy all by which he lived, all the world which had made him. He hardly noticed it.

His extraordinary gifts serving a limitless ambition put all men about him under his obedience: he chose his agents with unequalled skill, he grasped the widest field of fact and conjecture without confusion. He had no equal at intrigue. Yet he missed the motives deepest in their effect upon human conduct, and was destroyed by rival forces much less than his own but unperceived by him. The qualities which gave him so much external greatness were precisely those which blocked his sense of inward things and shortened all his range. Humbler and holier men than he, his contemporaries, divined much more and guessed the dim future as he never could. All he did resulted at last in what he least desired. Had he lived but a score more years he would have discovered himself to be an architect of ruin.

Conceive that figure, splendid in the scarlet of his office, with vivid pageantry about him, expressing in its gesture and poise complete domination and all the dignity of rule. Its ornaments of gold are all about it; its train of great men to do its bidding; its crowd of servitors. Let such a figure and its retinue be seen as upon a hill-top, brilliantly lit by an opposing evening sun. The majesty and brilliance of the group is violently impressed upon our sight because there lies behind it, in awful contrast, one dead curtain of black cloud. They are turned away from it; they do not feel its approach. It breaks and they are swallowed up.

Wolsey, the splendid court which he gathered about him, the complete dominion established by him over Church and State and held grasped in his own hand, is the supreme example of a man at issue with the unseen and overwhelmed by it, of the man who makes and whose creation is turned by forces of which he did not dream into a form utterly different from any he had imagined. He is the very model of those great men who stand in the very article of revolution and cannot guide or comprehend it. He lives to see his own failure, from a royal amour, an accident too petty and sordid for him to grasp its effect until it was upon him. Only at the very end, when the wreck is final, does he see vaguely but in its magnitude, the enormity of the things about to come upon Europe. Even then he does not grasp their power and mass, and he dies, the last of an old system which he himself had summed up in his own triumphant office, and quite unconsciously the builder of the new.

We are about to follow the career of a man who incarnated in England, and was the last to incarnate there, the united medieval hierarchy. The material splendour in which the Priesthood clothed itself upon the eve of its catastrophe, the absolute power which could be concentrated in its hands, its fatal absorption in the things of this world were present in him exceedingly; so that all that he did with all his caste could give him made for the destruction of that caste.

We are about to watch an eager pursuit concentrated upon the possession of the Papacy, just at the moment when the Papacy was challenged and its universal power suddenly shaken and thrown back. What is more strange (and what should be of special meaning to us modern men who idolize such things), we are about to see all those talents which we regard as the necessary elements of what we call success—industry much beyond other men's, clarity, right choice of lieutenants, unswerving object—lead to personal failure; while that mighty weapon of united national control which the mighty personality had forged, is snatched from the dying hands and used to cut down all that which it had been produced to defend.

There is not perhaps in history a tragedy more ironic, more full at least of that irony which lies in the spectacle of a man acting at his highest and having his action diverted, reversed, transmuted, utterly transformed.

Wolsey himself, the man who owed to the clerical organisation an advance from almost nothing to the summit of society, as the result of such advancement caused that clerical organisation to disappear so that no cleric in England could hold political power again.

Wolsey assembled and subjected to one lever the powers of the State, only to see the completed machine pass into other hands with other motives, attaining other ends. He had behind him, and in his progress perceived and used to the full, the vast economic powers of the Church—and it was due to him that those economic powers were dragged down, crumbled and disappeared.

Wolsey wove, as his chief interest, an intricate and yet more intricate pattern of diplomacy, watching and manœuvring a dozen contending rivalries abroad—and the great issue of the time to come, the Reformation, dwarfed those rivalries into insignificance.

He could not have been the prince he was had he not been wholly of his time, had he not been limited to the things close to him and seen on the surface only— and all those things were about to disappear. He would have told you himself that he knew men as no other knew them, but he knew them as instruments to be controlled by flattery, avarice, routine, or fear, or moral pressure, by the use of common and evident methods, and he knew men only so. Because he only knew them thus he missed one small abnormal factor, the secret control possessed over an abnormal character, the King's, by an abnormal woman, who came to possess his soul; and that detail, like the snare hidden in grass over which a giant stumbles, brought him down full length in one crash after so many years of uncontrolled dominion.

He was master of the State because he was the Chancellor come of the priesthood: yet on account of his action no future Chancellor would come of the priesthood, and within a time which he might have lived to see the supreme office of Chancellor had lost its significance.

He was master of the Church because he was Papal Legate with powers Legatine so absolute that nothing of the sort had been seen before: yet by his own action such powers Legatine were never used again. He was uniquely lord because he handled an unbroken Catholic England. By his own action that unity was shattered; and when after long years the nation recovered repose in a new religious unity, a common ethic, the essence of its new substance was (and is) its opposition to Catholicism.

All that Wolsey did was undone, and undone because he had done it; and he lived to see with his own dying eyes the perversion of the whole affair.

.   .   .   .

I have said that the story is of peculiar significance for ourselves in this our day.

We also, we, do not know what is upon us.

Some, noting the prodigies of our time—the collapse of tradition, the huge novelties of scientific achievement, the gathering of all economic power into the hands of an unworthy few, the management and creation of opinion, through the press, by fewer still—prophesy the coming enslavement of the world to a small class. Others prophesy our common reduction to the inhuman tyranny of Communism; others our sinking back into that savagery from which, they say, we rose before the beginnings of society.

Only one thing is certain: somewhat considerable is toward and what it is not one of us yet knows.

Among us also are many—especially those absorbed in affairs—who, vaguely conscious of impending change, still live wholly by the social system to which they were born and within the framework of which all their activities have been trained. They take for granted the continuance of what they have always known, and, in practice, presume such continuance for ever: the anonymous secrecy of financial operations, the control exercised by the great banks, the still orderly if unwilling labour of a vast proletariat, the invincibility of our present social organisation, its law, police and customs, are the air they breathe. In all they do they are lit by the clear light of the immediate past still shining brightly today, and all their considerable achievements are attained in the only world they know. One whole province of that world has crashed in Russia: elsewhere the intermittent refusal of labour grows ominous. An acute necessity for social defence reduces one society to accept dictatorship, another to offer subsidies to soothe the masses. All is changing. Yet these men, the principal figures of our day, continue to function as though all would endure.

Were there today, what there is not, one figure capable by genius and good fortune of combining in itself the remaining strength of society, he would be Wolsey's modern parallel. He would fail, as Wolsey failed; for the change would be greater than he. Were he to fail, as probably he would, through some petty accident unforeseen, as Wolsey did, the parallel would be complete.

III

THE PLOT

THE last of the great English Royal house, the house of Plantagenet, fell on the field of Bosworth, and the throne was seized by a usurper Henry Tudor, or Tydder, under the title of Henry VII. This usurper's mother, the Countess of Richmond, was a bastard Plantagenet (Margaret Beaufort), but his father was the son of a groom in the Palace whom a foreign princess, the widow of the great Henry V, had picked up to be her secret lover.

On the day when the battle of Bosworth was decided, an obscure schoolboy of twelve at Oxford was beginning his Latin for the priesthood: he was in the college of Magdalen, mixing with the young lads of the lower and lower middle classes of which the University then consisted. In due course this boy was, like principally his contemporaries, ordained a priest and was chosen to be a Fellow of that religious community.

He had the luck to find among his pupils the son of a great nobleman of Royal connections, Dorset, whom he visited, who gave him his first living in a Western parish and passed him on to be one of the Archbishop's Chaplains at Canterbury. There he served Nanfant the governor of Calais who recommended him to court. He thus became one of the usurping King's chaplains at the respectable age of thirty-five.

He was still obscure, but he had shown energy, industry and ability. He got an increasing income from benefices. He was used on official business, on at least one minor embassy to the Low Countries. Henry VII died shortly after and his young second son, also called

Henry (his eldest, Arthur, being already dead), came to the throne as Henry VIII of England.

Thomas Wolsey found himself in the new court, still in the background, but with a position and a good income. He had no longer to serve a ruler old in wiles, dry with worldly wisdom, implacable and the master of all his servants, but a boy of seventeen ardent in spirits, impulsive, and easily moved by companionship.

The chief of the old king's councillors had been Foxe, Bishop of Winchester, a man of wide, long and deep experience with all state business and crowned with high repute. The young king inherited Foxe as his wisest advisor. To this man Wolsey had long attached himself, gaining his patron's esteem by hard work and the flattery of imitation. Through him advancement was now certain. What made it doubly certain was the effect upon the lad of Wolsey's presence and character: a man nearly twenty years the boy's senior yet the best of comrades, full of jest and vigour and good talk, always in humour, yet full of experience. Wolsey began at once to advance.

The advance was rapid but not precipitate. He became in a few months King's Almoner. A great mass of official business began to pass through his hands. He organised the young fellow's first foreign campaigns, he became more and more that young fellow's admired elder companion.

But it was Henry's old grandmother, the Countess of Richmond, who had most effect upon the first months of his reign, and after that it was his wife Catherine who led him. This wife Catherine was the daughter of that very powerful King, Ferdinand of Aragon, who by his marriage with her mother, Isabella of Castile, had united Spain, who was also monarch of South Italy and Sicily and was already receiving the new wealth that poured in from newly-discovered America.

There was about this marriage of Catherine with young Henry one circumstance, then half forgotten, later to be of the utmost importance. Catherine had been nominally married, five years before, to Henry's elder brother Arthur. The marriage was not consummated. He was but a child of just fifteen and he died a few weeks after. The younger brother Henry, now heir to the throne, was then designated to be Catherine's future husband. But as the ceremony of his elder brother's marriage had taken place and there was no public proof that this marriage had not been a real one, a dispensation from the Pope was required: for marriage with a brother's wife was unlawful. The Pope of the day (Julius II) sent the dispensation and it was kept till the younger brother should be old enough to marry.

Catherine was therefore really married to young Henry immediately after his accession, and took full control of him. She was getting on for six years older in age than her boy husband—but a young woman of 23 is far more than six years in advance of a boy of 17— and with her firm though simple character excellently managed him.

But that state of affairs only lasted four years; Wolsey dominated the King more and more, and passed Catherine hand over hand in the business of managing a young fellow whose character then and throughout his life found the will of another indispensable to him. Wolsey, still protected by Foxe, entered King's Council in the third year of the reign, 1511-12, and began to get his great preferments, after having shown his unique ability

in the provisioning and organising of Henry's first foreign war, that of 1512.

So far the prologue and entry: the real drama had
not yet begun.

But a second campaign waged by the young man as
his father-in-law's ally was to bring the action on. This
campaign was that fought during the summer of 1513.
Wolsey organised that as he had the one of the year before, but unlike the earlier war this one was a triumph
and it made him. Thêrouanne was captured from the
French, so was Tournai; all was put down to Wolsey's
credit, especially by his King of twenty-two.

A further opportunity for him was the violent quarrel between his master and Catherine's father the King
of Spain, by whom Henry found he had been used,
abandoned, and betrayed in the campaigns on the continent. Wolsey, after so much success in the field, takes
charge of foreign business as well. He settles the peace.
He avenges the slight Henry had suffered from old
Ferdinand. He takes full advantage of it to push Ferdinand's daughter the Queen still further from her old
position of control. He negotiates a new alliance with
France, supports the marriage of Henry's sister to the
French king, and is henceforward in control of affairs.

The curtain falls upon the first act, the second opens
in splendour.

In that year 1514, the fifth year of the reign, Wolsey
had become not only the master of the King and far the
first man in England, but one of the first men in Europe,
and the great tragedy begins. He is given bishoprics, including the great metropolitan see of York (which he
never visited) and later all sorts of other vast revenues in
the same fashion. Bath and Wells, Durham, Winchester,

WOLSEY

From a Photograph in the National Portrait Gallery, London, of an Original
Drawing preserved in the Library of Arras, France

the great abbey of St. Albans, all these added revenues gave him a fortune greater than that of the greatest of the old nobility, and his wealth was at least half his power. He had grown so strong that he could disdain the whispered accusations against him of murder—for men said in private that he had murdered Bainbridge, Cardinal and Archbishop of York, companion of popes, chief English figure in Rome: the man who had barred his way to a cardinalate and to the great ecclesiastical revenues of the north. He had grown so strong that he could lure a rival in the King's favour, Charles Brandon, Duke of Suffolk, into a secret marriage with the King's sister in order to ruin his influence: so strong that he could prove his power to the same Charles Brandon by saving his head.

All through 1514 and on into 1515 he thus advances, till, in the end of that year, he is appointed Chancellor, that is, supreme minister exercising at will almost unlimited power in civil matters at home in the name of the King. Already the Pope, Leo X, needing support against the now overwhelming power which France had acquired in North Italy by the crushing victory of Marignano, had made him cardinal; two and a half years later, in early 1518, the same pope made him Legate— Vice-Gerent of the Papacy in England.

Already master of the State through the Chancellorship, he was now master throughout England of that twin power in Christendom which in those days stood at least equal with the State in the control of men.

All through this second act of his five, he had risen uninterruptedly until he possessed every source of government and was at last supreme.

In his ceaseless negotiation and intrigue with foreign

powers he had not the same hold nor the same perception. He would err. He was often foiled. But he had begun to make the English crown a partner in all that was
done in Europe, and whatever changes of policy he
was driven to, whatever miscalculations he made, did
nothing to diminish his unrivalled strength at home.
With his attainment of that highest office, the Papal Legatine authority in 1518, he steps on to the level summit
of his glory; the curtain falls on the second act to rise
upon the third which is one unceasing triumph.

For seven years, till 1525, Wolsey held in his own
hand all England. The King, though passing from youth
to the thirties, was still under his minister's will. There
was no such concentration of power elsewhere in Christendom, and though the English realm was a small one
compared with its great rivals, the Empire in Germany
and the Netherlands; Spain; France, yet this government by one man, raising vast revenues at will and able
to use them at will gave it an effect quite dispropor-
tionate. During those seven years Wolsey was watched,
listened to, often obeyed, by the competing sovereigns of
Europe and by the Papacy. He possessed what soldiers
call "a mass of manœuvre"; he could throw the weight
of great sums, wholly at his disposal, on to this side or
that of any quarrel. He could do it at a time when armies
consisted of expensively hired mercenaries, and when
all other governments were hampered in their resources
by customs and checks which forbade an indefinite increase of their revenue.

The Emperor, the King of Spain, the King of France,
had each four or five times the wealth of England in
their dominions, probably more; but of revenue available
for a single purpose continually, a free available "mass of

manœuvre" to apply to what part they willed, at what moment they willed, rapidly, during their struggles with opponents, they had nothing proportionate to that which Wolsey could boast.

All during those seven years Europe is full of Wolsey; England is identical with Wolsey; and Henry the King, in whose name he did everything and whom he controlled without question, was dazzled by the glory of it.

The Cardinal himself shone in a magnificence which had never been equalled in his own country and which rivalled the great courts abroad, even the court of Rome. His immense private income purchased glory and beauty of every kind, of tapestry, of gold and silver, and carven wood, of great new buildings. He went about in pomp that was more than a sovereign's. The crimson which he himself wore and which his hundreds of retainers and servants wore also in his livery, made, as it were, the central vivid patch of colour of his place and time; and the great golden crosses and the maces borne before him, the double insignia of the civil and clerical power, proclaimed his omnipotence. He desired, he thought he could obtain, there was a moment when he might have grasped, the Papacy itself.

Twice in the midst of the seven years, after the death of Leo X in 1521 and after the death of Adrian VI in 1523, he had proposed himself for election, and though he had wholly failed then, he had so far counted as to hold the promises of France and the Empire. He never visited Rome, but he was conversant with it. In his first advance he had followed the career of Julius II, had helped in the war promoted by Julius' "Holy League", and had marked the influence of his rival Bainbridge

at Julius' right hand. After Leo X had been elected in
1513, just as Wolsey was entering into power, he had
closely followed the new Pope's acts through the eight
years of his reign. The brief two years and less of Adrian
VI he less understood, for that high reformer's mind was
alien to him, but Clement, the second Medicean Pope,
who later was to fill all his anxious thoughts, he knew—
or thought he knew—thoroughly enough in his weakness and subtlety.

All the while Wolsey's driving power in administration, his unique capacity for detail, his strength of
memory, his capacity in co-ordination, gave the strong
foundation on which all the external splendour was
raised.

He had every talent of the ruler, and some of those
talents, notably the use of presence and majesty in mien,
he possessed to the degree of genius. But two things he
lacked, which would have been necessary to fructify his
boundless ambition. He could only judge men plainly
and especially as agents, that is, he missed their secret
thoughts, he never surmised in them anything but the
most normal motives, of fear, envy or what not. Therefore he was wholly unforewarned by any instinct when
hidden and abnormal obstacles were presented beneath
the surface.

The second thing he lacked was the cause of much
graver, more fundamental weakness: a weakness ruinous
to Europe as it first was ruinous to his own personal
career. He lacked the deep spiritual sense of what was
toward in the soul of Christendom; it lay within his
power to avert the revolution and disruption to which
Europe began to move in the midst of those seven
years: the vast religious quarrel in which all the unity

of our civilisation crashed to the ground: wars of more than a hundred years, ending in the final separation of Christian men.

On the eve of the moment when the Legatine authority was to make him absolute above his own people, Luther had raised his protest against the government of the Church, and the Reformation had begun. Before the seven years were completed the tide was already running like a mill race, the rebellious Princes and Cities in Germany had successfully defied the Emperor and the Pope, the medieval scheme, the permanence of which Wolsey had taken for granted like the air he breathed, was already imperilled and to eyes of better judgment might have seemed to be ultimately doomed.

All this passed him by. The religious revolution affected England very little; the long-drawn premonitory symptoms of it he had dealt with leniently and even contemptuously, rather laughing at the scattered and few heretics of England than repressing them. He had used his universal powers with adequate conception of the need for reform within the Church of his country (it needed reform less than any other ecclesiastical province in Europe), he had honestly intended to set right the disorders in the monastic houses, to correct abuses, to found new bishoprics that might be needed, and especially to advance learning with clerical revenues hitherto stagnant; but he had no conception of the intensity at which the fire of indignation was burning against the enormous corruption of the clergy. He did not even perceive what was already apparent to many, how that indignation would give opportunity for a riot of loot, how the endowments of religion which gave it half its strength were at the mercy of civil governments, large and lesser, landowners, princes and cities eager for the prey.

He suppressed a number of small monasteries, setting the example for what was to follow, but used the proceeds honestly for the endowment of learning in that time of expanse and renovation of learning. With the attack on celibacy about to be launched, he, the defender of strict orthodox discipline, took his mistress, his uncanonical wife, like any other great prelate of the time, bred a family and loaded it with ecclesiastical gifts. A defender of reform in the crying abuse of pluralities, he gave the very worst example of pluralities. A national figure if ever there was one, he found it normal to continue the diversion of the revenues of English Sees to foreigners engaged in his diplomacy. The dam had broken higher up the valley, the deluge was already upon him, and he could not hear the distant noise of the waters.

That third act in his tragedy, the seven years of unexampled glory, ends with the new presence—but not yet the appearance—of that which was to destroy him. Anne Boleyn in the spring of 1525 captivated the King. He knew nothing of it—but that moment marked his fate.

The next three years are a turning point not only for him but for Europe. The splendour of his own state, the shining of his own magnificence, is undimmed; indeed through the turmoil and rocking of those three years which shook the universal world, he seems greater than ever. They are the years when he builds his palaces and colleges and reaches the highest of his revenue. But there was piercing through them at point after point the elements of his fall and of that much greater thing, the coming of that religious war in Europe which was to end all he had known. For during those three years, when there rose the beginnings of a new mastery over the King of England, the conditions in Europe which had facilitated Wolsey's long-enjoyed opportunity for alliance and counter-alliance for playing—however imperfectly—upon the seesaw of the continental powers, disappeared.

Young Charles, the grandson of both the Emperor Maximilian and of King Ferdinand, had inherited Ferdinand's kingdom of Spain in the midst of Wolsey's advance early in 1516. He had been elected Emperor at the beginning of the great seven years in 1519. The crushing defeat of the French at Pavia at the opening of 1525 made Charles the apparent master of the continent and the Papacy itself trembled before him. In his anxiety the Pope had attempted secretly to support himself upon the chance of a revival which might come to the defeated French and especially upon the independent support of England coming in to help. An army, not directly commanded by the Emperor Charles V but acting in his interests, sacked Rome in 1527 and kept the Pope close prisoner, while months before, the King of England had begun to pursue Anne's plan for him, the obtaining of a divorce from Catherine, his Queen.

The fourth decisive act is the Divorce—1527 to 1529. Wolsey—blind to Anne's mastery over Henry—supported the divorce. He had begun to notice that the King was changed and acting independently of him, though he had not guessed that it was under the direction of a woman. He thought by using the threat of Henry's power he could bend the Pope to his will, he thought that if the divorce was granted he could make a new marriage with the French reigning family, he thought that Henry in his gratitude would at least help to make him Pope, he remembered how Charles V, when the last Papal election had been held in 1523, had tricked him: he directed all his powers, which still seemed supreme, to furthering Henry's plan. He would get the divorce and use it for building up an alliance with the French, a counterpoise to the now apparently over-whelming strength of the Emperor. He would get rid of Catherine and marry Henry to Renée, the sister of the French Queen.

The whole thing was a catastrophic miscalculation in every element of it. Henry, his character rapidly chang-ing under the effect of disease, was slipping from him. Henry had fallen into the hands of the woman who more and more controlled him. There could never have been question of a French marriage. There was never to be an English Pope, Thomas Wolsey, working with the English King for English interests.

While the Pope lay a prisoner, Wolsey for one brief moment, present as Ambassador in France, acted almost as though he were Pope himself. He granted their com-missions to the Cardinals present at the French court, he proclaimed loudly that with the Pope in the Em-perors' power Christendom must have a head free to act and that he himself ought to be that head. And all the while he actively promoted Henry's claim to be rid of Catherine the Queen, old Ferdinand's daughter, the Em-peror's aunt.

He and all his contemporaries had seen so many royal and half royal marriages annulled as a matter of course! He made no doubt of the issue.

Again he was wrong. The Queen was determined to resist. He had quite miscalculated her inflexibility and the strength with which she and hers could use the difficulties of the position. Even as he was thus playing the Pope and all but grasping the Papal power, even while he was, during that Embassy in France, negotiating for the French alliance and negotiating for the French marriage, he learned that Henry, for the first time in all those years, was acting independently of him. The King was sending secret agents to Rome to plead his cause; he had not summoned the moral courage to have it out with Wolsey, to insist upon his own view and make him privy to the arrangement with Anne. But Wolsey had discovered the plot and he now knew for the first time that he had a rival—how formidable a one he had not yet guessed, but he now saw that she was there.

Therefore when the curtain rises upon the fourth act —the divorce—it finds Wolsey, hesitating upon the stage, uncertain. One might almost say, if such a term could be applied to so active, decided and comprehensive a mind, that it finds him bewildered.

He has engaged himself in the divorce; he cannot go back; he knows that the object of the divorce is the marriage with Anne Boleyn; which is as degraded and absurd in his own eyes as in those of all his contemporaries. Besides this it ruins the whole scheme of international policy, offending the Emperor and France and the Pope all at once. But he cannot go back: he cannot go back. He implores the King to break through that woman's net. He fails. He is compelled to play the King's game ostensibly. But, while he presses for the divorce, threatens to break with the Pope in his apparent eagerness for it, does Henry's work with fervour in all outward acts, he is privately doing what he can, more and more against orders, and more and more doubting his success,

to prevent so ruinous an end to all the edifice he had
raised.

Anne suspects him. She makes the King suspect him.
She crowbars and levers him out of his real power while
all the façade of that power remains intact. The Pope,
Clement VII, adding delay to delay, is compelled to
appoint a Court to try the case in England; Wolsey and
another Legate, Campeggio, are to be the judges. Clement is even compelled to promise secretly that he will
allow their judgment to be final.

The trial goes forward in the summer of 1529, in
London. The Queen refuses the jurisdiction of the Court
and proclaims her intention of appealing to Rome. Still
Wolsey plays his double or his triple game, now thoroughly enmeshed in a snare from which he cannot escape. He insists on the dignity of his office, on his duty
to be impartial; he acts as little as possible and leaves as
much as possible to his colleague on that bench. And all
the while, of the alternative policies which pass through
his mind, he is still most possessed by the chance, the
possibility, the hope, that, after all, the King's miserable
subservience to Anne will come to an end and that his
own position will be fully restored.

He deceives himself. The very legal ground on which
he had advised Henry to stand—the imperfection of the
dispensation granted for Henry's marriage with his
brother's nominal wife—is struck from under them by
the announcement that Catherine's nephew, the Emperor, possesses a brief which corrects the imperfections
of the original dispensation. In the confusion thus
created, and considering Catherine's undoubted right of
appeal, the Pope revokes the case to his own court at
Rome, and at that moment—in the full summer of 1529

—even though he does not grasp the truth, Wolsey's career is ended.

The fifth act is no more than the lamentable winding up of all these earlier triumphs now ruined and all these later perplexities. It lasts for rather more than a year, during which Thomas Cromwell, the ablest man in Wolsey's service, exhibits a false devotion and betrays him.

From that midsummer of 1529 to the late autumn or early winter of 1530, the agony proceeds. Those sixteen months are a mere succession of Wolsey's desperation, destitution, failing efforts at recovery, illness, exile, and end.

To the last he intrigues. Even after he had been allowed to go north, to his Archbishopric of York, he was trying to keep strings of his own in his hands, and to play somewhat with the foreign powers and with the Papacy, who no longer heeded him; the habit of a lifetime was too strong. His health had broken; his last weakness was upon him; while his body thus failed the blow fell. He was suspected or discovered, all his combined enemies who had been so long at work were pulling him back to imprisonment, trial and perhaps execution.

He was summoned to return to London as a prisoner. He was mercifully released on the journey down south to the presence of the man he had so well served and so long governed. He broke down altogether under the roof of the Augustinian Priory in Leicester and there he died and there was buried, and there the curtain fell for the last time and the lights are extinguished.

.   .   .   .

After that tragedy, and by a dreadful irony, on account of its most brilliant moments, on account of that

very success, that summit of power which he had enjoyed to such extremity and which had lured him on to
his doom—Wolsey dead became the creator of all that
Wolsey living had worked to prevent or had ignored.

The very man, Thomas Cromwell, whom he had
picked out for service in suppressing the few small
monasteries, through his training and example supplanted him and became the destroyer of all the monasteries in England. That consolidation of the civil and
ecclesiastical power which he had so triumphantly
affected became the model for an irresistible tyranny
which destroyed in England that very pivot of Wolsey's
own station and ambition, the Papal rule. All that closely
woven fabric of international play, with England exercising her considerable part, was torn to shreds and
thrown aside, and the England which Wolsey left behind
sank out of Europe.

He was indeed dead and he had indeed failed; but it
was more than death and it was more than failure—it
was the negation and contradiction of his own mighty
labours; by his own act they were reversed, and he was
proved, in his own despite, the author of their undoing.

IV

THE CAST

The Chief Actor

WE MUST carry with us some picture of what Wolsey was when he entered into the fullness of public life (1510). It is a picture that should remain with us during the more than 18 years of his activity; for he was already in mature manhood, thirty-seven,[1] and of build, temperament and physical constitution upon which the succeeding years leading into middle age do not, with such, make any great change. Indeed, until his last illness (the worst effects of which were sudden enough, but the seeds of which may have been laid as early as the summer of 1529) Wolsey stands throughout the same strongly marked and vivid personality which has impressed itself upon the historical imagination of his countrymen. What he then was, in 1510, at the court of the young King, so many years his junior, that he remained almost to the end.

He was full in body, even stout, with a grandeur of carriage which impressed itself upon all who met him, and seems to have had about it nothing exaggerated or affected, but to have proceeded from the very midst of the man. He was genial at home, always animated and even perhaps on occasion witty, certainly jovial in all moments of relaxation. The hearty companionship which he could extend at will to those whom it suited him to please was the foundation upon which his power over the big lad reposed. Thereon did he securely build, at the outset, advice; later the growing habit of acting with, then for, and then in the place of the King: until at last it

[1] See note A, at the end of this book.

was he who ruled, and the other that watched, commented upon and admired him ruling.

The defect in him, which was the cause of his strength, was a furious but sustained and level intensity in the triple desire to govern others, to be eminent beyond all others, and to accumulate about him the varied emblems of splendour.

It was an appetite which grew by what it fed on. It was the product of opportunity.

It is most strange to note how devoid of any inordinate ambition is all the earlier half of his life; indeed up to an age when most men with a great desire to achieve have already accomplished their achievement or at the least thoroughly founded it. Yet his was no example of a talent waking late or of a function fulfilled when use for it arose. It was a mastering passion which did not possess him till it came suddenly, with his first considerable employment, his first taste of handling men and material in great masses and of command. It was something he had never known till he was given the organisation of the Spanish Expedition in his fortieth year. Till then he had been eager for minor preferments, he had pushed his fortunes, he had served the powerful well: but none had found him masterful. Then all changed: and the threefold appetite, for sway, for fame and for magnificence blazed up.

On this account did he show himself implacable in detail to all who opposed, or might have opposed, or seemed within any distance of opposing even the least of his designs. Therefore one by one did he accumulate the enmities of so many that at last one may say there was none to stand by him except such minor intimates as were either too loyal or too incompetent to take advantage of his fall.

On this account also did he attempt—for many years successfully—to stand wholly superior to all others. He depressed rivals great and small. He would have no subordinates, but only servants or mouthpieces. He created no hierarchy of office at the summit of which to stand. He had no marshals.

On this account, again, did he revel in costliness and beauty of apparel, furniture and ornament. York House was gallery upon gallery of stuffs and precious metals, like a museum of such luxuries. His servants, the beasts on which he rode in pageant, were a blaze of gold trappings upon crimson grounds. On this account he indulged in the daring expense of such men, building: the building of palaces to express and perpetuate his name. In this alone has he proved permanent.

In connection with that defect of permanent ambitions, there went what always accompanies it, a sort of forgetfulness of what time can do, a sort of illusion that what was would continue for ever. It is so with the vital. And vitality was his chief mark. He dominated men continually by a combination of energy and rapid thought, which his physical presence strongly sustained: his large firm face (wherein the blemish of a drooping eyelid was forgotten) and his decided voice.

Would that we had better record of that voice! How it would have helped us to understand! I can conceive it to have been not acute nor overdeep, but of a full rolling sort and very soon informed with the habit of command. I cannot doubt that it was exactly consonant to all his bearing and effect upon those upon whom his presence came. And the whole physical result of speech,

gesture, figure, decision, is summed in the phrase of
Acciauoli, who met him in Amiens during the embassy
to Francis not long before the end and who spoke of
"that talk, bearing and manner of affairs which mean a
large and enterprising mind," and added "I do not
remember to have seen since the days of Alexander VI
anyone who filled his office so majestically."

All this, in the days of his highest exaltation, his exceptional towering double office of Vice-King and Vice-
Pope—Chancellor, that is, chief and only acting Royal
Minister, Legate of the Holy See—rendered him over-
powering; but to these must also be added real and
worthy forces not dependent upon the effect of presence
or office, the forces of industry and intelligence.

Industry and intelligence he possessed and exercised
on quite another plane from those who surrounded him.
That he had not vision I must repeat continually, it is the
key to his failure and to his producing what he had never
intended to produce; but intelligence for dealing with
the problem immediately to his hand, that he had and
worked supremely.

Yet lack of vision is a fatal thing to those who govern.
It is not lack of judgment. Judgment is a sense of proportion in the elements of a problem, and a good estimate
of cause and effect. Vision is much rarer and much more
valuable. It is a perception of things distant in time or
place. It was Wolsey's lack of vision which made him
fail in all his efforts of his foreign policy, save in so far as
they made him grander at home. It was from lack of
vision that he was duped by Charles and by Francis, by
Clement VII, and even by old Maximilian in his day. It
was lack of vision that forbade him to see into the depths
of any mind—especially the mind of a woman. Through

this came his capital blunder on Anne's power over the King, which destroyed him. And it was lack of vision which forbade him to grasp the magnitude of the religious upheaval among the Germans.

As for industry, which is the necessary life blood of great administration, he had it up to the limits of possibility. He had it as Burleigh had it, as Richelieu had it, as Bismarck had it, as Napoleon had it, as Thomas Cromwell who betrayed him had it. It is a rare function, is industry upon this level. It is found attached to characters base and noble, to the mean and the generous, the dense and the most perceptive. He had it to the full, and without it no man can achieve that kind of greatness.

This dominating quality in him was best seen in the council: there he was not only master, but as it were an incarnation of the assembly; so that his colleagues melted into being but parts of his will and their signature to the unanimous advices were but copies of his own; but this unanimity we must also remember was conventional, it had by the early sixteenth century been for a lifetime a custom that the council should advise the King as a whole and with no divisions, not even on the most important matters, but with Wolsey in control the unity was real. It is a true miniature of Wolsey in action, that account which shows him clapping his hand down upon the table, and announcing his decisions with a perfunctory question to his colleagues that did not wait for an answer. But though the men around him felt themselves bullied they were also convinced. They knew in his presence a hundred things they had not known, they felt that he had been able to co-ordinate a mass of information whereof one or another only possessed disconnected fragments, and he would give his reasons, by which their minds were also drawn. Rancour against such mastery remained with them, and took its revenge when he fell, but it could not obliterate the memory of superior power; and when he had gone there was none to replace him.

He chose with skill the men who had to work for him; that is, though he had little penetration of character, he instinctively discovered those who were apt for the particular work he wanted done. To have great skill in that regard is rare, but that some measure of such skill should be accomplished by inability to understand character as a whole is common enough. One perpetually sees good householders picking out a butler first-rate at his business, but proving in the end dishonest. So through a whole list of Wolsey's agents you find just the talents required, but not one is really devoted to him. Even Gardiner, whom he sought out and made, takes his fallen master's place as a matter of course.

His limitations gave him a perpetual confidence in himself which was also no small part of his strength; but it would have been useless had it not been accompanied by great suppleness of mind. He could bend himself, even in age, to studying and supporting by flattery or friendship and acquiescence, any other person, however hitherto hostile, whom he thought necessary so to treat. We find that in all his dealings with the King for the better part of twenty years; we find that in his final ambiguous alliance with Anne Boleyn. The verdict which Shakespeare, if it be Shakespeare, has recorded upon his courtesy to inferiors is just. Those who were too low to affect his course were treated by him with close and generous attention. It is not right to say that this was only the emphasizing of the distinction that lay between them and himself, it is clear that his heart was in the matter; for when all the important men that he had formed and used abandoned him it was the unimportant ones who were still faithful. He gave the best proof of his character in the way in which in the midst of all business he was at pains for poor suitors in his court, and in the last months before his death his graciousness to them quite changed the people in the north to whom he came, and with whom his name had hitherto been odious. For we must always remember that a note of Wolsey's whole life was his intense and increasing unpopularity. As early as 1512 the soldiers curse him for being the author of their misfortunes; in all the succeeding years he is more and more the tax-gatherer and the inquisitor into men's affairs; and, after he had fallen, even such a man as Sir Thomas More delighted to record his opposition and called the broken Cardinal "a scabby sheep."

Of his lesser weaknesses that which most lessened him was a way of reducing all things to a personal issue. A great part of his motive for working ceaselessly against Charles V in the latter years was personal annoyance at the Emperor's having betrayed him over the last Papal election. He took personal revenge when he was all-powerful upon a man who had put him in the stocks during his obscure and perhaps riotous youth as a parish priest, and he showed a curiously persistent determination to "score." He would sacrifice points of policy to the satisfaction of a personal triumph. With this considerable foible went a rather absurd haste and clutch for money. He could never have too much of it. He got it by every means, he put pressure upon those to whom he could give official favours, and as often as not they had to buy them. He was so eager in this pursuit that he made no concealment of it. Perhaps the most comic instance is his perpetual fussing about the revenues of the Bishopric of Tournai which he had been promised, and which it was very difficult to get paid, because Tournai was never really his. Indeed his collector there was excommunicated, which did not help matters.

In his advance to power he was without restraint and may have been guilty of murder. In his exercise of it he deliberately ruined those who might be rivals, however worthless—such as Suffolk: or had them put to death as in the case of Buckingham.

His religion was upon the pattern of his position and time. It is not true to say that it was mere convention; he was devoted to the external Church, and at the end of his life he certainly prepared well for death; but he never felt, he never expressed to another, regard for the perilous contradiction between the then common life of a great worldly Prelate and the express doctrine and discipline of the Catholic Church. A Cardinal and a Bishop who makes the brother of his mistress his confessor and who finds nothing strange in that relation, who says his Mass regularly as a matter of course in spite of such relationships, in spite of avarice, in spite of violent worldly aims, explains to us what the Church had become upon the eve of its great peril. Gardiner, when he came to die, said of himself (remembering his services to the King and the schism) "I denied as Peter did, but I have not wept as Peter wept." In other words he repented.

I have said that Wolsey made a good death and so he did; and yet it is difficult to use of him the word "repent." There was perhaps in his view nothing to repent of. He had lived as men of his sort then lived. He had served his Prince; the paradoxical union of duty and ambition troubled him no more than it has troubled thousands of other lesser men of the kind. How all this affected his fate when he had got rid of this world and came to greater things we do not know.

I have said little of his passion for building, because it was not peculiar to him: it was common to all the great of his time. But one indirect result it had of profound effect. To build the colleges he had planned, and particularly the great Oxford foundation, he suppressed certain small monasteries and took their revenues and lands. Thereby he trained the men, he set the example, he inaugurated the policy which ended in a prodigious economic Revolution: the greatest England has ever known. The dissolution of all monasteries after his death, and the distribution of their lands among the new adventurers and the old families was what made the restoration of Catholicism in England impossible. It was the foundation of that complete change in English religion, that transformation of the English mind at the Reformation, which to Wolsey was inconceivable.

Hampton Court, which is the most famous monument to his love of externals, he had in mind from the very beginning of his advance, in the first months of 1514. He signed the lease of the site, holding it for 99 years of the Knights Hospitallers, at a ground rent of over £1,000 a year. He began to build at once, and in about two years had it fit for beginning to live in part of it. It is a very good living record of the sums which were passing through his hands even in that very earliest part of his career. They were evidently far larger than what could be accounted for by his official endowments.

Towards the end of that career he gave the great palace to the King, but there is some difficulty in saying exactly when the transaction took place. Wolsey was living there till the end of 1528, that is, up to the very beginning of his last troubles which came with the divorce. Yet as early as 1521 he writes to the King of Hampton Court as "your manor." You find Henry living in Hampton Court as though it were his own, but then you find Wolsey living in it again, even close up to the end of the abortive Legatine Court in the summer of 1529. What seems to have happened was this (and there are parallels to it in other parts of Europe and in later dates of history when a great ecclesiastic had accumulated too great a fortune): he made over the palace directly to the King (who was of course ultimately overlord) at least before the middle of 1525, that is, rather more than ten years after he had begun building it. For in that year the joke was made by the Imperial envoy "that having given his house and all his furniture to the King he might say 'Here is a sucking pig from your own sow's litter, which pray take as my humble gift'." As much as saying that Wolsey had only grown rich through the King's bounty. It is not until after the Cardinal had been exiled to Esher that the King began to treat Hampton Court as entirely his own.

But in connection with Hampton Court there is one interesting little point to be noted, something which I think is very much in Wolsey's favour: in favour of his intelligence, in favour of his imagination. He had a violent superstition against the name of Kingston. He would not go through Kingston if he could help it. Now that superstition must have been a strong one, for it forced him to make a detour unless he went by water.

HAMPTON COURT PALACE

For the straightest road to London and from the Court would have led him across Kingston bridge. We shall find that superstition meeting him again at the end.

HENRY VIII, THE KING

What struck contemporaries most in the matter of the King, the man upon whom Wolsey's whole life depended, by whose power he ruled and through whose final disfavour he fell, was his physical appearance, especially in youth. He was exceptional in his rank, which of its nature may have any kind of man within it, hearty or feeble, big or small. Moreover the inbreeding of royalty rendered his hearty bearing, his early strength and stature, and breadth of shoulder, his excellence at sport and riding something exceptional. All through the first third of his reign and nearly to the end of the first half even hostile observers dwell upon that mark in him. Though he was struck by disease early, it did not affect his character or his frame for some time.

He had contracted syphilis; but his vigorous constitution fought the results for long. The first effect was seen in the perpetual miscarriages of his wife (though it is true that she was of far less vigorous blood than he) and still more in his children, upon the cause of whose abnormalities modern medical research appears agreed. It is partly due to this that Henry seems almost a different person in the later part of his life from what he was in the beginning of it. He becomes callous, excessively irritable, as coarse in mind as he grew gross in body. The change came when, at his own volition, after the first ten years of his marriage he lost the companionship of Catherine. But whether in his earlier and healthier phase, or in his later diseased and at last disgusting one, certain mental characteristics run consistently through the changes and mental deterioration in his character, and to understand these the essential is to study the nature of his will.

Henry's was not the will of a man principally impulsive. Impulsive he was, and unstable. Yet instability was not his leading character. It was a result of another weakness—the inability to master himself. His will was not the will of an indolent man. His physical exercises were continual, and so was his reading and attention to details of State put before him. The key to the anomalies of Henry's will is this: it was the will of a man permanently immature; concerned, as are the immature, with immediate objects alone, and those objects individual always and usually mere appetites.

It was not a weak will in the sense that it collapsed in the face of opposition—on the contrary, opposition inflamed it and it had to be flattered; but it was a will not excited to action save by some pressing feeling of the moment concerned with nothing grander nor more permanent than enjoyment—in the extended sense of the word enjoyment. Often this will was exercised at its greatest pressure for some merely physical enjoyment, sometimes for a pageantry, or a diversion by night at Court; sometimes it would be exerted for a larger object, the satisfaction of revenge or the assuagement of a peevish ill-humour born of offended vanity, but there is hardly a case in which we find it externalised as it were, directed to objects which are those of society or of the State or even of the dynasty—save as the dynasty was represented by himself. There is hardly a case in which you can follow a plan of which Henry's will is the initiator and the constant promoter to its conclusion. In the breach with the Papacy there is nothing of the kind:

KING HENRY VIII
From the Portrait by Holbein
Drawn by William Derby and
Engraved by T. A. Dean

he is led on the whole time by others. In domestic and ecclesiastical legislation there is nothing of the kind. In the relations between the English Crown and the continental states there is nothing of the kind, he is then wholly in a minister's hands. Where any plan seems consecutive it is always somebody else's and this leads us to consider the most striking effect which Henry's temperament produced upon the political history of his time: I mean the successive abandonment of initiative to others and the sharp and sudden catastrophe in which each such delegation of power concludes.

In very early youth he is strongly influenced by his wife; next, everything passes into the hands of Wolsey, and during all those years when a man is entering maturity and should most exercise his own powers this Renaissance King with no limit to what he might do of himself leaves all to another; he does not neglect public business, on the contrary he is assiduous in it, he listens to arguments and he suggests. He is interested and he is active, but it does not concern him to control, still less to originate.

He allows himself to be managed, he stands in some dread of his manager. He shirks conflict with him even when his sense of dependence grows severe. There follows what invariably follows in characters of this kind, a crisis in which the superior will guiding his own has piled up too large a weight of dominion over him, provokes, at last, such resentment against the sense of intimate subjection as is intolerable. The rider is shaken in the saddle once and again, irrationally, as in a fit of temper. Then there is an outburst of rage, and the rider is violently thrown. It happened with Catherine, it happened with Wolsey, it happened with Anne, it happened with Cromwell.

The saddle does not remain empty long, another rider succeeds, and another. When Catherine's indirect gentle and steady manipulation had been dropped Wolsey succeeded. When Wolsey's overmastering activities were leading him to ruin, Anne Boleyn took control. It was she who devised and Henry who fulfilled her plans. There follows resentment to that in its turn; the object of the resentment is put to death. Cromwell, the ally of Anne Boleyn, succeeds to complete power. It is hardly a Ministry, it is another delegation of the kingly authority into the hands of one subject. Then comes, more conspicuous than on the earlier occasions, the regular process of irksomeness, resentment, a violent reaction, and the destruction of the offending mastery by the death of him who exercised it.

We have a sharp direct index to Henry's insufficiency when we consider the attitude women adopted towards him after he had lost the steady companionship of Catherine. They are in terror of his power, yet they make a fool of him when once they have become familiar with his nature. He was as absurdly amative as he was defective: a very butt for women and the more did they mock him. The story of Anne Boleyn holding him on a leash for years, then indicted for every sort of adultery, including incest before his very eyes under his own roof, is repeated in the still greater contempt shown for him by Catherine Howard, by the willing absence of Anne of Cleves, by the nagging (and theological at that) of Catherine Parr, who, on the instant of his death, takes up at once with his brother-in-law.

One instance or even two of ludicrous misfortune in

such affairs might be explained by the vivacity of the
ladies rather than by the character of their mate, but a
whole succession of them is too much for such an explanation. The truth is that men so easily led by their
imperfection in sex, so easily captured, are also men easily
despised. And we have good tests of Henry's lack of
stamina in all this, none of which is more characteristic
than his wretched public tears on hearing of his misfortunes and his absurd proclamation forbidding men to
talk in taverns about his matrimonial troubles. Let it be
noted with all this that Henry never risked his body in
a fight. The reputation of Francis I for high courage in
the press of battle, leading charges, was one cause of
his jealousy.

It is true that for the last seven years of his life Henry,
suffering the final effects of his disease and half maddened by the mixture of disappointment, blind power,
appetite and the betrayal his insufficiency had suffered
at the hands of women, does not again let any one person
take the helm. But the essential of the thing remains.
He is still swayed by the nearest force about him, he
can still be managed and is managed by those who see a
little farther, desire ultimate things, and pursue their
objects steadily. At last the Seymours rule, and particularly his eldest brother-in-law Edward who mainly con-
trols, and maintains himself to the end. It is true that the
King was no longer under one hand and even in his
last Testament he attempts to check the power that his
brother-in-law might have after his death. Still he cannot act alone; and that other will at his side is sufficient
to achieve its ends. It procures the condemnation of the
Howards, it secures the Regency.

An exception may be found in the policy of Henry

towards Scotland. It is continuous and it is his own. But even here the action is personal, it is a family affair, and though continuous, it is capricious. It has a central principle running through it, the subjection of the northern kingdom to the supremacy of the southern: a principle inherited from his predecessors through the centuries; yet it is not of one piece—for he destroys with his own hand and for one personal, almost domestic, reason, the chance of uniting the two kingdoms under one head.

The talents of Henry must not be underestimated upon the ground that they were misused; thrown away upon personal objects, when they should have served his office and the state. His vanity and unbalance, his lack of self-control, his irrational fits of temper hurt the use of his talents, but those talents were remarkable. He could and did carry in his head a considerable mass of detail, and even in his last days, when the worst and fullest effects of his corrupting disease were upon him, that talent persisted. He was multifarious in contrivance, as we see especially in the ceaseless string of suggestions and counter-suggestions during the manœuvring for the divorce. He was fairly gifted in the art of drafting a document—a rare thing in rulers, commoner in their servants. The best example of this is of course the memorandum by which he duped and betrayed the Pilgrimage of Grace. But there are many others, such as the recasting of Cranmer's hortatory letter preceding the divorce. It is also in connection with Cranmer that some have thought they could discern another faculty in Henry, the right selection of agents. They are wrong. All the agents which we know to have been of Henry's own choosing after Wolsey's power was shaken are inferior.

Cranmer came from the Boleyns. It was they and especially Anne, who had had experience of a character suited to do her work: a man at once servile and well instructed.

Of lesser aptitudes all Henry's contemporaries noted, and we can still admire, an incongruous group whose only common source was the early education he had received, when he was destined for the Church. He was something of a musician, he was a passable theologian, he was a good linguist. He had excelled in youth at much requiring skill above strength; he rode well, he played tennis well. He could even write and speak, for though he may have been helped with his theological disquisitions, they are lucid and in good order and some of his angrier outbursts make good reading. He had the power of expression, and, without wit, he had raciness of language, some humour, a good use of idiom in speech.

Among the weaknesses of Henry's character we must note an odd incapacity for handling money. He was the sort of man who in private life would have been perpetually out at elbows, and in the great part he had to play he was startlingly incompetent in the use of what must always be the chief instrument of such a part; for political power can only act continuously and permanently through money.

The blame falls in some degree to the vast expenditure of Wolsey upon foreign policy while Henry was still young, a man in the late twenties and early thirties. The spectacle of these huge sums, the experience that it was possible to raise them, the ease with which they were expended, all struck Henry at that moment in life when he would be most impressed by them. But it is mainly his own defect, that, to the day of his death, he squandered pitifully. He stands here in such abrupt contrast with his father that the example might belong to two men of different blood. This spendthrift character does not appear in particularly high Court expenses. It appears rather in his inability to keep the stuff within his fingers, and this impotence of his was profoundly to affect the future of England.

The monastic and other Church endowments which he looted were dissipated, as to two-thirds of them, in the course of less than twenty years. Not only was he always so pressed for money that he sold the confiscated land and goods hurriedly at inferior prices, but he gambled much away, he gave much away, he allowed much to be filched by his subordinates, and it is directly his fault that the English Crown became impoverished, lost its economic power to the gentry, and was by them in a little more than a century devoured. Henry's orgy of loot was hardly in full swing before 1540; Charles the first was put to death in 1649.

Nor had Henry the excuse, as had his successors, of a ruinous and continuous rise in prices. The loss of the purchasing power of money due to the flood of precious metals from the New World was only just beginning to affect prices in England in the very last years of his reign. It was effective under Mary and became ruinous under Elizabeth. Yet Henry, apart from the squandering of the Church lands, debased the coinage, repeatedly and without recovery.

In religion he was genuinely devout: it is the best thing about him. He rigidly maintained the full faith he had inherited. He was determined that his country should not lose it. He had a special veneration for the Real Presence in the Blessed Sacrament and for the

Blessed Virgin Mary. Rather than not kneel in the Presence of the Sacrament of the altar he risked his health in his last years.

Go to Walsingham, whither he had himself gone on Pilgrimage, and see the gaunt broken archway still standing of what was once a great shrine in Europe. Henry ruined it for gain. But as he died he recommended his soul to Our Lady of Walsingham.

CATHERINE OF ARAGON

Catherine of Aragon, the Queen and second figure in the drama, is better understood through her simplicity than through any other characteristic. It was to her disadvantage in her early efforts to order the State during the first four years when she was fully in control of her young husband. It was wholly to her advantage in the final struggle.

She was a short, fair woman, squat even in youth and tending to become fat after her thirtieth year, equable in temper and perpetually seen in smiles. Tact she never attained or attempted. With more of that quality she might have prolonged her husband's subjection to her. She had great manners, of course, for she came from the very heart of what was most dignified in Europe, the houses of Aragon and Castile. She had all the courage of her famous mother Isabella, none of the astuteness of her father. She had no pretence to beauty, such charm as she possessed was no more than the charm of youth, it passed with youth. Nor was there (as one might imagine with so great a woman in so exalted a station) a natural sympathy, if only bred of conventional courtesy and breeding, between her and those whom she met.

Her sense of duty was as firm as the rest of her, and her general firmness all noticed and admired. She decided quickly, once and for all, in every main cause of her life. She had the fixed will of the placid, and, in the three or four matters upon which her life turned, an iron sense of right. It was this that caused her to bear so faithfully and with so much sorrow those difficult middle years when Henry was leaving her, though the last years of complete abandonment and betrayal were supported rather by her sense of rank and what was due to it. There was no trace in her of that nervous weakness which in her sister's case ended in madness. But her health, ruined by such a husband, was early destroyed and she died too young, barely over fifty, with a constitution broken down long before.

A character so straight, so free from all complexity, grasping so strongly those few main principles which for her were the whole of life, was wholly unfitted for negotiation. Had she been better fitted for it she might have conquered the plot which Anne Boleyn her rival had laid against her. She was all "yes" and "no"; and unless a situation could be explained to her in the shortest terms, she could not see the outlines of it. If it were in any way multiple or complex she could not deal with it at all.

Twice in her life she was duped and saved in spite of herself. When her cynical father-in-law, Henry VII, got her to write to her parents suggesting the incredible marriage with himself, when she had been left a nominal widow on the death of his own son, her mother Isabella saved her. Once again, when her enemies tried to use her against herself and to make her write to Charles V for the original Brief of dispensation (which, if ever it had got into England would certainly have been destroyed), her nephew, the Emperor, saved her.

She never learnt English properly, yet she never did anything to offend the English people, and she was extremely popular, especially with the Londoners; though her affections remained Spanish, she was always loyal to the crown she wore.

There was only one phase in her life during which her simplicity and lack of judgment risked her dignity. It was in those five years between the death of the boy, Prince Arthur, when she was not seventeen, and her marriage with his brother just after his accession. During those years, in the loneliness of her exile, in the detestable company of her father-in-law, the victim of perpetual bargaining between that father-in-law and her own father, Ferdinand, she so clung to the only friend she had, her Spanish confessor, that there was danger of a scandal. Such a scandal would have been unjust, but the episode illuminates the emptiness of her youth.

Some years of happiness she had, perhaps half a dozen, between her crowning and the beginning of her trials. They profoundly affected her; they became a memory with her; the more cruel to her was the neglect and desertion that followed.

Her religion, steadfast and unchanged, austere, fixed, as was everything about her, sustained her at the end.

It was her inflexibility of purpose and of standard which more than any other factor decided the great business of the English schism, of her husband's breach with Rome. Had she yielded, England would be Catholic today. Her unswerving honour led her to that ignominy in which she died; and the symbol, I think, of her complete isolation is that too simple slab of dark stone which marked her grave in Peterborough, without so much as a name on it, for three centuries. Today the name is indeed inscribed but there is nothing more: no monument of any kind; no mark that here lies buried the woman upon whose determination turned the transformation of England, and the daughter of such mighty kings.

ANNE BOLEYN

Nearly all those who play a considerable part in history owe as much to circumstance as to their individual powers. So it was with Anne Boleyn. We must keep continuously in mind the essential point that she was a Howard. That alone does not even begin to explain her. So was her wanton and futile little cousin Catherine who followed her to the block a Howard, but if Anne Boleyn had not been a Howard the whole story would have been different and Anne could never have assumed the part she played. It is the neglect of her Howard connection which has misled so many in their judgment of the King's aberration and its consequence.

The Howards were semi-royal, they represented the Plantagenet line from Thomas of Brotherton, the younger son of Edward I, whom his brother had made Earl Marshal, an office which the head of the Howards exercises to this day. Thomas' line had ended in an heiress whose claim to the Marshalship and the Royal tradition passed to the Mowbrays. The Mowbrays had ended in an heiress who had married the first Howard of any conspicuous position. But in spite of this double passage of the descent through women, the tradition was still of the greatest effect. Howard took on the title of Earl Marshal, his son was given the then Royal title of

Duke, coupling with it patent of Norfolk. He and his descendants were much more than the first peers of the realm, much more than Earls Marshal of England; they were a branch of the Plantagenet tree, and men thought of them as of something separate from the mass of subjects, even the greatest.

In a fashion the Howards were senior to the Tudors; for though the Tudors had confirmed themselves also by a Plantagenet marriage, yet they were of very base blood and always nervous of their position. The Howards were certain of theirs.

Anne Boleyn's father Thomas Boleyn, was the son of a successful merchant who had retired from a business inherited from *his* father, a Lord Mayor of London; but Thomas Boleyn was descended on the mother's side from the great Irish family of Ormonde. Thomas Boleyn had sufficient talent to be useful in public affairs, but it was not from him that Anne derived the qualities she wore in the eyes of her contemporaries, it was from her mother. For Boleyn's wealth had been such as to permit his marrying Elizabeth Howard, the daughter of the victor of Flodden and the sister of that Thomas, third Duke, who was so great a figure at Henry's court, who was the challenger and hater of the upstarts, and whom the King himself secretly felt to be a rival. And real rivalry there was between the Howards and the Tudors right on until the chief of the new millionaires under Elizabeth, Cecil, saw to it that the fourth Duke should be put to death and end such rivalry for ever.

When, therefore, Henry Tudor became entangled in Anne Boleyn's net he could plead to himself inwardly that he was not looking too low. The grotesque spectacle of such an infatuation led men to exaggerate the differ-

ence between them. It was in reality no great gulf.
Henry, in his abandonment of his first and Royal wife,
of the high line of Aragon, degraded himself sufficiently
in the eyes of those about him, but he had not yet taken
the step which he could and did take later when he had
turned despot and chose a Seymour. He had not taken
a subject at random. He had made something of an
alliance.

As to Anne let us get her picture.

Bald above the eyes, lacking in brows, and with a
stupid but very obstinate mouth, flat chested, with a long
thin neck, not too upright in carriage, she has not left a
word of wit or warmth or personality whereby she may
be remembered. What a wretched lanky pin on which
to hang the destiny of the Christian world! Who would
have said, watching her ungainliness and silence in the
throng of the Court, even though he were noting Henry's
inability to remove his eyes from her, that this figure
would unloose such a change in England? Yet there was
that about her—what we know not, because such subtle
things cannot be recorded—there was that about her
which caught those men, though a hundred others would
pass her by without recognition. Hardly had she come
to England from her education in France when Wyatt
was caught and Percy—then the King. It was perhaps
a calculated momentary gesture of sympathy, when she
thought such a gesture worth her while (Wyatt complained that she solicited him before the Royal opportunity came along). It was perhaps a calculated glance
from the bald brow and dark, probably intriguing eyes.
It was perhaps her voice, of which we have no record
that I know. Her speech was French and her manners
those of the French court—perhaps that counted.

ANNE BOLEYN
From the Portrait by Holbein
Engraved by E. Scriven

Whatever it was, she flew for high game.

One most illuminating point in the miserable relations between Henry and Anne is the incomprehensibility of it to all contemporaries; the woman was no longer young, especially as youth was counted in those days; she was twenty-seven,[1] certainly not beautiful, and apparently slightly deformed in one hand, and before she got her way and admitted Henry, under the certitude of being Queen, she was thirty-two; while it is the very nature of these oddities in the business of violent and merely physical attraction that they are so often incomprehensible to outsiders. That her dark eyes fascinated, all would admit; for the rest she seemed rather repellent, and perhaps the beginning of her double chin was the most healthy thing about her.

Yet, as we have just seen, she had already shown the capacity for catching and holding a man; she had certainly caught and held Wyatt, he wrote verses to prove it; so she had young Percy, and years after they had been pushed apart at Henry's command and with Wolsey as his agent in 1522 he still spoke with passion of the memory.

She does not seem to have had modesty. She would insult when she felt herself secure, and she early acquired a fair number of enemies. Yet she would conquer.

What she probably had—but that is just one of those negative things which exasperates us in history because of their nature positive evidence is absent—was an ability—when she chose to exercise it—to be as silent as death and as fixed in purpose, in spite of physical inclinations.

It went with all the rest of her; it was part and parcel of that astonishing capacity of hers (until she was struck

[1] See Note F at end of this book.

by the Furies after her first childbirth) which gave her that extraordinary self-control whereby she kept the King on tenterhooks for seven mortal years.

Now strength of this sort in a woman who is ensnaring a man is a weapon of the first class; it at once entices, intrigues and enslaves, and by ever so little a relaxation here and there it enhances indefinitely the power the woman possesses over her victim. He must on such occasions think that for him alone out of all possible men there are occasional distant promises of favour. It flatters his vanity as much as it urges his passion.

She never slipped, she never wavered, she had full command of the situation from the beginning, not indeed until the very end, but from the beginning until Henry had been fully satisfied, until the coming of her child was certain, and until his anger at his own wretched servitude had turned into that exasperation which was at last to bring her to a violent and contemptible death.

Thomas Howard
Third Duke of Norfolk

Thomas Howard, third Duke of Norfolk and second Earl of Surrey, was the first and most pertinacious of Wolsey's enemies, and triumphed with the triumph of his niece Anne Boleyn, the daughter of his sister.

He was a small spare man with black hair, astute, curiously ambitious of leadership, which he was incapable of exercising, even when he possessed it. For, of the gifts required to replace or even to imitate so great a rival as Wolsey, he had none but tenacity. He was unscrupulous, he proved himself courageous. He had, as was fitting, a very high feeling for his rank, a feeling

exasperated by the disabilities of his youth. For though
to be a Howard was to be a semi-royalty, representing a
younger branch of the Plantagenets, yet the great family
had struggled since Bosworth with difficult and sometimes mean conditions.

When Richard III, last of the Plantagenets, was killed
at Bosworth and Henry VII usurped the throne, the first
Duke of Norfolk, who had fought with him in the battle, and, like his master, had been killed, was called a
traitor and his blood attainted. His son was kept
in prison three years, then released and allowed to call
himself Earl of Surrey but not Duke of Norfolk. He
was over forty when Bosworth was fought; it was as an
elderly man that he was admitted to the Court of
Henry VII and as an old man that he served young
Henry VIII.

All this had badly impoverished the Howards. The
daughters of this Surrey made comparatively small
marriages, none of them into the great families; one of
them, as we have seen, being given to Boleyn, the others
to Thomas Bryan, Sir Henry Wyatt and Rice.

The old man's victory at Flodden (he was seventy at
the time) earned him the restoration of the title. He was
called second Duke of Norfolk and he lived on until
nearly the end of Wolsey's famous seven years, dying in
1524. Then it was that the man with whom we have to
deal here, called Thomas like his father, became third
Duke of Norfolk. He was just over forty, and from
thence onwards filled the rôle of titular head of the old
nobility.

The impoverishment of the family still hampered him.
He had, what with his name on the one side and his early
embarrassments on the other, a sort of dual position

which strongly affected his character and accounts for most of his actions. It made him grasping, it made him unscrupulous, it spurred him to activity, it combined in himself so famous a title and lineage with the humiliations of his early years. To a man in such a mood the greatness of a small grazier's son risen suddenly through the Church, the despotic power of that "new man" to which he had to bow, were an irritant beyond bearing.

He had confirmed his position by a great marriage. As the grandson of the man who was the first support of the Plantagenets, he had been given the daughter of Edward IV for a wife; he was therefore brother-in-law to Henry VII and uncle to Henry VIII. He inherited his father's official posts. He had been present at Flodden with his father and had reported the capture of the Scottish artillery in a famous letter written in French from that field.

In the Council he chafed continually under Wolsey's pride. His ambition was to be head of that body, an ambition which was fulfilled on Wolsey's fall; but he was unable to fill the place for he was not of that stature. He stood continually behind his niece Anne Boleyn in her effort to reach the Crown and in her final duel with the Cardinal.

Those who do not allow sufficiently for the power of intrigue which Anne possessed, for her strength of purpose and capacity for holding out indefinitely, for her exact judgment in playing the fish she had hooked, tend to exaggerate Norfolk's rôle in the business. Some almost make him the author of it. That he certainly was not. But he was a powerful support for the woman whose first claim in that society was that, through her mother, she was a Howard.

He was not of a calibre to fill the stage even when the greatest parts were assigned to him on the Cardinal's fall; but what with his rank, his descent, his connections, the way in which the older nobility regarded him as their symbol, he counted for more than, as a personality, he was worth. And his determined and tireless hatred stands high in the factors which combined to drag Wolsey down at the end.

CHARLES BRANDON
DUKE OF SUFFOLK

The Duke of Suffolk, the second figure of the pair who dog Wolsey's end, is a character so fascinating that I compress with regret my description of him into these few lines. Perhaps the most characteristic sentence written of him in modern times—a sentence not wholly accurate but very just—will help to introduce him. "He married five women, of whom the first was his aunt and the last was his daughter-in-law." He was handsome, he was specially and remarkably brave; and he was a lover as ready, eager, and, above all, successful as any man in that crowded story of the Renaissance amours.

From the earliest years of his hot youth to the end of his exceedingly active life he is for ever risking his addresses and nearly always triumphing. There was something in his personality which had this effect. To the old nobility he seemed an upstart. He was of good territorial stock, but no more; his grandfather being a knight who had served under Henry VII before that adventurer captured the throne. His father had been standard-bearer to Henry VII at Bosworth and on this account had been singled out and killed in the battle by Richard III. Charles must have been born before that date but probably not long before; he was therefore of much the same age as Queen Catherine and some six years older than the King.

Tall, upstanding, quite unscrupulous, stout in build and agile and comely, with fair beard and, as it would seem, humorous eyes, he pushes, elbows, struts, marches through the crowd of the time. He was impetuous in battle, he led the assault on one of the gates of Tournai and captured it: he was as impetuous in making hot love to Margaret of Savoy, the Regent of the Low Countries, to whom he had been sent for the negotiation of a treaty. It seems to have been because it was believed that she would stoop to marry him that Henry gave him the semi-royal title of Duke; at any rate, after some fairly violent flirtation she was shamed out of it—and all the while he had two other wives alive, one of them that Mary Brandon whom some called his aunt, and who was at least his cousin.

His impudence was enormous. We shall see how when the young widowed Queen of France, Henry's sister, insisted upon marrying him he might have lost his head; how Wolsey saved him, and how he showed his gratitude —for he also was in at the death and a leader of the pack.

Leo X

Three Popes cover the period of Wolsey's active control over English foreign affairs. A fourth, Julius II, was on the throne when he first entered public life, and was the centre of that policy which produced Henry's early expeditions to France wherein Wolsey was so considerably employed. But it was not Wolsey, in those early years before 1513, who decided what the alliances and enmities of the English throne on the continent should be; it was the Council at large, to some extent the boy King's own caprice, and very largely—much more than is usually recognised—the influence then very strong upon him of his Spanish wife. Julius II died just at the moment when the first state of affairs in the reign was turning over and Wolsey was beginning to direct; for he died in 1513; and from 1513 to Wolsey's fall in 1529 three names distinguish the Papacy. First that of Leo X, next that of Adrian VI, lastly that of Clement VII, who long outlived the Cardinal.

Of these three, Adrian's reign was so short (unhappily) that it is barely more than an interruption to the two long reigns between which it falls. Leo X ruled for eight years, from early 1513 to his death at the very end of 1521. Adrian, only elected in the first days of 1522, died at the end of the summer of 1523. Clement VII, who succeeded him, is Pope during all the remainder of Wolsey's career and for some years after Wolsey's death.

What we are really dealing with, therefore, as a consecutive influence throughout the period, the Papacy with which Wolsey was directly and ceaselessly concerned, was the Papacy of Leo X and Clement VII.

Now the essential mark of these two reigns was that they were a family affair, and the family of which they were an affair was the immensely rich merchant Medicis of Florence.

Clement VII was first cousin to Leo X, was not only first cousin but also bound up with him in as close and intense a family feeling as could be found in Europe. The Medicean bond was of this intimacy and strength from the nature of the Medicean tyranny: the way in which the family had arrived at power and the way in which it maintained power in the Republic of Florence.

It had arrived at power because violent city democracies can only end in Caesarism. Someone would have been Caesar anyhow, at the end of the factions, but what made the Medicis absolute was money. Their position was one of the very rare examples of mere money dominating life before these our modern times, in which it is for the moment supreme. They were of no territorial lineage: wealth (combined of course with the adventurous spirit among them and with energy) had made them what they were. Their hold was never perfectly secure; their title they knew, and all the world knew, to be insufficient; yet their ambition had come to be a tradition with them, as it was also their condition of survival.

It was all this which bound the Medici clan together. Therefore did the two successive Medici Popes act rather like an elder and a younger brother than like two cousins. Giulio Medici was the right hand of Leo during the latter's Pontificate, managing everything, and regarded as a sort of Vice-Gerent. When he himself came into power not two years after Leo's death, it was but a continuation of a briefly interrupted sequence.

Of a hundred vivid events which illustrate the closely knit unity between the two men, let one suffice: the famous scene in the Cathedral of Florence on the Easter Sunday of 1477. Lorenzo the Magnificent, tyrant of the Republic and princely patron of the arts, was at Mass in the Cathedral of Florence with his brother Guliano. Conspiracy against the rule of these millionaires was ready to break into flame. At the Elevation of the Host, as the signal, the conspirators rose; the huge building was filled with clamour and tumult, the brothers fled through the struggling mob, Lorenzo just escaping, stabbed to death

before he reached the Sacristy door by which he would
have fled. On that day little John, the great Lorenzo's
son, was a child of three years old.

Guliano's mistress, whom he had perhaps intended to
marry and with whom he lived openly as a wife, was
with child and about to give birth to that posthumous
boy who was to be baptised Giulio. The child John,
Lorenzo's son, was the future Leo X; the baby about to
be born Guliano's bastard son, was the future Clement
VII. Such was the community of origin: one strand in
the strong bond between them. Such episodes form the
background of a Papal policy wherein Florence and the
supremacy of the Medicis therein came first, to the lasting hurt of the Christian world.

For the succession of Clement VII to Leo X, the occu-
pation of these thirty years and more by one Medicean
interest on the throne at Rome, was fatally contemporary
with the bursting of the Reformation storm. It was Leo
who witnessed, failed to understand and neglected, the
original protest under Luther; Clement who failed to
compose that tempestuous quarrel arisen in the Germanies, who suffered the breakaway of England, and
who lived on almost to that decisive date when Calvin's
book appeared. Just when the Church most needed impartial and just guidance, wholly superior to persons and
their ambitions, the Church suffered the guidance of two
successive brothers, rather than cousins, of one family;
two men born, bred and steeped in the conceptions, not
of the Faith Universal, but of an Italian Principate.

Leo, the elder of the two, was born at the very end of
1475. He was therefore young for the office when elected
to the Papacy—only thirty-eight. He was Lorenzo's
second son, destined for the Church as a cadet, given the

highest culture of his time, and well fulfilling his father's hopes from such an education. His childhood and youth remain a standing example of the family spirit in which the Church was governed in that generation which fore-ran and produced explosion. He was loaded with abbeys and benefices under the control of the immense Medici fortune. He was only eight years old when the Pope gave him his first Abbey and made him Apostolic Protonotary as well. He was not nine when he got his second Abbey. He was little more than ten years old when he got his third—and it was no less a foundation than St. Benedict's and Monte Cassino! He was made a Cardinal at thirteen, and actually sat in the Consistory as a child of sixteen.

But though he was an example of these absurd pro-motions, of what religion had come to in the agony of the Middle Ages, the man himself was worthy, so far as personal character went, of the great office to which he came. No monarch has done more for material civilisa-tion on the side of the arts than he. But he neither under-stood nor attempted to restore that for which, had he known it, the soul of Europe was athirst, I mean the spiritual greatness of the awful office he filled. He came in the very day when something ruthless in active holi-ness was required, and what he gave was the spectacle of great pageants, of admirable but excessive feasts (himself a temperate man), good music, though too much of it, and masques and stage plays perpetually.

As you read of him you must figure to yourself a man whose health was never good, very fat in the face though not without energy in the brows, and indeed of a corpu-lent body ill supported on half-twisted legs. But this uncouth figure had great dignity. He kept an even temper and for the most part a smiling and happy one, and with money he was generous exceedingly. It was his generosity which hampered him throughout his reign, but it included a mass of great foundations, and though he doubled the cost of the Papal establishment and though he made it too splendid, it was but a fraction of his expenditure.

ADRIAN VI

Over the name of Adrian VI, Adrian of Utrecht, one may murmur the word graven in the town of Besançon, the single word "Utinam!"—"Would that!"

Utinam! Utinam! Would that Adrian had lived! He was sixty-two years of age. The strain would have been heavy upon him, yet had he lived but ten years all might have been saved. He lived for less than two. He exercised the Papacy actively for barely more than one.

His origin, his character, the direction to which he had given his holy will, his fixity of purpose, his separateness from the welter into which the court of Rome had fallen, his unswerving love of doctrine and unity and of the living Church; these combined would have done what was needed.

He was poor, where the Medicean Popes had come out of a very cesspool of riches. He was humble where they were delicately proud. He was zealous where they were cynical.

He had been born the son of a small man living in a town cottage, a pious father who left him by death, as a child, to a still more pious mother. She stinted herself to give him some schooling; his industry was noted; he was sent to Louvain, among the many glories of which university he is, with the late Cardinal Mercier, one of the first glories. A rigid ascetic, deeply learned, lowly and authoritative with a just authority, he had been wisely chosen, for the fame he had acquired and for his reputation in virtue as well as in scholastics and the humanities combined, to be tutor to that little Charles of Hapsburg, who was to be the Emperor Charles V. It was perhaps the best thing Maximilian ever did.

He took over the task when the boy was six; some ten years later when the young fellow became King of Spain, Adrian Dedel, Dutchman of Utrecht, lived side by side with Ximenes, the great Primate of Spain, he who had denounced the fatal indulgence of Julius, and Leo's more fatal continuance and marketing of it. For Adrian had been made, through the influence of his young master, a Cardinal, and from his see he was called Cardinal of Tortosa. There was no one in Europe more fitted for the dreadful burden of the Papacy in such a moment than he—but what a moment and what a burden!

The Germanies were breaking away. The Turk had carried Belgrade. Rhodes, the last bulwark against the Mohammedan upon the seas, was in daily peril of falling. Should it fall all the eastern Mediterranean would pass into the grasp of the infidel, and from that base, as also from the Danube valley, he could begin a last and perhaps a fatal attack upon Christendom.

It was upon the 29th of August 1522, in the worst season of the year, that Adrian made his solemn entry into the town of Rome. He died upon the 14th of September 1523, not before Rhodes had fallen. The Christian princes had grown contemptuous of Christendom and would not unite to defend it.

He died with nothing accomplished, and, he being dead, all the evils returned.

He had attempted in that brief space to restore the purity of the Roman court, to begin—at last to begin—the correction of those enormous abuses which were undermining all Europe wherever the organisation of the Church was to be found. He had for his reward abuse and ridicule, the hatred of those whose interests his indignation for justice had impoverished, and at the passing of his saintliness there was one sigh of relief from all who could return to their vices and their follies and throw to the winds the spiritual inheritance of a thousand years.

The earth did not mourn for him. Whatever spirits are the protectors of our ancient, still precariously enduring, culture must have mourned indeed; but no one hears such mourning for it is beyond the boundaries of the world.

They put up his effigy in the Church of the Germans in Rome with a modest motto to remind future generations that the best are condemned to live in the most evil times.

They would have done better to have inscribed three words, words from the prophet Daniel; or three sombre texts in which Our Lord predicts the fall of Jerusalem.

CLEMENT VII

Clement VII was one of those men excellent in organisation, defective in power; good ministers, bad kings.

He could organise, and had for years managed the affairs of the most important government in Europe—so much so that men thought of him as though he were the

Papacy itself when he was acting for his cousin before his own elevation—so much so that he was still the soul of Papal action on its temporal side during the brief interlude of Adrian VI. Yet when he himself wore the crown his action was perpetually paralysed by two very different faults which met in him, indecision and attempted counter-insurance through intrigue.

I mean by "counter-insurance through intrigue" that habit some men have, when they are menaced from a particular quarter, of defending themselves not by a parry nor by direct counter attack, but by an outward pretence of friendship coupled with an attempt at secret alliance with the attacker's apparent enemies. This habit of carefully discounting risks does not usually accompany indecision, but in Clement both were present.

He was otherwise a good man, sincere in his concern for Christendom in spite of his too great concern for the Medicean house and for Florence. He desired with all his heart to unite Christendom against the fearful Turkish menace; he desired with all his heart the restoration of peace within the body of Christian men, distracted by the new doctrines and old corruptions. He was a man also of refinement and taste, as a Medici should be, almost as great a patron of the arts as Leo had been. His inability was an inability to be sufficiently angry, to stand firm, and go forward to meet an enemy or a peril. He always hoped to escape one or the other by some combination. He would yield too much, he would temporise too long, and therefore throughout he disastrously failed.

He lost England—he failed to appease the German quarrel—he suffered the dreadful sack of Rome, he achieved nothing.

His calm, long-nosed, bearded face, somewhat low

forehead and level brows would give a false impression of him, an impression of greater serenity and power, were it not for the troubled eyes. It is in his expression rather than in his features that you find the man who was perpetually hoping when hoping was useless, perpetually conceding after concession had ceased to be fruitful.

It has been said that whatever character had been in power during those tumultuous years of Henry's divorce and of the formation of Protestantism in the German diets, the unity of Europe could not have been saved. I doubt it. It is individuals who make and change history, and it was an evil fate of enduring consequence that Clement's refinement, essential virtue, but lack of heroism and square principle, coloured in such a moment that government upon which all Europe depended.

FRANCIS I

Of the three Kings who stood up like a trinity of youth before Europe in the five years, 1515-20, Henry of England, Charles of Spain, and Francis, the last, the King of France, merits a particular attention because it is so easy to caricature him. It would be equally easy to make a fancy picture to his advantage.

He stood in age between Henry and Charles, his two young contemporaries in that time of youth. He was born in the fifth year after Henry's birth, just over five years before that of Charles. When he triumphed in the blaze of Marignano he was a little over twenty, the King of England not yet twenty-five, Charles hardly fifteen. He is central, not only in time, but in the part he plays. When he wins a great battle all western Europe takes on one aspect, when he loses a great battle all that aspect is reversed.

There are characters which advance the strength of their nations by some moral effect as much as do others by direct action, and Francis was of these. Of diplomacy he had none: he was a charging man who won or lost. He was advised as to the preservation of the French realm, consolidated by his predecessor Louis XI, and he followed that advice in a not very perspicuous way. But that was not his effect (and he had a great effect) upon the increasing unity and centralisation of France. He had rather the effect of a symbol, he suited the national temper; he filled to perfection that rôle which was the very essence of the Capetian monarchy, the incarnation of the people in one man.

He owed something of this glamour which he exercised, coming so suddenly after the premature age and senile death of his cousin Louis XII; and here comes one of those innumerable "ifs" to history. What would have happened if Mary Tudor had borne a son to her ill-matched dying husband?

He was adored by his women-folk, his mother and his famous sister, later the Queen of Navarre—"Born" says Rabelais "for heavenly love."

"The pearl of pearls"—for Margaret means pearl. (And what an understanding it is of the Reformation to know that such a woman was aflame against the Church!)

They helped him to become a sort of God, and his mad valour, his brazen energy in arms (though not in thought) his scorn of consequence, his long-nosed but handsome challenging Valois face crowned with brown hair, his tall strong figure more manly than his years, drew all his subjects to him. Each wished that he had been made in the same mould and each saw in him the Gallic leader. That damascened armour of his, worth a ransom, dented in the countless shocks of battle where (unlike Henry) he was the active fighting man, risking his blood hand-to-hand over and over again, tell you, I think, as much about him as can anything else. He talked admirably, he moved with strength and grace, alertly. His gestures were also alert, and his eyes. He could play with death as carelessly in hunting as in war; he was generous, admirably. Of scruples he had none, of conscience very little, though he did feel a certain sincere attachment to religion in the perils through which it was about to pass: "Were my right hand heretic I would cut it off." When he forced the mountains in the famous march of his first campaign, not only the Spanish engineer whose genius did the work but the thrust of his own character also achieved the result. Whatever is loved, whatever is despised or hated in the French character, he clearly showed.

Yet has he not remained a national hero, for he determined nothing of himself, nor did he become the figurehead of any final movement. One last quality he had, and I will not leave him without giving it its name; he was a poet. He was a poet on a very small scale, but at any rate spontaneous. Not one of all the others who ruled Europe in that day could say the same.

CHARLES V

Charles V, the Hapsburg, the youngest character in the list, was also he who held longest the greatest place in Europe, for he was the heir to that marriage which we have seen to have so consolidated the mass of Christendom into one hand and to have threatened the very existence of the French kingdom and the independence of the Papacy. He inherited madness plentifully on both sides; the instability of his grandfather Maximilian, the admitted lunacy of his mother Joan, heiress of Castile. His age goes with the century for he was born in 1500, so that he was ten and a half years younger than Henry, his uncle by marriage, five and a half years younger than Francis. He was brought up by his aunt Margaret, the Regent of the Netherlands, and owed to that education his strongly Burgundian tradition and the Flemish formation of his character and acquaintance. He owed to it also his language, which was French, perhaps in some degree his heaviness and taciturnity. But it is remarkable that the nervous taint never appeared in him, he was perfectly sane, one might almost say too sane; sedate even as a child, and, till the beginning of his active life, slow-witted.

He took little exercise. When he was constrained to go hunting the event is so important as to be specially noted; while he was yet in his teens he would sit up far into the night reading and writing dispatches, and at the same age he would solemnly chide servitors of his whom he found wanting. In physical appearance he was remarkable not for beauty but for an individual stamp which singled him out from others and which he passed on through four generations at least of Hapsburg monarchs in Spain, his descendants; while one feature, the big pendulous lower lip, has been a boast in the family from that day to ours.

He had been difficult to nurture, grew up sickly in temperament and never, even in his more robust later years, matched the physique of the rival princes. He was intelligent, with a good taste for mechanics, and if tardy in arriving at a judgment, strong in holding it. He was a man of firm and fixed principle throughout his life, he took very seriously every duty to which he was called, and particularly that title of Caesar, Emperor, Lord of Christendom, which in itself had become so shadowy a thing, but which was given some substance when the man who bore it was also master of the great Hapsburg inheritance among the Slavs and South Germanies, the great Burgundian inheritance which gave him the Jura, Luxemburg and all the rich towns and active commerce of the Netherlands—by far the wealthiest district of Europe—and Master also of South Italy, Spain, and the New World.

In all that tedious cats-cradle of falsehood and betrayals which makes up the endlessly complicated pattern of rivalries between France, England, Venice, the Empire, Spain and the Papacy, his must still be called the most direct and the most honest mind. Though he played off one rival against another as all did, and were perhaps compelled to do, though he used the Lutheran menace against the Pope and was half responsible for the hideous sack of Rome and the imprisonment of Clement VII, yet he fixedly desired the maintenance of religious unity and the saving of the Catholic Church, and he was always at heart the champion of our race against the Mohammedans. He was the last crusader upon Moslem soil, and might have recovered North Africa, whereon he landed his forces; just as his bastard Don John of Austria, the victor of Lepanto and saviour of Europe, was the last crusader by sea, the last crusader of all. He could not but be actively alive to the Turkish menace, which was upon the very borders of his ancestral land; Vienna became the outpost of Christendom after the fatal day of Mohacs. Just as the court of England was the most remote from and cared least for the Moslem peril, so he, after the Popes, cared most.

Among all the actions which make him worthy of enduring fame the greatest and best was the last, when, like Diocletian before him, he voluntarily resigned the headship of the world. He retired to a monastery and made his soul.

CAMPEGGIO

Laurence Campeggio, the colleague of Wolsey in the great business of the divorce, his co-Legate, the name chiefly associated with his own in English history, was in Europe at large a much greater figure than appears in the story of this island. He merits a very close attention. He merits also a high degree of admiration; for he was learned, steadfast, and of high integrity.

He was not, indeed, in those days of unrestrained intrigue and falsehood, indignant with his time (as he should have been). He was too much sunk in affairs to show any revolutionary emotion, but he was strong for reform, he tried to put at the service of reform the very great gifts and acquirements which he commanded. His gifts were many; poise in judgment, a sort of solidity in all he did, which characteristics were backed by a good inheritance of fortune, good family tradition. He had also the gift of an equal temper in negotiation. Upon the whole he understood far better than most of his contemporaries the coming of the deluge, the advance of the Reformation. But since future things are never grasped, he did make one very bad error, when he reported before the end of his life that the affairs of Germany were in a fair way to settlement. They were not; nor have been from that day to this—religious unity has never yet been recovered among the Germans nor (for that matter) in Christendom at large.

He was of an age with Wolsey, probably born in the same year, possibly a couple of years later; of a resolute calm face and figure, square in brow, steadfast in regard, his face covered with an exuberant but well-trimmed beard.

He was from a family of Bologna, that famous mother of civil law, wherein his father before him had been a great lawyer and had trained his son to the same profession. Laurence Campeggio was soon among the first jurists of Europe. He had married in youth and his wife had given him five children. On her death he took orders—in the same year, 1509, which saw the accession and coronation of young Henry VIII—and thenceforward his high talents and strong undisturbed character were at the service of the Papal See. He was given the Cardinalate some few months after the nomination of Wolsey to the Sacred College, that is why we find him junior in rank to Wolsey at the beginning of the inquiry on the divorce.

The whole weight of his high fame in law, canon and civil; of his high and deserved repute in personal character; was thrown into two allied directions—the reform of the evils within the Church and the settlement of disruption in the Germanies. In both he failed, as all men failed, but in both he deserved to succeed. He it was who stood behind the brave effort of Adrian VI, which might have saved the commonwealth of Christendom, but did not sufficiently endure. He perpetually urged the reform of the monastic houses, the vigorous purification of the Roman Curia, especially on its shameful financial side wherein he spoke rightly of bloodsuckers but might have added with even more justice the modern epithet of "fossil"; and yet better the unchanging epithet of soulless. He would have reformed that process whereby the granting of dispensations and the rest had become a mere routine for payment. He would have let in fresh air and moral responsibility.

Vigorously did he denounce the abuse of indulgences, singling out those that had led to the explosion in Germany, and the proceeds of which had been applied to the building of St. Peter's.

Laurence Campeggio was that kind of man to whom all men listen with respect and whom—since the fall of man—nobody follows. When such men, by inheritance or otherwise, are given the opportunity to govern, the evils of mankind are for some short moment relieved. Opportunity for government he had not; but he advised well.

As against what we have to praise in him, and it is much the most, must be set that something inevitable to the man of one trade, and great industry and regularity in that trade: professionalism. He was a diplomat, an envoy, a negotiator, a faithful servant of his state and Prince, which was the Papacy and the Pope. He had therefore something too much of caution, something too much of the acquiescence in whatever that government did. Upon the supreme necessity for reform he never compromised, but in the details of his profession he was bound to compromise or he could not have followed it: his profession was to work throughout Europe as agent of the Roman Government. He carried it out well, all men respected him, his character was a great asset to the

Papacy of the day—had it acted in the main through such agents it might have avoided its catastrophes.

We shall find him, in the part he plays in the great drama, steadfast, wary, and always keeping things in focus, never allowing personal emotions under insult or delay to influence his general line, not even allowing ill-health to cloud his vision.

Yet in health he suffered cruelly. He survived his exact contemporary, Wolsey, by nine years; yet Wolsey was still untouched by age in that autumn of 1528 when Campeggio, journeying to England, was already crippled with gout. But Wolsey was stricken down, and his final illness and death were, as like as not, the action of the mind upon the body. Campeggio went through no such ordeal.

Before we leave him, if we are to understand the part he played, we must remember that he held after having been elevated to the Cardinalate, the position of "Cardinal Protector" of England. It was a lucrative position, worth some solid thousands a year, and there were added to the revenues of its endowment the revenues of an English bishopric, the See of which he nominally held; first Hereford, then Salisbury.

Herein his functions must not be confused with those of another compatriot of his, Giglis, who held the same position towards the See of Worcester. Giglis was the active agent or ambassador of the English Government with the Papal See. Wolsey, for instance, acts with Giglis, as he might act with any other agent to a foreign court, receiving secret dispatches, sending orders, treating the Ambassador as identical with the Government which created or used him. Campeggio's position was much more formal and in no way subordinate to the English

Crown; it meant only that through him went the demands of that Crown to the Holy See, that to him were referred the cases arising, and that from him was expected the presentation of the best case that could be made out for the English demands.

When what seemed to the men of his time the very important, but subsidiary, business of the divorce no longer concerned him, Laurence Campeggio was engrossed for the remainder of his life in the larger general European business, the stemming of the break-up among the Germans, the still hoped for and always baffled common action of Christendom against the Turks.

It is characteristic of him that he said before he died a thing, diplomatic and juridical, yet of lively interest to those who are concerned with this pivotal moment in English history: he said that, had the business depended upon the proving of Catherine's virginity upon her second marriage, all would have remained at least doubtful; but that on the Papal power to dispense, whether the first marriage had been real or not, there could be no doubt at all. In that sentence spoke the legist, always willing to doubt human evidence, however passionate, however sincere, always concerned with abstract principles of law.

BAINBRIDGE

Bainbridge, Cardinal and Archbishop of York for the last six years of his life, was about eight or nine years older than Wolsey. He was of better birth—a Westmoreland family—and had risen rapidly as one of those bureaucrat clerics of the new Tudor dynasty who were paid for their services by appointments to great Church revenues.

Henry VII had made him Dean of York before he was thirty, Master of the Rolls immediately afterwards, then Bishop of Durham, finally Archbishop of York with its great revenues in the autumn of 1508, the year before the King died.

When Henry VIII, the new boy King, came to the throne in the April of the next year Bainbridge was sent (probably in continuation of some plan made in the old reign) to Rome, to represent the English government more or less permanently and as Ambassador. For though the Ambassadorships of those days were not, as they are today, careers and posts involving long regular residence, yet in this case longer residence than usual was probably intended.

He arrived in Rome just at the critical moment when Julius II, the aged warrior Pope, was in the thick of his action against French power in Italy; just at the moment when Henry, following the wishes of his wife, had joined the Holy League with Spain and Germany and Venice to drive the French King from the Milanese. He got to Rome on November 24, 1509.

He is thenceforward the right-hand man of Julius; his character and talents marked him out, in spite of a violent temper, for command in the field; moreover it was he who gave Henry VIII's adhesion to the Pope's coalition against France. When it became necessary to make a batch of new Cardinals rather more than a year later, in the spring of 1511, to counteract Louis XII's schismatic council at Pisa, Bainbridge was included. He got the hat on the 10th March of that year, while Wolsey was as yet no more than a minor though important figure at court, the Almoner who was, the year after, to organise the expedition against Europe.

The Pope made Bainbridge Legate to the Papal armies, made him commander of them, sent him to besiege Ferrara. When, in the violence of the quarrel between the French King and the Holy See there was question of taking away Louis XII's title of "Most Christian King" Bainbridge urged that it should be given to Henry, and after Julius II's death Leo X might have given it but that the war was brought to an end and Louis reconciled with Rome after Henry's great and successful campaign of 1513, wherein Wolsey appeared for the first time in real power.

Bainbridge therefore at this moment, the end of 1513 and the entry of 1514, was the principal immediate obstacle to Wolsey's further advance. He was Cardinal, and it would be difficult for a second English Cardinal to be named while he lived. He was Archbishop of York, and that great revenue would have put a coping stone on the arch of Wolsey's new financial fortunes. He was able to serve the English Government to great purpose at the Court upon which all depended—the Court of Rome— he was very famous as a Churchman and a soldier; and he stood in flank, as it were, of Catherine's influence over the King. With a few more years of life (he was barely fifty) he might have been the first subject of the English crown.

Just at that moment, in the middle of the year 1514, he suddenly died by foul means, and we shall see later what that meant in the story of Wolsey's life.

RICHARD FOXE, BISHOP OF WINCHESTER

Richard Foxe, Bishop of Winchester, is an early and secondary figure in the drama of Wolsey, so far as national politics are concerned. But if we are considering

Wolsey the man, the way in which Wolsey's life looked to Wolsey himself when the dying Cardinal gazed back on it in the Priory of Leicester, then Richard Foxe takes a very great place, for it was upon him that Wolsey half consciously modelled himself. He worked with Foxe all his first years; he drew from Foxe the tradition of diplomacy which he himself followed; he discovered in Foxe the secret whereby an exact negotiator, secret in keeping his own counsel, open in his manner with the foreigner, can become necessary to a government. He observed in Foxe what great revenues could do to support a career, and though he vastly exceeded Foxe in the race for wealth and though he had not Foxe's anxieties of the soul, Foxe stamped himself upon Wolsey and Wolsey never lost the impress.

Wolsey had seen Foxe during all those years as a great Prelate, he had marked the effect of a crowd of livery about him, and a retinue longer than any other man's. He copied these also.

Richard Foxe was born slightly higher in rank than his pupil and a quarter of a century earlier, a Lincolnshire man. Because at Oxford he belonged to Magdalen there was here a link between him and Wolsey, but he was at the summit of his power long before Wolsey appeared on the scene. He rose, as so many have, in the revolution which Henry VII's usurping of the throne produced. He was one of those partizans who gambled upon the Tudor adventure, as men in our time, during Prince Napoleon's exile, gambled on his success and became great in the Court of the Tuileries when their leader was called Napoleon III. His fortunes then may be compared to Brandon's and a whole group of others.

He was in Paris when Henry Tudor was meditating

his final raid, and the adventurer left Foxe behind to keep on negotiations with the French King. It was his first piece of diplomacy and a successful one. It was very secret. In the very year of Bosworth Richard III did no more than suspect that this silent man already somewhat in the public view was secretly linked with his enemy, "That great rebel, Henry ap-Tuddor", so that Foxe did not get his benefice until after the battle (the vicarage of Stepney). But Bosworth once decided he went ahead at once; he was made principal secretary, Privy Seal, and before the end of the year Bishop of Exeter—a see he need never visit, and the revenues of which made him great at Court.

He was immediately used in further diplomacy and was always successful in a time when everything depended upon the ability of the Government's distant agents. He not only worked the precarious neutrality of Scotland but he justly foresaw how later on in the Perkin Warbeck business the King of Scotland would attack the Tudors. He was just on forty then, when those Scottish negotiations were afoot; he was forty-five when he conducted more important Ambassadorial work in Paris.

Like Wolsey, he passed from addition of revenue to addition of revenue. Getting Bath and Wells in place of Exeter, Durham in the place of Bath and Wells, and at last—like Wolsey—that wealthiest see in all England, Winchester: a princely income. And it was he who married Prince Arthur to Catherine of Aragon and who baptised Henry VIII.

He was identified everywhere with the Crown, as later and more thoroughly was Wolsey, and was entrusted with the execution of Henry VII's will. Like

Wolsey, he could make appointments by recommendation (Fisher, the great Bishop of Rochester to be mar-
tyred in the next reign, was his nominee). Like Wolsey
he dominated the Council—where, against the advice
of the Archbishop, he favoured Henry's marriage with
his brother's widow. Like Wolsey he was eager for the reformation of the monasteries, against the corruption of
which his indignation was loud. Like Wolsey he grasped
the Renaissance and was for founding colleges: Corpus
Christi at Oxford is his. He paid for it from his private
revenue. I believe you may still see his altar plate there,
and in the quadrangle is the pelican, the symbol of the
Blessed Sacrament, which he had taken for his emblem.

It is remarkable how faithfully he helped the beginning of the Cardinal's public life. He had no jealousy
of the younger man, their most famous relation was when
he showed astonishment at his pupil's enormous industry. Nor is it true that Wolsey attempted to oust Foxe
in his old age. They corresponded continually, and their
correspondence was affectionate to the end.

Foxe, whom Henry VIII kept on as a matter of course,
an inheritance from his father, during all his first years,
was himself desirous of retirement and rest—and his
motive was religion. He was nearer seventy than sixty
when he was allowed to take his repose. Wolsey had
been in the saddle for more than four years, he had been
prominent for half a dozen, he had been Cardinal some
months, when his old master slipped back contentedly
to the work of his diocese and to the making of his soul.
A foreign Ambassador, noting him in this his age, used
two words fitting him exactly, "authority and goodness".
That authority his famous pupil exaggerated, that goodness he did not attain. When his last phase was upon

him he grew blind; he lived to see the beginnings of the storm, for he did not die until the October of 1528 when already for nearly two years "the King's great matter" had been afoot. From all this God spared him. You may see his tomb in the exquisite little chapel, a worthy memorial of himself, which is in his own Cathedral at Winchester.

THOMAS CROMWELL, THE SUPPLANTER

The last considerable figure to come upon the stage of this tragedy is Thomas Cromwell, the supplanter. For he was indeed the supplanter. That he planned to take the place of his former master, that not chance but a successful intrigue explains his advent, I make no doubt. He was one of those few men who *do* plan their lives, or at any rate plan them after the arrival of their one great opportunity, seize it and use it, keeping to a thought-out method.

He was a man of great strength over others, particularly vile, exceptionally cowardly in the face of death, conspicuous even in such a time for his avarice, still more conspicuous in any time for his vast talents in affairs. He was the only rival to Wolsey in capacity for work, for covering a wide field of detail, for co-ordinating a mass of multiform action. He was far inferior to Wolsey in the comprehension of Europe, though Wolsey himself had no great capacity in this; yet he had travelled, which Wolsey had not; he had gained cynicism (into which Wolsey never fell) from too considerable acquaintance with too many kinds of men. He had not Wolsey's loyalty or suppleness, but rather, when he had discovered, as he soon did, what kind of character he

THOMAS CROMWELL
From the Portrait in the National Portrait Gallery, London

had to deal with in the King, he treated it with contempt, and that was his ruin.

He was born the son of a public-house keeper in Putney near London, over the river from Fulham.[1]

He went off as an adventurer, seems to have been a
private soldier in the Italian wars, and to have come
across Machiavelli's book "The Prince" which his powerful intelligence could worthily understand. He then
became intimate with a banking family and entered into
several forms of negotiation and commerce, the principal of which was money-lending.

It was as a money-lender that he had become a substantial man when Wolsey chose him as the very character upon which to depend for secretarial work and
advice. We shall find him Wolsey's right-hand man in
the suppression of the smaller monasteries, and we shall
see how it was his training therein that founded the
ruin of all monasteries after Wolsey's death. He was
a man of sturdy figure and square head, steady but secre-
tive expression, with little sunken pig's eyes, firm and
decided in their glance. The more striking because it
appeared in a face pasty, pale, and too fat.

One indication may serve to fix his character with the
modern reader. When he fell, he fell so suddenly that
the great mass of his papers remained undestroyed. Well,
everything came into that office in writing—complaints,
petitions and, above all, bribes. The debtors to whom he

[1] His sister married the son of a neighbouring publican and black-
smith called Williams, of Welsh origin. The child of that marriage,
Richard Williams, was particularly favoured by his uncle; given a vast
mass of Church loot when that uncle broke up the monasteries, and so
founded one of the very wealthiest families in England. He assumed
the name of Cromwell side by side with his own. His vast wealth continued through three generations, and a cadet of that millionaire family,
founded on the spoils of the Church was the father of the famous Oliver.

had lent at usury, others who fawned for advantage, others who trembled from fear—all discharged letters at him, and his spies helped to swell the vast correspondence. But as for him, the answers were verbal and take the form of directions, leaving as little record as possible. For more truly than of Foxe might Bacon have written of him that he watched all men silently and opened himself to none.

Such men commonly die well, satisfied and full of honours. It is a happy exception that Thomas Cromwell died otherwise—by the axe and whining for life.

SECOND PART

THE ACTION

V

THE FIRST ACT

THE ENTRY TO GREATNESS
1472-1513

THOMAS WOLSEY was born at Ipswich in the latter half of 1472 or early in 1473. No record has survived to give us the date.[1]

The stock of which he came was middle-class, and what we should call today rather lower middle-class, but not unsubstantial. His father was probably a butcher, certainly also a grazier in cattle, who may have killed his own meat. The family left bequests to the town and owned property in two of its parishes, which shows it to have been not without some modest competence.

It is a commonplace that men taking up the clerical profession rose through the organisation and spirit of the Church from any post, low or high, to any post low or high within that organisation. The clerical body was not entered by purchase nor was the education necessary to a priest expensive. The colleges were endowed. The ranks of society were not separated in those days by differences of accent and of daily hours as they have since become. There was therefore nothing exceptional in a lad of Wolsey's birth entering the clerical profession and rising in it to any degree. That when he fell the baseness of his birth should have been made a reproach against him was common form: it was what always happened when any one fell from high estate.

Of his family we know hardly anything, except that he may have had at least two brothers. They are mentioned in the notes of a foreign Ambassador. One of them

[1] See Note A at the end of this book.

may be a Wolsey who was attached to the Court in a minor capacity. But there is no mention of them in the will of the Cardinal's father, Richard Wolsey, which was deposited with the Bishop of Norwich when Thomas Wolsey was a very young man, twenty-two or twenty-three years of age, before he was ordained priest. Nor is there any mention of a sister, either in the will or by any other contemporary allusion. His affection for his native place we can judge by his foundation of Ipswich college.

We know nothing of his boyhood except that he was destined for the Church and was sent to the University of Oxford to the College of Magdalen. The university of those days continued to be what it had been from its origin in the great spring of the Middle Ages, until all England was transformed by the change of religion. It was a group of wealthy, clerical, teaching corporations whose pupils were largely brought up at the expense of this foundation, the great bulk of them sprung from the populace. Membership of an Oxford College did not suggest, as it came to suggest after the great social revolution following upon the Reformation, any privilege of wealth or rank. Men came to their University as children, they were taught the "arts", that is the Humanities, their Latin and Greek, in their teens. The proof or record of their study was given them after three years, when they were fifteen to seventeen. It was a degree called Bachelor of Arts, which did not mean that they had achieved their full University training, but rather that they were beginning it, for they were made Bachelors long before they were grown up. They then passed some four years in the more serious studies proper to the higher learning, and after the full seven years were given the certificate of such learning in the Degree of Mastership—they were Masters of Arts. This, the term of university instruction, left them ready for the priesthood if they would be clerics, and they could be elected by the corporate body of the college to membership therein. They were henceforward, if so elected, called Fellows of the corporation. And this position came before the canonical age for ordainment to the priesthood, a young man's twenty-fourth year.

Through this regular curriculum young Wolsey passed with his comrades, most of them of the same low rank in life, most of them destined as he was to that clerical status which then covered three quarters of the administrative and official work in Christendom.

It is characteristic of Wolsey, and a thing to be seized at our first reading of him, that just as he was without large vision on the Europe of his time, though of acute perception in details beneath his hand, so he had no vision of his own career; at least none that we can discover from any intentions of his youth. It is true of course that most men destined to rise to great eminence from small origins begin with no fixed plan and see nothing at first of their goal. But many such men, though they are not born to opportunity, seem to have had a vague sense of coming greatness, though it may have been no more than a vanity which helped to push them forward. With Wolsey there is not a trace of this. He makes himself useful, he does all his work with energy, he impresses those whom he meets, and it is by these characteristics alone that he goes up the first steps in a progress which is not very rapid, still less anything extraordinary. He did not seek opportunity at first, but when opportunity came he recognised it; and during the long years of early manhood there is nothing to show that he was even as yet touched by that ambition which inflamed him after his 40th year.

He passed slowly from his first degree to his second at Magdalen; he seems to have allowed more than the conventional space to intervene between his B.A. and his M.A., for he was, if his own memory served him well, only fifteen when he took the first degree. He was ordained priest in connection with his Fellowship in his twenty-fifth year, and was Bursar of his college in the year following (1499). As Bursar, he was responsible for the building of Magdalen Tower, that last and famous complete monument of medieval beauty which marks the ancient entry to the town. There were vague stories told of him later on when he was famous, probably distorted as all such stories are, but already an indication of his character. They said that he got into trouble for spending upon the fabric college money beyond his warrant.

So far the young man had already advanced half way through the twenties, was of no account, and had no name of any kind beyond the narrow circle of the corporation which he had joined. His first passage into the world where advancement could be found was accidental.

In the children's school, of which young Wolsey was master, were the three young sons of Lord Dorset. And with that name of Dorset we can appreciate the chance which fell in the way of the young priest.

Edward IV, Edward of York, the last great Plantagenet and the last but one of the Plantagenet line of English kings, had been captured half a lifetime before, himself vigorous and beautiful in youth (and a great soldier) by a young woman well suited to him in body as in mind, for she was of his own kind, as vigorous, as beautiful, if not as young. Elizabeth Woodville was her name. She was a widow, whose husband had been a Grey; and Thomas Grey, her son by that first marriage, thus fell under the protection of the throne. He was given a quasi-royal title after fighting for Edward at Tewkesbury, being made Marquis of Dorset (the title Marquis, rare and of recent origin, somewhat alien still to English ideas, connoted some close connection with the royal blood by alliance or adoption). He was Keeper of the Tower under Edward IV and when that King's young sons were murdered, presumably at the orders of their uncle Richard III, he fled and a price was put upon his head. Thenceforward all his sympathies were with the oversetting of the Plantagenets by Henry Tudor. He proclaimed Henry in the first abortive effort, fled abroad, was not present at Bosworth, was somewhat suspect even after Henry VII's triumph, but was accepted at last, and stood among the greatest names in the kingdom. For, after all, he was half-brother to Henry's own wife, and virtually royal. He was, at this moment when Wolsey first had the good luck to come across him, a little under fifty years of age and not far from his death, for he died just after, in his fiftieth year.

This was the half-Prince whose children had, by Thomas Wolsey's lucky star, been put under his mastership in the school of Magdalen. He went down to pass a Christmas in the great house of his pupils—presumably the Christmas of 1499. Dorset so liked him that he gave him his first benefice, that of Lymington, in Somerset. On taking that benefice he had to give up his Fellowship, and for the moment it might seem that no greater advantage lay before him. There was nothing so far to mark the beginnings even of a humble administrative career. He was no more than the parish priest of a country living.

But the great patron upon whom he had thus fallen by accident (and who perhaps barely remembered his name among so many others) did at least notice some such talents about him or enjoyed from him some such sober flattery, that immediately after his death Wolsey advanced by the next step towards the future for which he was destined.

Dorset died in September 1501. Two months later we find Wolsey one of the Chaplains of the Archbishop of Canterbury—on what was probably recommendation of Dorset, or of the President of Wolsey's old college of Magdalen, Richard Mayew. This man was Almoner to King Henry VII, was a member of the Council, and became later Bishop of Hereford, and this is presumably why we find Wolsey granted later on the important revenues of the Deanery of Hereford, to hold with his other benefices.

Thus in the opening year of the sixteenth century, 1501, when Wolsey was 28 or 29 years old, the first modest door towards advancement was opened to him.

Having passed through that door, the two minor talents, which are of minor worth in government but of supreme advantage to personal advance, were brought into play. He proved amenable and cheerful to his superiors, and he showed that he could do their work for them—and better than they could. At once his income rises, and his reputation within the still limited circle which had heard of him. Two months after Dorset's death, and while Wolsey is occupying the Chaplaincy

in the Archbishop's Palace, he gets a dispensation to
hold two more benefices besides Lymington, and when
his new master died, little more than a year later (1503),
he passed on as Chaplain to that old knight, Sir Richard Nanfant, who was Deputy-Governor of Calais.

Here he made himself still more useful, for he had
the luck to have a master well past work, yet deeply
involved in affairs not only public but private: the affairs of a very rich man. His private income Wolsey administered, and amply earned his gratitude. Nanfant
died in January, 1507, but not before he had recommended Wolsey to the King. This recommendation was
backed up by Lovell, who of all on the Council was
most listened to by Henry VII, for Lovell also had suffered exile for the Lancastrian cause, had fought at Bosworth and at Stoke, and was in the very heart of the
Court. He had come across and appreciated the priest
and supported his claim.

All this while Wolsey had increased rapidly in the
esteem of his employers, more rapidly in the revenues
by which he supported his new station. He already held
more than one living before the end of the reign, and
could maintain a minor station at Court.

There is hardly any other instance of a man in the
first rank of European affairs appearing so late in life
with such absence of record upon his youth. Not a few
have shown their talents very late and were unsuspected
of them earlier. Marlborough and Oliver Cromwell are
the two classical examples in English History of unexpected genius appearing at the moment when the careers
of most men are half over. But of Cromwell's youth, the
cadet of an immensely wealthy family, born in the heart
of the new Reformation millionaires, we know all that

need be known; of Marlborough's a great deal more; of Wolsey's hardly anything. There did indeed exist a diary of his, though whether it would have included any memorials of his life before he appeared at Court we may doubt. That diary apparently, and a mass of his letters, were burnt by a clergyman who possessed them, who thought them of no value and who indeed, regretted to learn, too late, that they might have fetched £50.

The foundation which Wolsey was laying at this moment depended upon his reputation for efficiency in missions.

Henry VII had formed something of a new bureaucracy. It was not, of course, either in structure or personnel, an innovation, but it was a fairly rapid development of older things; and an essential part of it was the use of numerous agents sent by the Crown to negotiate with foreign courts. Now in this particular function of foreign agency two talents at this moment were of especial value; these talents were expedition, and an instinctively just interpretation of the policy entrusted to the agent. The general talents always demanded by diplomacy had of course to be present as well; the agent must know how to persuade, how to conceal, and the rest of it. But *expedition* and *interpretation* were of particular moment in this height of the Renaissance kingships for this reason:—that intrigue was far more multiple, far more complicated, than it had been a generation before; while the Princes were individually more powerful and their power more centralised and concentrated into their own hands. The consequence of such conditions was that to be first in the field when there was a race for an understanding or alliance made all the difference, while interpretation of one's employer's intentions was especially necessary from the rapid and perpetual shifting of interests. The King would send the agent, giving general instructions, let us say, to dissuade a foreign prince from a particular course of action: the presence of that agent before those of rival princes at the foreign court, his forestalling of competitors, might turn the scale. Again, having arrived at the foreign court he might discover elements in the situation upon which the government at home had had no information. To refer back to that government was to lose time; to act on one's own responsibility, so to achieve the result desired and return in possession of it, was to make oneself invaluable to one's employer. These were the key points which Wolsey had grasped, and there is a famous story which vividly illustrates his understanding of them. This story was told by Wolsey to Cavendish many years after, recited only from memory, and suffers from the inaccuracies inevitable to that kind of record; but the essential quality of the feat was what had remained so strongly impressed upon the mind of the man who had achieved it, and that quality is not obscured by slight lapses of memory upon its minor particulars.

Henry VII had occasion to send Wolsey to deal with the Emperor, who was at the moment on the frontiers of his dominions in the Low Countries, near the English town of Calais. The chaplain was not dispatched from Richmond until mid-day. He seems to have discovered that he could catch the barge for Gravesend at London at the turn of the tide, if he made all haste. He pressed over the few miles, caught the barge just as it was starting on the first ebb in the mid-afternoon, and was at Gravesend in three hours down-stream, with a westerly wind to help as well. He got post horses at Gravesend, posted with relays to Dover through the same night, was aboard the packet for Calais in the morning, posted immediately on landing to the Emperor, did his business that day, was back in Calais that evening, reached Dover just over twenty-four hours after leaving it in the morning again, and, by further relays of post horses, was at Richmond by night. When upon the morning of the third day he saw his king, Henry was prepared to upbraid him for his delay in starting. But he learnt that in the short interval Wolsey had done all that was demanded, had supplemented his general orders, and had procured for the English crown what only a man on the spot could so procure, reading into his instructions just what was needed.

That was the story as told by Wolsey in age to young Cavendish, and set down by him many years afterwards in his record of the Cardinal's life. It is probable that the whole transaction took longer, it is probable or certain that, as nearly always happens, when one records in age a feat of youth, the feat was exaggerated; but what is reasonably certain is that the example was unique, and remained as strongly impressed upon the Court as upon the man who brought off the successful stroke.

The point to seize, then, in these beginnings of his career is that Wolsey was making a reputation for industry and energy and grasp of detail and exact performance which would make him indispensable. He was bound to be left as an inheritance from the old King to the new.

Henry VII died on April 22, 1509. The son who succeeded him was not yet eighteen and for the first few months of his reign, while his grandmother, the Lady Margaret, Countess of Richmond, through whom came the Lancastrian claim, still lived, her influence may somewhat have retarded Wolsey's progress: but the check may be exaggerated, for during those months we find Wolsey getting yet another benefice, a Prebend of Lincoln, and made Dean of Hereford. And by the autumn, on October 9, he had already been granted a fine house with large gardens at Bridewell at the end of Fleet Street, held of Westminster Abbey; and a month later, on November 8, he was nominated Almoner to the King in place of Hobbs who had just died.

It was a further accession of income and consequence, but still more of consequence. There went with the post sundry perquisites, the confiscated goods of suicides for instance, and the *deodands*,[1] and what was much more important a very considerable body of patronage. It was a post which an energetic man could use for his advancement, though a slack man need make little of it. Wolsey certainly used it to the full, and men began to apply to the Almoner for this and that, finding that he was more and more in the confidence of the inexperienced, hasty, popular and vain youth who governed.

The strongest influence by far at the moment and for two or three years to come was of course not Wolsey, who was but just beginning; it was Catherine, over five years older than her husband and managing him. But Wolsey throughout the next year, 1510, and the following year 1511, is already on the fringes of the administration. We have a sharp glimpse of his increasing influence in a note appended by Archbishop Warham,

[1] Objects which had caused the death of a man by accident and were confiscated.

the Lord Chancellor of the day, to a royal order which had been passed on direct to him through Wolsey, without going through the regular routine of the Privy Seal. Wolsey was already of sufficient influence for Warham himself to accept his authority, and the Archbishop writes on the order the new man had passed to him a phrase to cover the irregularity of the action. He puts it on record that the King's wish had been vouched for by Wolsey, and apparently that was enough.

It was about this time, in the first year or two of the new King's reign, that Wolsey, following the precedent of the time and what was a common practice for such of the greater ecclesiastics as wished to follow it, took a regular mistress.

We understand him better if we appreciate the conditions under which he settled down in his privacy as a family man.

We have to note to begin with that there is no tradition of any previous attachment. There was not in his case, as in the case of so many great clerics of the time, a rather wild youth, followed by a steadying down when they reached great affairs. He had made merry at fairs down in Somerset between his ordination and his 30th year, like other parish priests of his day. He had even been put in the stocks for excess of such merriment. He was always a jovial companion, and in his first growing friendship with Henry, though he was eighteen years older than the boy whom he served, he made a first-rate boon companion, singing, they said, and dancing at his feasts. But no one connects his name with that of a woman. His first affair, so far as we can judge, and discounting for what they are worth a few vague rumours, was his only one.

Next let us note that the action was undertaken late in life. It was a bit of clear-headed planning such as one would expect of him. He would not undertake the responsibilities of a family until he was solidly established, nearer forty than thirty, and possessed of a first-rate income. But the last and most important thing to note in this connection is the character of the act.

Since the drastic and profound cleansing of the Church in the great reforms of the later 16th Century (half a lifetime and more after Wolsey's death) the celibacy of the Catholic clergy has not only been the rule that it had been for centuries but the practice. Scandals lingered, particularly in the French Church, during the 18th Century. But they were the exceptions and they *were* scandals; they shocked the general conscience. Now it is to be emphasized that in this last lull before the great upheaval of the Reformation, a connection between an ecclesiastic, especially a highly placed ecclesiastic, and the other sex, had ceased to have the effect on public opinion which it had formerly had, and which it was to have so strongly after the great cleansing of the Church by St. Pius V. Irregularity, vice, all that could be blamed in laymen, was duly blamed in a cleric, but not a constant alliance with some woman; indeed for such was invented the term "uncanonical marriage". There was a conventional glozing over the situation, but not any horror of it, nor any real pains taken to hide it.

When Pope Alexander VI (at a time when Wolsey was already in Holy Orders), went down to the gates of Rome in great array to greet his young mistress whom he had just ransomed from her capturers the murmurs which rose against him were not due to his relations to the lady, but to what was thought a lack of dignity in that he, being the sovereign of Rome, and middle-aged should appear in a jaunty little cap. When Campeggio, who had been lawfully married as a layman and only took orders after his widowerhood, alluded to his children the allusion was sometimes mistaken by his hearers for the children of such an "uncanonical marriage". They saw before them an elderly Cardinal, heard talk of a grown-up son, took it for granted that the Cardinal had had a mistress. They saw nothing extraordinary in such a thing.

The real gravity, therefore, of Wolsey's thus entering what was in the eyes of his day, more like a secret misalliance than a liaison, and of all the other similar cases throughout Europe, was that it rendered futile the general talk of reform. After all, celibacy was the rule of the Church. It was enforced, with penalties sometimes, against humble men. It was never allowed to be so flouted as to permit of the presentation of these "uncanonical" wives, or their presence upon public occasions. After all, the vows of chastity had been taken; and how should great Prelates pretend to restore the prestige of the Church and to avert coming disaster if their own example flew in the face of their precept? Wolsey genuinely desired to play a great part in such reform; he knew, as everyone at the time did, that reform was a crying necessity and that it was mere common sense in every great ecclesiastic to range himself upon its side; for if reformation, already perilously delayed, were delayed much longer there would be a crash.

Yet Wolsey, in common with any number of others of his kind up and down Christendom, contradicted in his own life the very elements of that policy.

To us who today have left that atmosphere long behind the thing seems paradoxical, but every age presents a parallel. Our own presents a glaring one. Europe is full today of rich men who talk Socialism, who are perfectly sincere in their talk. Some of them take office as politicians, many actually subsidize Socialist publications and institutions but not one of them gives up a fraction of his millions.

The lady upon whom Wolsey's choice fell was a certain Miss Lark, whose father probably kept a public house in Thetford. By her he had a son and a daughter, Thomas and Dorothy by name. The father advantaged them both without concealment, and especially of course, the boy. Dorothy was made a nun in the great convent at Shaftesbury, and is presumed to have lived on till long after the dissolution. Thomas (who was called Thomas Wynter) was made a particularly flagrant example of the misuse of Church endowments, and there again we have that universal contrast between the profession of reformation and the practice, which was to lead to ruin. Even the tutor who brought the boy up was given several livings, and the boy himself was given later the Deanery of Wells, a Prebend in Beverley (worth £2,000 a year),[1] the Provostship of the same place, Archdeaconries in York and Richmond, and no less than seven further Prebends, in as many separate dioceses, as well as the Chancellorship of Salisbury. What is more, Wolsey also got him a coat of arms. He was given the advantage of the lectures of Louvain, he travelled in Italy. It is remarkable that Wolsey only failed in the attempt to make him Bishop of Durham. And as for Lark herself, Wolsey made an honest woman of her at

[1] See Note B at the end of book.

last by marrying her with a great dowry to a Mr. Lee[1] of Aldington in Cheshire, a substantial landowner with several thousands a year in rents.

But it is to be remarked that he did not take the dowry out of his own purse, he pressed it out of one John Stanley, who in his turn was the bastard of yet another Bishop. One of her brothers was Wolsey's own confessor (a combination not without humour), and was made Royal Chaplain. His influence with Wolsey was remarked everywhere. They died in the same year, but not before he had become Master of Trinity Hall in Cambridge. Another brother, Peter, ended with Gardiner, whom Wolsey also had made.

From this side glance upon the rising man's private life let me return to his public.

The patronage of Foxe, which had already helped Thomas Wolsey when he was Henry VII's chaplain, continued to urge him forward under the new reign. How much came of Foxe's initiative, how much of Wolsey's own pertinacity we do not know, but the older and younger man worked together; and in the autumn of that year, on September 30, 1511, the first letter of Wolsey's hand remaining to us is addressed to Foxe, and shows clearly how much the subordinate already counted. The principal use of Wolsey to Foxe was the support a man tireless at work and quick of character could give him against old Surrey. For Surrey, who should by rights have been Duke of Norfolk, had his family not been attainted for their support of Richard III at Bosworth, who was head of the Howards and, in spite of impoverishment, the natural leader of the old nobility

---

[1] The ancestor of, or at least of the same family as, Robert Lee, the General of the American Civil War.

against the officials, was Treasurer; a post almost hereditary and held by him all his life. Further, his son had
married the King's aunt. But the opposition of Foxe to
the Howards was not only the opposition of the official
to the noble, it was much more the opposition of the
man who was learned in policy and had conducted it
so long to the man whose aims were personal and might
therefore interfere with policy, especially with foreign
affairs.

Surrey's whole aim was the restoration of his blood
and of the family fortunes. In pursuit of that aim he was
indifferent to the wider view of Europe and England's
position therein, which was Foxe's chief concern. Now
in this very letter of Wolsey's we find him intimately
linked with Foxe in the business, and suggesting that the
temporary absence of Surrey from the Court might be
used to exclude him permanently. We find also something more, and something very significant. Wolsey was
as yet no more than a secondary official, though already
an important one; he was rising through the patronage
of a higher official and through the way in which his
lively company and perpetual readiness to act influenced
the King, yet he takes it upon him to move in a very
great matter.

The Pope Julius II, an old man whose demands were
calling all Europe to war, was thought to be dying;
and Wolsey in this letter tells Foxe how he had talked
with the young King at Mass upon the great importance
of providing an English candidate for the Papacy if it
should fall vacant. It was an early, and the first, sign
we have of that concentration upon the Holy See as
the pivot of all European policy which was Wolsey's
fixed principle thenceforward to the very moment

of his fall, eighteen years later. But the mention of Julius
II and the impending war, which raised Wolsey to the
first rank, demands an explanation of the state of Europe
at the moment.

Just before Henry VIII's accession, was launched the
League of Cambrai.

The solidity and strength of the Venetian aristocratic
Republic had frightened both Maximilian the Emperor
and Louis XII of France, who at the moment held
Milan and had challenged the Papal States.

It was while Henry VII of England was approaching
death at the very end of 1508 that this combination
against Venice, "The League of Cambrai," was made.
The Pope Julius joined it, angered against the power of
Venice which had encroached upon his own territories.
Secretly he intended when Venice should be humbled to
drive Louis of France from Milan. For old Julius II
was a fiery, intensely military man, who had determined
to drive all that was not Italian out of Italy, to confirm
for ever the power of the Papal States as the chief thing
in Italy, and to make himself famous and the See of
Peter intangible, through the sword. He was a man also
who had a violent appetite for personal power—"He
loved to be lord and master of the world's play."

Now just after Henry VII had died on April 22,
1509, and his son had succeeded, as a boy of 17, the
French King, acting from the Milanese and on the eastern boundary of that district, on May 14, 1509, had won
the great victory of Agnadello against the Venetians.

No one else in the League of Cambrai, though it had
been joined by the Emperor, the King of France and
the Pope, had moved. The League (which was nominally
gathered to oppose the Turk) had won a victory, French

and only French, and it lay therefore in the power of the King of France to say whether the places Venice had held before that victory should go back to their former owners; Verona to the Emperor, Ravenna to the Pope, the south Italian port of Otranto to Ferdinand of Spain.

The republic of Venice, with its unfailing political sense, saw that the allies would be rendered uneasy by the French victory. The next year, 1510, the second phase began. The Pope forgave Venice (which he had put under an interdict). He began to move against Louis of France to drive him from the Milanese, and Ferdinand of Spain, King Henry's father-in-law, began to rally to the Pope. Wolsey, already with some power, advised his King, for what his weight was worth, to join the movement.

The French King was getting isolated as the very result of his victory. The Pope, at great expense, had bought up the mercenary troops of which the now virtually independent Swiss cantons were full; men well-trained, brave, large-bodied, enduring, indifferent to particular governments, out for hire; the chief reserve of mercenary troops of those days of salaried armies.

The French crown in its danger conceived the idea of calling a General Council against the Pope; so opens the second phase.

If there was one thing the Papacy dreaded it was the calling of a General Council against itself. The King of France relied, with insufficient judgment, upon the old conciliar movement, which was really dead. He argued from the Decree of the Council of Constance that a General Council should be called every ten years, and on the oath taken by Julius II himself upon his accession

7 years before, promising to call one. The King called such a Council at Pisa. It was a fiasco. The Pope denounced the Cardinals as schismatic and made new Cardinals to support him (including Bainbridge—the Archbishop of York—who was ever at his side) convoked a true Council to meet at the Lateran the next year, and meanwhile formed what he called "The Holy League", which got its title from the idea of defending the Papacy against the power of the French in North Italy. Venice was with him, of course; Ferdinand of Spain, and the young Henry VIII, Ferdinand's son-in-law, were to join in before the end of the year. General war followed.

It was on November 13, 1511, that Henry, the King of England, joined the League, and henceforward was allied with his father-in-law, Ferdinand, and the Emperor Maximilian against the French power.

Knowing what Wolsey was to become there has been a temptation for modern historians to regard him as the author of England's entry in force upon the battlefields of Europe for the first time within the memory of man. It is an error, Wolsey advised of course, as I have said, for what his advice might at this early stage be worth, and, as we shall see, the war gave him a new opportunity and before it was over saw him the first man in government. But so early as the end of 1511 it was not Wolsey who decided such affairs. It was Ferdinand of Aragon, master of Spain and Southern Italy, working presumably through his daughter, the Queen, who brought Henry in. But we must note that at the same moment Wolsey enters the Council, it is in these last days of 1511 that we first see his signature in Council, "Wolsey."

He comes in as but one among many and a junior.

But he is at last officially of the administration, and how strongly and immediately he used his new position we shall see.

I have said that already, before the death of the old King, Wolsey had acquired through ecclesiastical preferments a permanent income which had some effect upon his position. That financial basis was now increased. The income which Wolsey enjoyed upon this his first entry into the Council at the end of 1511 was considerable. It did not make him a rich man as the more important men were counted, but it gave him a substantial position from which to rise. He had what we should call today about £4,000 a year from parish benefices alone.[1]

It is true that this was a gross income subject to considerable deductions from the charges of collection over considerable distances, and for the cost of keeping substitutes to do the actual work of the parish. One of these benefices, Lydd, was only three days off in Kent, and the next nearest, Redgrave, was five days off in Suffolk. His original parish of Lymington was quite a week away, while his latest endowment at Great Torrington was further still. Still, the net residue left him with the income of a gentleman, apart from what he received from his offices.

To this had been added before the old King died the

[1] Here, as throughout this book, I quote the sums of the day in terms of modern money, its purchasing power in goods and services. It is the only way to convey a true impression. For this purpose I multiply the original sums in £.s.d. by 20 to 25. I think the real multiple ought to be rather higher, but as the old-fashioned academic rate of calculation is still current (calling "Henry's penny the Victorian shilling"), I have deliberately chosen a multiple rather too low because I know that, even at this rate, it will sound unusual. In a note at the end of this volume, Note "B," I have given the full argument in support of such a conclusion.

Deanery of Lincoln and a Prebend in that Cathedral as well, his perquisites as Almoner, his new property in Bridewell, a Prebend at Hereford, a Canonry at Windsor, and the Registrarship of the Garter. For a man who agreed with Foxe on the necessity for correcting the abuse of pluralities he was doing well. He had acquired that taste for wealth which later on was to be an adjunct to his power and to feed the splendour in which he delighted.

But as yet the sums of which he disposed were not upon a scale to render him remarkable amid the great riches of the Court and of the Council itself. With his patron Foxe holding the vast revenues of Winchester, with Suffolk at his side, and Surrey at the Council board, it was not a few modest thousands a year that distinguished him, it was the sudden burst of industry which marked him, the grasp of affairs that he at once showed, and his lightning swoop upon opportunity.

A great war was afoot, the first great war of the generation. He had not made it but he would use it. Parliament voted the necessary subsidies, not guessing what was to come. By the spring and early summer of 1512, fifteen thousand men had been gathered and armed, and it was Wolsey who organised. No one else seems to have volunteered for the work or no one else to have been competent for it. It was he perhaps who gave the command of the expedition to Dorset, the son of his former patron; it was certainly he who did all the "Q" work; to him all the letters were addressed; he gave the orders, bought provisions, organised transports, controlled all the mass of detail of what was, remember, for an English government of that day an experiment without precedent and without tradition; something that had to be made all of a piece out of nothing. To have proved himself suddenly capable of such a work was Wolsey's title to all that followed. He was in his fortieth year, and acting in the plenitude of his great talent.

Wolsey then was the business side of England's first great continental expedition, but he was not the political side of it. Had he designed *that side*, it might have been less disastrous.

Ferdinand, who had called the English contingent to Spain, desired to use it for his own ends. He had joined the Holy League, not from any affection for the Pope, nor any orthodox scruple against the schismatic Council the French had summoned at Pisa, but to make certain of Navarre. Navarre was that disputed Basque kingdom on the Pyrenees, with its capital at Pamplona on the south side of the mountains, over which the French or the Spanish crown could claim suzerainty. The bait held out to the then romantic and always unstable youth on the throne of England was the possession of Guienne, that is, of the country of Garonne and Bordeaux, its vineyards and its wealth. His ancestors on his mother's side the legitimate Plantagenet kings of England, had held that land for centuries, it had been finally lost only within living memory. The loss of their English market was still regretted by the inhabitants, there was still an appreciable memory of an older and more prosperous time before the King of France had swept Guienne into his net. The great Talbot had died less than 60 years before in the last battle fought for its recovery.

But Ferdinand cared nothing for all this. Whether he believed that the English force, large as it was, could hold such a conquest is doubtful; what he was certain of was that with so great a force between Navarre and the sea his left was secure and he could secure his own hold over the disputed province which alone concerned him. When he should have secured that possession the fortunes of his son-in-law on French soil were indifferent to him.

Dorset and his 15,000 very miserably failed. They found themselves under the very worst of a southern summer attacked by disease, and they effected nothing. The men mutinied and compelled their general to bring them home that autumn. It was disaster. And even as they mutinied it was Wolsey whom they cursed, imagining him to have launched the expedition (in which imagination they were wrong, as were many others), but knowing him to be the man responsible for their provisionment and pay and therefore in their eyes the author of the whole affair. It was the first launching of Wolsey's unpopularity, an unpopularity which grew unceasingly even as his power grew, spread to every rank. It broke upon him at the end, when he lost the King's support, and swept him away.

The disaster was of no effect, nor was the unpopularity, upon the man whom they chiefly concerned. He was the more determined to advance in his strength, and what he next did by way of compensation for this defeat put him once and for all in the saddle and made him the right hand of the King.

He set to work to organise a new expedition, and this time to control its policy, as well as its staff work, provisionment, transport and pay. Not only a new expedition but a much larger one, and now that he was to be consulted on the essential things as well as the material side, he advised a plan very differently thought out than that abortive stroke across the Bay of Biscay which could serve no end but Spain's. The attack was to be delivered at close range on the immediately opposing shores of the Channel, with Calais as its base. The immediate political ally was no longer to be Ferdinand but the Emperor Maximilian, whose frontiers of the Low Countries stood within a ten days' march of Paris. It was to strike at the disputed cities, the wealth of which was important to the French power, and which were symbols of the undying dispute between the Empire and the French for the control of the belt of Flanders; for the French claimed feudal suzerainty over it; the Emperor, as the heir of Burgundy, was actual sovereign.

Of these towns on the edge of the Netherlands two were principally aimed at, the two great commercial cities of Thérouanne and Tournai.

On the Feast of St. Peter and St. Paul, or, as it was called in England, St. Peter's Day, the 29th June, 1513, it blew so hard from the north that nothing dared venture out from Dover into the white sea beyond the lee of the cliffs, and the shipping in the offing took refuge by running before the wind to the ports of the French coast.

On the next day, the 30th June, the wind, still favourable, had dropped to a strong breeze, and men saw from the walls of Calais, "the King of England coming with his fleet, such as Neptune never saw before." Three weeks later he set out with his great host, his guns, his baggage, and the fine retinues about each leader; Charles Brandon, Lord Lisle, with a whole battalion, Thomas Boleyn with a hundred men; and a score of others the same, John Seymour among them. Foxe, Bishop of Winchester, came with a hundred men, but Wolsey had double the number.

They sat down before Thérouanne, and Maximilian,
the Emperor, was there, he for whom all was being
done. For if Henry was to get the glory, Wolsey the
advantage, Maximilian was to gather the results. The
Emperor went about amongst them "of middle height,
open and manly countenance, nose in the air, pallid com-
plexion, and grey beard," very well pleased, absurdly
professing to be but a private soldier serving under
Henry's command, but getting £1,500 a day for his
pains.

After the French had been beaten off in the rout of
August 16th, the "Battle of the Spurs", the town could
not be saved. On the 23rd August, St. Bartholomew's
Eve, the garrison of four thousand marched out, and on
the next day, the St. Bartholomew, the King and the
Emperor entered with all imaginable pomp.

In the destruction that followed it was again Henry,
or rather the English taxpayer, who was paying; for
only two days later nearly a thousand labourers were
at work pulling down the walls, though it was the Emperor's soldiers who finished the burning and destroying
of the whole place.

It was Maximilian who demanded that Thérouanne
should be destroyed as an example to rebels (for so he
held them) and the town was utterly razed to the ground.
We can follow today the big mounds which are the
relics of its walls, we can go down what was its great
High street, now a country road, to a wretched village
which still bears its name. On either side of us as we
go are ploughed fields where once stood the crowded
wealth of stores and burgess houses, and a tree-grown
hillock marks the ruin of its magnificent cathedral.

By the middle of September the triumphal army had

already pitched their camp by Tournai. The news had come in from England that the Scotch had been completely overthrown at Flodden on the 9th, and they said Te Deum in Lille Cathedral eight days after the victory. The surrender of Tournai followed at the beginning of the week. Brandon after a conspicuous feat of arms was made governor. The Bishopric was promised to Wolsey. On the 21st October the King sailed again from Calais. In those four months Wolsey had been made.

The whole of that few weeks of fighting in a wet summer had been a triumph, and in it Wolsey shone with the beginning of that magnificence which was to distinguish his later years.

Henry had desired glory, and glory had been given him, and Wolsey was the man who had bestowed it. Henceforward he and the King were one; very soon he was doing all that was done in the King's name.

It is to Wolsey that all write, it is Wolsey whom all recognise as the new leader; for it is he who by his ceaseless labours during that rainy seige of Thérouanne, by his exact organisation, has brought victory. There is not a detail which he does not watch. You may find in the papers of the day such a little note as this: "Two great culverins with 28 mares to draw them at 1od. a day per mare" and the item is not countersigned by any subordinate, it bears the name of the director in chief, "Thomas Wulcy." It is Wolsey who writes to the Queen on the very day of the surrender of Thérouanne, the 23rd of August. It is Wolsey who receives the Queen's answer in forty-eight hours, telling him that "Almighty God helps here our part as well as there." And she puts it down to Henry's devotion to the Faith. It is to Wolsey that she writes again a week later, closely and intimately, and a fortnight later again, begging him to continue writing, telling him what comfort his letters are to her, giving him the news of Flodden, excusing herself for writing late, saying she had waited for a sufficient account. It is to Wolsey that Ruthal, the Bishop of Durham, writes begging for aid, seeing how heavy his expenses have been through the Scottish war, and crying "For the love of God, maister Almosner, rembee this matter and keep it secrete." It is Wolsey whom Maximilian sees to be the centre of all things, even as early as the first victories. It is of Wolsey that Henry writes to Bainbridge in Rome, Archbishop and Cardinal of York, begging him from the camp before Tournai to find preferment for his Almoner.

There also, after Tournai had fallen and been occupied, passed a detail hardly noticed at the time but to be of ironic interest in a few years.

The King of England received a letter come from Rome, written a fortnight after the Te Deum in Lille, a week after Tournai had surrendered. It was written by Giulio de Medici; the conventional announcement to a sovereign that the writer had been made Cardinal, and assuring Henry of his services. But what were those services to be? The man who wrote was to be Clement VII, the Pope of the divorce.

Meanwhile upon the other front, against Scotland the ally of France, Queen Catherine, Regent at home in her husband's absence, had sent Surrey to win the great victory of Flodden, whence dates the gradual absorption of that country by the English crown. King James was killed, his wife, Henry's sister, was left precariously Regent for her infant child. But Catherine's successes at home did not counterbalance the presence and the acts of Wolsey abroad, and when Henry came back to her she found that she no longer governed that malleable man. Wolsey now held him, and would hold him tight enough for fourteen years.

Such was the work of Wolsey in 1513. Such was his gift to his new young master, in whose eyes he now seemed so great a figure. He had given Henry what Henry most desired; the toy of military renown. Henceforward the Almoner was to take over much more than staff work. He had entered into power.

VI

THE SECOND ACT

WOLSEY at the turn of the year (1513-14) was already master. He was master through his conduct of the military triumph which had filled the young King with a kind of awe: a wonder that any man could do such things—and that they had been done for him. Henry, not yet knowing the world, with such a character as we know, hitherto managed by his wife—only twenty-two years old as yet, and considering only his toys with no conception of foreign policy or of organisation —had fallen upon a genius; and a genius in his fortieth year, and a genius who was at once respectful, gaily companionable, and as it seemed endowed with an amazing universal aptitude. The young King was captured, and had a new master before whom Catherine sank into the background.

That new master went forward with plan and decision. In the new year he got the promise of the Bishopric of Lincoln. The Pope went through the formality of provision (it was of course in Henry's gift) on the 6th of February, 1514; within a month the temporalities had been made over to the man who was now virtually the only minister. On the 26th of March he was consecrated.

But he was moving for much more. Indeed there was nothing more remarkable in Wolsey's life than the rapidity with which he makes the gambit. In that same week in which the Pope had signed the provision for Lincoln, on the very next day, he was suggesting that he should be made *Legate a Latere*.

How extraordinary the demand was, even later when his power was known throughout Europe and when the Papacy was in desperate need of allies, I will tell immediately; that he should move for such a thing now when that name was only just piercing, when men had hardly grasped what he was, is astonishing as a flash of manœuvre. He had to wait for the post long and anxiously. It was strange that he should have expected it at all; but he had sown the seed thus early; and not much later he sent the Deputy Collector of the Pope in England, Polydore Vergil, to intrigue subtly at Rome for him in another matter. He would be a Cardinal. This also was early enough, in all conscience. He had but just exchanged the Almoner's post for a Bishopric, and he was asking for the Hat! Polydore Vergil was warned not to proceed as though from Wolsey himself, but to have quiet suggestions made, to get the thing talked of in a roundabout way, so that when the offer came it should seem the spontaneous gift of Rome.

There is another new thing apparent in this early moment of Wolsey's progress, a thing which continues throughout his life. He used more than one agent, and he was careful to keep each agent ignorant of what the other was about. While Polydore Vergil was thus suggesting and sending the word round that a Cardinalate for Wolsey would be a strengthening of the Papal policy, that it would secure the support of Henry against whoever might threaten the Papal States in Italy, Wolsey was giving the same task to Sylvester de Giglis, the resident at the Papal Court who permanently represented England and was endowed with the revenues of the Bishopric of Worcester. This man had appreciated in those early months of 1514 what Wolsey had become, and that to be agent for Henry VIII meant to be agent for Wolsey.

Leo X, the new Pope of somewhat over a year's standing, had a mind to give Bainbridge a legacy *a Latere* for the court of Henry VIII. He had inherited Bainbridge from his predecessor Julius II; Bainbridge held the second See of England, York, he had a very great name, he was a Cardinal of some years standing. Had *he* been sent as *Legate a Latere* to Henry it would have been normal enough. A *Legate a Latere* was a Papal Ambassador and Lieutenant at once. He was sent into distant countries with plenary powers to act locally as the Pope might act. He was sent for a special occasion. He returned after a brief visit. Such Legates had been sent to England in the past more than once, but their stay in England had been short because only critical moments demanded their presence. Their function was special and brief, and it had been of the essence of their mission that they had come straight from the Pope himself and returned to him.

Wolsey, on hearing that this idea of sending Bainbridge to England as Legate was in the air, put up the strongest opposition. He seemed to make it almost a fundamental law of the realm that such a visitor, though himself English, should not land in the island without particular precautions, and at any rate (he said) the appointment was unsuitable, and then again there was no call for it at the moment. Yet he himself only recently a Bishop, unheard of in Europe till yesterday, already designed to be Legate—in the end to be Legate for life.

The audacity, the enormity of the demand, lay especially in this, that Wolsey was a permanently resident subject of the King, an Englishman, living in England and ruling there. If he were made Legate it would be handing over the Papal power to the King whom Wolsey served and already almost replaced.

But while Wolsey was thus reacting with all his strength in the spring and early summer of 1514 against the appointment of Bainbridge, and beginning himself to make the extraordinary demand for his own appointment, there happened, in the midst of that summer, something which, if history could be written from full evidence (it never is) would be the chief episode in Wolsey's life. It was the strange and sudden death of Bainbridge.

What followed is typical of the energy with which Wolsey pushed himself upwards. The campaign of the year before, 1513, gave him for the first time chief influence over the King; only at its close had he begun to outdistance Catherine in that field, for Henry was always under the control of the stronger character in his presence. Absence freed him.

The winter of '13-'14 is the opening of Wolsey's full power over the King. Yet in half a year this incident of his ambition is upon us and Wolsey is already taking full advantage of it. It is a rise more rapid than Napoleon's.

We have seen who Bainbridge was. We have seen that in this first half year of 1514 Bainbridge was the principal bar to Wolsey's further progress. Seniority, long fame, the great revenues of York, the great position of Archbishop, the chance of the Cardinalate, the claim to legateship—all these made Bainbridge the rival, all these combine to give the strongest motive for the removal of Bainbridge. There must be added one other motive, special to the hour. The opening of 1514 was the very moment in which the lad who was King of England (barely 23) was in high passion against Catherine's father, Ferdinand of Spain, who had made a special peace behind his back. If that anger could be made to last, Queen Catherine's control over her husband, which had now lasted four years, might be eliminated and leave the field clear for Wolsey. But the influence of Bainbridge, devoted to the Papal policy, appointed to Rome in the days when Catherine first managed affairs, might have set back the whole plan. Bainbridge might have appeased the young man's wrath and have reinstated the Spanish connection, if not in its old strength (for the Pope had already proposed the French marriage of Henry's sister and was determined on peace) at least so much as to restore and maintain Catherine's rivalry against the new minister.

In the middle of July, 1514, when all this was at stake, Bainbridge died of poison.

Was Wolsey guilty of the murder?

We shall never know. The Cardinal of York had been poisoned by his Chaplain, Rinaldo of Modena. The murderer said that he had been urged to the crime by that same Sylvester Giglis who was doing the most secret of Wolsey's work at Rome.

Giglis vehemently denied the charge. The murderer killed himself. It was given out that he was a madman, that he had acted in revenge for a blow which he had received from the dead man; and though Pace (who was Bainbridge's executor, and who knew nothing of Wolsey's intrigues with Giglis) was pressing for a full inquiry, the thing was hushed up and Giglis left free.

Wolsey had promised to defend Giglis, *as he would*

defend himself. It is more than probable, one might almost say it is certain, that Leo believed the charge, at least as against Giglis. When, later, pressure was put upon him to make Giglis Cardinal in his capacity of English envoy at Rome, Leo refused, saying: "It would be an infamy!"

The very moment the news of Bainbridge's death reached England, Wolsey, already Dean of York, was proclaimed his successor in the Archbishopric; and let us remember that Bainbridge before his death complained of interference by Wolsey in the gathering of the revenues of the See, and that he had denounced Giglis for a traitor. On the 5th of August the temporalities of the See were given to Wolsey, and it is worth noting that the money which the new Archbishop borrowed for the charges of the transference and for the Pall, some £80,-000 of our money, was repaid not out of Wolsey's new revenues, but out of the dead man's estate.

A week later young Henry wrote personally to the Pope begging that Wolsey should be made a Cardinal, as Bainbridge had been. But Leo would not be hurried, partly perhaps because the scandal was too recent; mainly because he had no inclination to give away all the assets he held in hand for bargaining with the English Government (which now meant Wolsey himself). The three-cornered duel between the Pope and France and the enemies of France, the ever-changing predominance in Italy of now one power from beyond the Alps and now another, made it essential for each of the players to keep in hand his best cards as long as possible, and we shall see how Leo did not yield on this matter of the Cardinalate until, more than a year later, the sudden victory of French arms over Milan constrained him to the hurried purchase of Wolsey's support.

Such was the singular introduction of the new controller. He now appeared in this year 1514 as a deputy-king. His name stood for England. With a vast personal revenue to be added to unceasingly for years by gifts, new endowments, foreign pensions, some secretly extorted, and bribes; with a sure grasp on the whole machine of government, he set out to direct in full the affairs of the country. His confidence was as boundless as his energy. He felt himself possessed of a material he could handle at will. He did so handle it—and with this result, that in Foreign Affairs he missed his aim without exception, with unvarying error: that each such failure raised him by one step more in his power and its grand accoutrement at home; that in England itself he gathered all the ropes of administration into his single hand, put the lay and civil executive, the making of laws and ordinances, the ecclesiastical world into one, and, when he fell, left to the Crown an unchecked mastery. He had made possible the raising of taxes hitherto unheard of —for he had destroyed the power of resistance from below. He had made possible confiscation and loot of sacred endowments. He had left the way free for a lay prince to be supreme over the Church itself.

We are about to follow the action of Wolsey in the affairs of Europe.

It was this activity which made him the famous figure in history that he is. Even had he not attempted to influence the main affairs of Europe and confined himself to mastery over England, to the reformation of the church there, to the management of his king and to the creation of a despotic central government, he would take the full place that he does in the story of his country; but undoubtedly what gives him his stature in the general story of our civilisation is the effect he produced upon contemporaries outside, and that effect he owed altogether to his powerful intervention among the great interests which were dividing the world. For this he is everywhere remembered—yet it was especially in this that he failed. He blundered in every foreign effort he attempted. He was always either too late or ill informed, or unable to judge the proportions of a problem. No single object of the dozen or more he set before him in 15 years of active intrigue throughout Europe was attained. None the less Wolsey as foreign minister was renowned over all the world and his fame filled Christendom.

Why was this? It was because his work was so incessant, his action so universal. All were perforce preoccupied with it. The noise was continual and the pressure unrelieved. His attack was continuous. That it was always beaten off men half forgot because it was always renewed. And all this came suddenly in a time when Europe had ceased to expect force from England.

England was not yet upon a scale of population or even wealth (though she was wealthier in proportion to her numbers than most districts) to preoccupy continental minds as a rule when Wolsey appeared upon the scene. She had ceased to be for now a hundred years a general part of Anglo-French civilisation, for a hundred years her governing class had ceased to be French-speaking. The attempted combination of France and England into one realm—an effort which had filled the Middle Ages—had been abandoned for a lifetime; only the oldest men could remember the last feeble efforts to maintain a Plantagenet upon the French throne, and already 25 years had passed since the last Plantagenet had fallen and the usurping Tudors had succeeded. It was Wolsey who unexpectedly thrust England again to the forefront of interest. To the forefront of power he could not thrust her, for even had *he* had the qualities required the nation had not sufficient resources for that. It could not rival France or Spain. But his sudden new unique capture of all the springs of government put into his control far larger sums of money than could normally have been raised from a nation on such a scale, and at the same time this unchallenged individual power permitted him to act always directly and swiftly. The effect upon contemporary opinion in Spain, in France, in Germany and Rome was the greater because it came after so long a period during which no one had thought of England save as a place declining under continual civil war or, later, given a brief peace by an adventurer who had made himself King, but who certainly would not venture abroad.

The interests into which Wolsey now thrust England appear upon the surface such a tangle of twining and untwining alliances, of open treaties broken, renewed, secretly denounced, of private understandings and betrayals, successive defeats and victories, often within a few months one of the other, that, unless we find the directing principles which give unity to the whole it is almost impossible to follow it. The confusion is made worse by Wolsey's own lack of any one directing principle. By so much as he had one clear aim of personal dominance, personal wealth and personal glory at home, by so much he lacked any constant object in dealing with foreign powers. But there are three main facts which determine all this jumble of treaties and wars.

The first of these main facts was the persistent effort of the French nation and Crown to thrust forward into North Italy, and later to react against the overshadowing House of Austria, the German and the Spanish power combined.

The second was the determination of the Papacy during this quarrel between France and the Hapsburgs to prevent itself from falling into complete subservience under the one or the other. "The Pope would not be chaplain to the King of France or to the Emperor."

The third was the pressure continuing and increasing all the while, of the Mohammedan in the Mediterranean and up the Danube valley.

The whole sequence of Wolsey's action turns *not* (as is too often imagined) upon any attempt to strike a balance between the conflicting forces abroad, but upon his following and supporting of the Papacy in those shifts and changes whereby it kept up the wrestle for independence both in spiritual power and as a temporal state.

One thing he left aside: the Mohammedan pressure. Of all Christian states England was most remote from that menace, and Wolsey, a man always confined to the thing immediately under his eye, hardly let it enter his calculations. He mentions it and Henry mentions it, for the time was full of it. The defence of Christendom against the Infidel appears as the conventional motive for one diplomatic arrangement after another, but it never took a serious part in the general scheme.

As to the resistance of France to the growing Hapsburg menace, the conditions were these:

Maximilian of Hapsburg, the head of that house, was Emperor in the years before Wolsey rose. He possessed, that is, was directly sovereign over, various inherited states centring round Vienna. His was "The House of Austria" and Vienna was his capital. We have seen how he had married the heiress of Burgundy and got with her the French-speaking Burgundian possessions in the Jura country and also the mixed French- and Flemish-speaking Low Countries, that is, not only what we call today Holland and Belgium but a large strip of what is today Northern France, going as far as Arras. To be Emperor meant to be nominally the Head of Europe and more really the overlord of what was called "The Empire"—a mass of states and cities (including his own) nearly independent of the person set over them and yet regarding that person with awe, providing fitful subsidies to him and occasional armies. The bond was a weak one, it was not even strong enough to produce a sufficient force to meet the Turk on equal terms in the Danube Valley and Vienna was repeatedly in peril.

Meanwhile, in those same years before Wolsey rose, Spain which had been formed into one country by the marriage of the King of Aragon with the Heiress of Castile and by their common conquest of Grenada, became possessed, through the discovery of America, of a New World; and the gold and silver of that New World were beginning to pour in, making the power of Spain increasingly important.

Now for this great power there was no heir, there were only two daughters; Catherine who had married the King of England and had no more right to the throne, and Joan who was to inherit the vast kingdom. Maximilian married his son Philip to Joan. But he was a man of fifty, and had bad health at the time of which we speak. When he should die (and in point of fact he died before Wolsey had held power for quite five years) all this great bundle of sovereignty—direct rule over so much in South Germany, Imperial power over the rest, immediate sovereignty over Burgundy, Flanders and the east of France, the nominal right to appoint a ruler in Milan, all South Italy called the Kingdom of Naples, all Spain and all the immense new wealth of the New World, would be Hapsburg. It did not fall to Philip because Philip died, but it fell to Philip's son Charles, who was born in 1500, who was to become the mighty Charles V and who failed by but a little to become the master of the whole western world.

Such was the menace of the Hapsburg power, and wedged in between the two branches of it lay France. Necessarily the French effort, even as an effort of mere survival, was resistance to this overwhelming thing.

Now in what direction could that resistance be most effective? In Italy.

Northern Italy was the wedge thrust in between the two halves of the Hapsburg dominion. The immixture of the French in Italy was not the result of the situation created by the Hapsburg menace; it was far, far older. The French kings would in any case have tried their adventures beyond the Alps and had already begun doing so before it was appreciated what Spain was to become, and what therefore the Hapsburg intermarriage with Spain would produce; but it remains true that the existence of the French claims in Italy (Louis XII had claimed Milan by descent and had seized it) led to the use of that situation as the main weapon of the French

monarchy for resisting the Hapsburg power when the
full menace of that power was apparent.

The word "Italy" meant at that time politically (north
of the solid Spanish block which governed the Kingdom
of Naples in the south) a number of States some very
small, none of them on the scale of a nation; and these
states played and were played one against the other perpetually during the whole of this time.

The most important, the most necessarily permanent,
was the temporal dominion of the Pope, with Rome for
its capital. It stretched right across from sea to sea in a
belt cutting off the lesser principalities to the north, from
the Kingdom of Naples holding the whole south. Of
these lesser principalities in the north the central one, the
richest and the keystone of all the group, was the Duchy
of Milan. At one moment the French seize and hold the
Duchy of Milan, at another they lose it. The Emperor,
who nominally had the right to invest claimants with
the Duchy, attempts to assert his power, succeeds and
fails alternately. And all the while it is the holding of
Milan by the French which makes them for the moment
the dominating power between the Alps and Rome, or
the loss of it which brings back the predominance of the
Hapsburgs.

In the see-saw between those two struggling strengths,
a see-saw of which the Milanese is the shifting weight,
one major interest remains fixed, and if we concentrate
our attention upon that interest we can understand the
whole apparently inextricable tangle. That interest is the
interest of the Papal States, the district of which Rome
was the capital and the Pope the King.

Just as the Pope in his larger function as spiritual head
of Christendom struggles against subservience alternately

to the Hapsburgs and France, so does the Pope as sovereign of the Papal States struggle to maintain and increase his temporal power lest it should fall under the
virtual overlordship of Paris or Vienna. Of all the war-
ring powers, small and great, the Papacy in its temporal
sense "Kingship of Rome and the Papal States" is that
which lends unity to the whirligig of those twenty years.

The Pope stands thus the fixed centre of the whirlpool
in Northern Italy with four main qualities attached to
him which secure his position and make him the perpetual centre on which all pivots. First, he has still by
far the highest prestige; secondly, through payments
from all over Europe he has an immense and certain income. Such income was a great importance in those days
of war waged with highly paid hired soldiers, days in
which great monarchs like Maximilian and Francis find
themselves at times suddenly without resources. Thirdly,
the Papacy was a state certain of continuance in spite of
an antiquity compared with which those of all others
were negligible. It was vigorously continuous. There
were no minorities, there were no appreciable inter-
regnums, there was no longer any danger of Anti-popes
and disputed succession or civil war. Most important of
all, there could be no counter hereditary claims to its
possession, as there was with Milan, Navarre and fifty
other towns and districts of Christendom. Lastly, the
Papacy could pay for a support in a coinage which no
other power commanded: it could grant highly coveted
titles, benefices more coveted still, and spiritual jurisdictions ardently desired both for their revenue and for their
power. It could purchase an alliance by calling a King
"Defender of the Faith", by making a distant Prelate a
Legate or Cardinal or both, by adding to a Cardinalate

the privileges of a special Legateship: that is, deputed power enabling its holder to act as Pope abroad. Conversely Papacy could excommunicate. It could summon, with considerable remaining moral force, the succour of a Christian Prince or City as in duty bound to maintain the Holy See. It could ask for such succour in the name of Christendom itself, for Christendom was, remember, in all men's eyes still one sacred thing and the Pope the necessary symbol and active agent of that unity.

To complete an appreciation of the forces in Italy we must see what was meant by the "eccentric factor"— Venice.

Venice was a State unlike any other in the bundle of the Italian states and cities because it passed for being in the eyes of others and was in its own eyes invincible; because it was founded on a sea power which none could seriously challenge, because that sea power gave it a commerce which filled it with immediate and available wealth, far beyond its needs, liquid, disponable at a moment's notice; and because it had by far the best diplomatic machine, the best foreign office. All this peculiar strength of Venice reposed on one moral basis, the same as that on which the power of England until quite recently depended and Venice was, after the regular model of great commercial societies based on sea power, an aristocracy. A wealthy governing class cheerfully obeyed, skilled in managing its inferiors, native and foreign, never dying, all its personalities in touch one with another, was the soul animating the whole.

Therefore did Venice stand permanent, whether as a stumbling block to any other ambitious power or as an ally; and therefore it is that you find the Papacy and every other unit in the game alternately opposing and approaching "The Most Serene"; "The Mother of the Cities", "The Republic". And Venice, Mistress of the mainland along the Alps right up to the confines of Milan, holding the issues of all the eastern Alpine roads to Germany including the all-important Brenner, yielding a little here and now recovering what it had yielded, certain at its heart that it was secure, plays a part entirely its own in all the competitions of the time.

There you have the elements of the foreign field which Wolsey must deal with. Already before his advent Louis XII had invaded Italy and taken Milan with the aid of Venice. It was against that preponderance of France that the Papacy had called the league which Henry like his father-in-law Ferdinand and Maximilian had joined, and which had pushed the campaigns of 1512 and 1513: the victory of Thérouanne and those wars in which the young king of England's Almoner had first taken the reins. That coalition had succeeded. Louis had lost Milan. The Papacy was free of the French menace. It did not want to strengthen the Allies further. Julius II had died, Leo X had succeeded him and all was ready for peace when the Campaign of Thérouanne was accomplished.

But Wolsey did not understand. He allowed himself —and Henry—to be duped.

All was done in spite of him. Before he was back in England Ferdinand caused to be signed by his envoys at Lille a solemn Treaty in which he promised to invade Southern France in the next year, while his son-in-law again invaded it from the north, and Henry was to pay £125,000 to aid the Spanish campaign.

Not a month later Maximilian in his turn was promising most faithfully to renew the war in 1514, and

Wolsey was busy preparing to raise again the most enormous sums for that coming campaign.

He was the man now so unquestionably supreme in his own country, and by these vast levies of money, which the greater rivals and leaders could not match, so able apparently to impose his will abroad, that he should have had the game in his hands. Yet he allowed Henry to be deceived, for he himself was deceived as well. It is a proof of what he was in his person and manner, that Henry's anger after the betrayal was to fall, not on him, but on his fellow-princes. Even at this moment, while D'Arcy was writing to Wolsey (in the beginning of the next year), "Sir, every man will now seek to be your friend," the allies were beginning to make peace behind his back.

A week before Christmas, 1513, the Pope Leo had written to Henry urging peace, and Maximilian and Ferdinand were playing their own game as though neither Wolsey nor Henry was worthy of consideration. Before the end of February the King of England was writing angrily to Margaret of Savoy in Flanders complaining that there were rumours of her father's desertion of him and of the King of Spain's desertion as well. He was right. The thing was afoot. But neither he nor Wolsey had been made a party to it. They were completely taken in. More than a month before, the Emperor had written to his daughter telling her of the proposal, and she had written vigorously protesting: *"Car je vous asseure, Monseigneur, que en lui"* (Henry VIII) *"n'a nulle faintise . . . . on doit aller de semblable maniere et ne lui rompre nulle promesse."* ("For I assure you, my Lord, there is no guile in him and one ought to treat him answerably and break no promise.") But her plea was not heard.

Similarly Wolsey's plan (for as it was Henry's, it must have been Wolsey's) to retrieve the position by forcing a marriage between Brandon, the handsome favourite, and Margaret the Governess of the Netherlands, and so getting a hold on the Emperor her father, failed altogether. In vain was Brandon made Duke of Suffolk, in vain was he urged to a violent wooing, which she favoured. The Emperor put a stop to it, making her ashamed of such a match, and while Wolsey was assuring Maximilian through Henry that only a *mauvais esprit* could have put it about that any such marriage was proposed, his duplicity was so patent that it had been guessed almost before it was written down.

By April 1514 the thing was settled. The Emperor and Ferdinand had determined to make peace. And the King of England was left to undignified tirades and shoutings against the perfidy of his allies—he had made such huge and such expensive preparations for the renewal of the war!

Even the matter of the French marriage was not Wolsey's doing. It seems natural to think it was, coming after such a disappointment, and it has been repeated over and over again that it was Wolsey's. It was nothing of the sort. It was the Pope's. And the Pope alludes to it later as a matter of common knowledge that he had suggested it and pressed it.

The matter had stood thus. While Wolsey's policy and the King's was still a fast alliance with Maximilian against France, Maximilian's grandson Charles, a boy of thirteen, had been affianced to Henry's younger sister Mary, four years older. When he wrote to her he signed, *vostre Mari* (your husband). He was that silent, studious, awkward boy, already rightful king of Castile, soon on Ferdinand's death to be monarch of all that was Spanish, in five years, upon Maximilian his grandfather's death, to be Emperor as well. Well on in that month of April 1514, Foxe was writing from Esher to Wolsey (on the 17th), urging the marriage, as the young prince would soon be of the canonical age of fourteen, at which date by solemn treaty it was to take place. Yet only three days later Gattinara was making fairly sure that Louis XII, not Charles, would marry Mary. The initiative had not come from England, it had come from Rome. And the elderly Louis XII himself was thinking of it before it had entered Wolsey's head. Wolsey did not lead here, he followed. Maximilian himself, I think, knew what was toward before anyone did in England.[1] It seemed to him natural enough, after having thrown Henry overboard, that Henry should make his sister jilt Maximilian's heir, and his daughter Margaret, who had brought the boy up and looked after him, followed suit.

Though the proposed marriage between Henry's sister Mary, a girl of 17 and the elderly Louis XII of France was not Wolsey's idea,[2] though as I have said he followed

[1] Now, and again somewhat later, the elderly Maximilian showed signs, for all his astuteness, or perhaps as one might expect from his astuteness, of being a little touched in the head. He wrote to his daughter just about this time that he proposed to make himself Coadjutor to the Pope, and after his death *he was to be canonised*, and gloats over the way in which she will have to worship his bones. *"Il vous sera nécessité que, après ma mort, vous seres contraint de me adorer."* "You won't be able to escape it! After my death you will be compelled to adore me."

[2] Ludovico Canossa was the Pope's great diplomat who worked the marriage of Mary Tudor with Louis XII. Hence it may be said of Henry VIII, to the contrary of that other German Henry centuries before, that he did not go to Canossa but Canossa came to him.

and did not lead in the matter, yet it exactly suited his idea of what Europe was and would long continue to be.

Here was France defeated and driven out of Italy, her claim to control Navarre beyond the Pyrenees destroyed by the success of Ferdinand, and her efforts on the eastern frontier broken. The alliance of France with England, now that France was no longer a menace, would be a fitting answer to Maximilian and Ferdinand's duping of him. There would no longer be French pressure against the Papacy. The French King had yielded to Leo, the schismatic Council of Pisa was dissolved, there was no French army to overawe the Papal States from Milan. Further, in smiling upon the Pope's idea of an English-French alliance he made himself an especial friend of Leo and might expect from him those gifts, the Cardinalate and the Legateship, which he so intensely desired. He was perhaps already thinking of a higher ambition and of succeeding to the Papacy itself when Leo should depart.

The arrangement would last. Louis XII of France, though over 50, had plenty of years to live; as like as not he would have a son by Mary (as yet he had no son) who would succeed him, be ruled in minority by a Tudor mother and continue the advantage of the English Crown. It was all perfect. Mary was promised to Maximilian's grandson and heir, Charles of Austria, a boy of 14, but they had got out of that. Mary was sacrificed (she seems already to have had something of a love affair with Brandon) but that was inevitable with royalty. In the first week of October she had met her future husband at Abbeville and she must have noted, what so many others had, that he looked prematurely old, sitting on his high Spanish horse and his mouth

mumbling. It was stipulated as part of the marriage contract that the French Crown should give up Tournai:
and the revenues of the See of Tournai occupied Wolsey
not a little—none had yet been paid him. Everything
was thus settled apparently for the best, and all fitted in
exactly with what Wolsey might himself have chosen.
He half persuaded himself that he had planned the
whole thing. He spoke as though he alone were conducting it and, at any rate, he reposed in it as a final and
successful piece of diplomacy.

Whereupon, after some eleven brief weeks of high
revelry on the part of the young bride, of late hours and
misery on the part of the elderly bridegroom (whose idea
of a healthy day was to take his principal meal at eight
in the morning and to be in bed by six) Louis XII died
on New Year's day, 1515, and the whole scaffolding
crashed to the ground.

Those who had relied so much upon the permanent
weakening of the French throne, and at the same time its
support through the English alliance and Papal favour,
could console themselves by making sure at least that the
new King of France would be too much of a boy (he
had only just entered his 20th year) and too much afraid
of combination against him, too much afraid of hostility
from all around including the head of the Church, to
renew any French adventure. Italy was safe and the
peace. And in that firm assurance Wolsey could face his
second year of power, the year 1515, and his future
advance.

Meanwhile, someone must bring Mary Tudor back, in
her widowhood, from France. She would be a valuable
asset recovered in the diplomatic game. If it should ever
be necessary to veer round away from France and to the

Hapsburgs again, she might be held out as a bait. Wolsey concurred in or decided the choice of the messenger. Who should be chosen but Henry's boon companion, the conquering, the irresponsible, the very brave and handsome, and very scoundrelly Charles Brandon, newly-made Duke of Suffolk in the hope that he might have captured Margaret of Savoy.

It was imprudent. The promiscuous man had already had no little effect upon the girl before her marriage. Whether Wolsey knew of this or not, it may be doubted, for all his subtlety, whether he actually planned what followed. But at any rate he made use of it.

Suffolk was sent over on embassy to the French Court, met the King on February 1st, 1515, and on the 2nd, Candlemas, was given his formal reception at Noyon.

Now Francis was only 19, but he had good advisers. It was important that Mary Tudor should not be free for another royal alliance.

That same night Francis took the handsome Englishman aside and told him most cordially but very privately that the widowed Queen of France, Henry's sister, desired nothing better than to marry this, his new guest; and what is more, he told Suffolk certain things about them both with regard to their relations in the past. It would seem that Suffolk blushed, perhaps for the first and last time in his life. Francis added that he would do all he could for them both. Men thought he had himself been attracted to this widow in her 19th year, and it would have been no wonder if he had been, for she was not reticent, nor he scrupulous. But now he would help them!

The very next day Mary proposed to Suffolk, and Suffolk wrote off at once to Wolsey. He could not resist her. But indeed Suffolk never resisted any woman nor, apparently, any woman him.

If it was important to Francis that Mary should be prevented from a new Royal perhaps anti-French alliance, it was important to Wolsey that Suffolk already too influential with Henry should be pushed aside.

So Wolsey wrote back a long cordial letter assuring the Duke that Henry (as well as himself) thoroughly approved of his sister's plan, and encouraged them to go ahead! But had he said a word to Henry?

But for that letter Suffolk's fears would have conquered. It was a desperate risk. One does not tamper with the blood royal, nor did one in the sixteenth century make a King one's brother-in-law without his leave; especially a King with no male heir and fearful for the succession. Doubly must one hesitate to play such tricks when one is a favourite of little lineage, of sudden promotion, jealously hated by all the old names of the kingdom.

However, Wolsey was everything, he was more than King, and under this assurance that he as well as the King was all in their favour, the young woman and the man with whom she was infatuated were secretly married. Suffolk wrote again to Wolsey confessing that he was now Mary's husband.[1]

He begs Wolsey to show his letter to the King. It was March 5, and he tells the all-powerful man that in him is all his trust, and he sends a great diamond.

Now comes the revealing stroke. Wolsey wrote back in quite a different tone from his first letter. He had

[1] Everyone spelt words in those days as they sounded to them, but Suffolk's phonetics are out of the common. In this letter the word "our" when he speaks of himself and his wife becomes "howar," for he loved an extra h. And he calls himself Mary's "wosbound."

shown Suffolk's letter to Henry and he was sorry to say that Henry was extremely angry! He took the thing "grievously and displeasantly"; and Wolsey professes that he can "devise no remedy"—however, if Suffolk will pay back nearly half the Queen's jointure, surrender all her jewels and her plate, things may possibly be arranged.

Suffolk was so near the King and so dear to him, so thoroughly his companion, that he must be got rid of somehow, and the trap laid by Wolsey's first letter, snapped down by his second, was a very good way. On the strength of this letter Suffolk and his bride started out on April 16, leaving without regret "this stinking city of Paris"; but badly frightened in Calais a week later where the mob bellowed round their house, threatening to kill him for tampering with the blood royal. He saved his head and Wolsey apparently had saved it—as also, by the way, Wolsey had imperilled it.

Therefore does Wolsey appear with every advantage, reaped by this unfailing cunning of his which it would be moral pedantry not to admire and moral perversion to praise. In the King's eyes he was the negotiator who had compelled Suffolk to return and to pay such splendid forfeits for his misdeed. In Mary Tudor's eyes he was the kind friend who had not frowned upon her adventure and the man she had desired. In Suffolk's eyes Wolsey was the man who had saved his head. In Wolsey's own eyes Wolsey was the man who had driven three fools in blinkers.

What was to have followed, according to plan, during the summer of 1515 was the easy manipulation of Francis. He had proved himself awkward in meddling with

Scottish affairs, but there seemed no serious danger in him—though he must be watched.

What actually followed was no clever manipulation of this young God in armour such as had been designed in London. What followed was the lightning-stroke of Marignano.

Francis had gathered into Dauphiny on the French side of the Alps 35,000 men, most of them from his own people, others mercenary and hired. Gather them though he did, and though it looked like the preparation of something mighty in the way of arms (60 to 70 great guns of bronze, hundreds of smaller pieces) Henry and Wolsey knew better. The King of England said to an ambassador: "The King of France will not cross the mountains; he is too much afraid of *me*."

On the far side of the Alps the only two roads, that by Mont Genèvre and that by the Mont Cenis, were guarded at their descent into the Italian plains by solid bodies of Swiss—too strong to be forced by any invading column before it could deploy. The way from France to Milan seemed blocked. A Spaniard of genius, engineer to the fiery lad who was French king, a man who would face anything by way of his trade, said the position could be turned by the defile of the Argentière.

There was no road. Rocks must be blasted, trestle bridges over chasms extemporised, heavy ordnance slung down the precipitous cliffs by ropes. The astonishing thing took five days, but on the sixth the host was down upon the plains at the Italian foot of the mountains, the lands of Saluzzo. Colonna had sat down to meat. A messenger arrived all dusty from his gallop, "The French are across the hills." And immediately after Bayard came riding at the head of the vanguard, trooped into the market place, and the forces facing those empty roads across the Alps which Francis had not used were trapped. There was nothing between him and Milan, he had but to go forward and seize the prize. On August 12th he captured the Milanese cavalry, ten days later Alessandria had fallen.

The news of the French army falling like a thunderbolt, prepared to recover the Milanese bastion of Louis XII, reached Rome.

The news had, among all its other effects, one which especially concerns us. All hesitation on the advantage of English support was forgotten, and on the 10th Leo in Consistory named Wolsey Cardinal. Three days later Francis, baulked of Milan by a new rush of 20,000 Swiss, come down from the mountains, was engaged all day and all night confusedly and violently before Marignano, fighting under the moon, and sleeping the last hours before dawn on the carriage of one of his great guns. The next day, September 14, broke with all undecided, but there was heard to the east the battle-cry of the Venetians advancing, the battle-cry of St. Mark, and the Swiss were broken between two fires. For the first time that invincible infantry lost its name, and 10,000 of them lay dead in proof thereof.

Far off in England, while these things were happening before Milan, Wolsey was saying *first*, that Francis would never go into Italy; *next,* that if he did he would be defeated; and when that "Battle of the Giants" of Marignano had been decided a full eleven days, Wolsey was still calling the hero of it a misguided young man, whose unhappy fate he must bewail.

As for Henry, his attitude was more remarkable still. When Wingfield sent him the news from Calais exactly a fortnight after the battle, on September 27, he refused to believe it. When he was shown the actual letters of Francis' mother, Louise of Savoy, he said they were forgeries. All these ineptitudes he delivered at Greenwich, until at last Surrey brought him to his senses. It was not done by rebuke but by suggestion. Said Surrey: "After all, if the victory had been won over the Swiss and so many of them killed it was a good thing, for the Swiss were vile fellows who ridiculed all princes and nobles, basely republican," and Henry, ever amenable to suggestion, veered round, admitted that something had happened after all, and agreed loudly that the Swiss were villains.

But it must have rankled to remember that this young rival king over the water, not 21 years old to Henry's 24, had risked his body in battle and had achieved such a triumph that Thérouanne and Tournai would be forgotten.

See how Wolsey's miscalculation in Foreign affairs bred at once a new glory for him at home. He had been hopelessly wrong about Francis I's intentions and power! Yes. But he had got the Hat, the Crimson Hat with Tassels, the Cardinal's Hat. He made the most of it, prepared its journey to be a triumph and its reception a radiant day: a national feast.

When the Hat came out from Rome it started with particular pomp, it journeyed with the same, and its passage through south England to Westminster was a pageant and a triumph. Never was a dead object, of dead stuff and stiffening, brought nearer to idolatry. We shall assist at a sort of Worship of the Hat.

But let it not be imagined that this, one of the early examples of "The Magnificence" which blazed round

In the Possession of M.ʳ Kingsley. ___ Impensis I. & P. Knapton London. 1738. J. Houbraken Sculp.

WOLSEY
From a Portrait Bust Engraved by Houbraken
In the London Library

Wolsey henceforward, was calculated. Wolsey did not put on these things for the purpose of strengthening himself, of ruling more thoroughly; he put them on for the sheer love of splendour. All those shouting liveries and heaps of sculptured gold, great houses, arrased rooms, were an end in themselves. And this Procession of the Hat, this apotheosis of what a clothier made, was all one with the rest. Giglis, the man who the year before had been pointed at in Rome as Wolsey's agent in the murder of Bainbridge, had orders that the Hat should leave the city with solemnity. It was Giglis's own secretary who set out with it on the 7th October, 1515. He carried with him a Plenary Indulgence for all who should be present at the ceremony in England.

So the Hat went splendidly north, a month on the way, and came to Calais on November 7th. The Hat was the fruit of that great fear which had fallen over Rome when the news came of the French invasion. Marignano was eight weeks past, the news of it in England more than a month old; its fruit, the great Concordat, was little more than a month ahead, but to the England of Wolsey the Hat, the tasselled Hat, meant more than all these things. It came to Blackheath by Thursday, November 15th, and there was met by Lord Essex and the Bishop of Lincoln, in full pontificals.

At the gates of London stood the Lord Mayor, the Aldermen, and the Guilds with their banners lining the streets. It made its splendid progress to Westminster and was received at the Abbey like a hero returning from battle in laurels and with bronze. The Abbot came out to greet it, with eight other Abbots flanking him, and solemnly did they lay it on the High Altar to wait the final scene on the following Sunday. For it was on Sunday, the 18th, that the Hat was at last to be put on. Colet preached before the dense crowd, wherein the chief nobles and the pride of the realm had assembled. In his sermon he compared Cardinals to the order of Seraphim, the angels who burn with love—hence their scarlet. The Choir was crowded to the altar steps; all the great Abbots, Westminster, St. Alban's, Reading, Glastonbury, and the rest, seven Bishops in attendance, and with them Warham of Canterbury to officiate. As he put the Hat on Wolsey's head like a crown, a loud Te Deum filled the Church as for a victory. Norfolk and Suffolk, standing on either side of him who was their master and whom they had already begun to hate, led him to the door, with eighteen Lords in train to do reverence, while before them was borne the Mace and the Crosses of his Archbishopric and of his new office: all this in the presence of Warham, Primate of England, whose cross was put aside as though he had not been and as though all were today and henceforward the Cardinal's.

They made procession to Whitehall and to the great feast at York House where, in the Great Hall, after they had passed through room after room of successive grandeur, were Henry and Catherine, with the Queen Dowager of France. And thus ended that famous day, the day of the Hat—and meanwhile in Italy the Victor of Marignano was preparing the Concordat, which in the next month was to cut the ground from under the coming of the Reformation to France.

By the Concordat between Francis and Leo, the King was given a new mastery over the French Church, its appointments made over to him, its national character enhanced: but the Papal position and Unity maintained. It did both good and evil. It has been well said that "the

Pope and the King each gave away what was not his to give: the Pope the liberties of the Church in France as against the King, the King the liberties of the Church in France as against the Pope."

But seeing what was to happen, seeing that within two years the storm of the Reformation was to break and within five to be raging, it was the Concordat which saved—in the long run—the communion of France with the Church Universal. Had Wolsey planned for such a thing in England the schism would have been saved. He preferred to plan for a reform to be accomplished in the English Church by his own power and to his own renown, so that when he passed and his delegated papal power had passed with him, Pope and King stood opposed.

When Wolsey rose from the shock of Marignano, and when Henry had been persuaded that Marignano had really taken place, there was a question what next to do.

Here were they allied no longer to a power which the Papacy had ceased to fear but with a power which worked its will and again over-shadowed Italy and Rome. "All is French from Rome to Calais." The Alliance must not be broken lest worse befall—for England could make no league against Francis. Yet the papal policy was Wolsey's one guide: to free Rome from foreign pressure, a necessity to his career.

Wolsey decided on a policy obvious enough, but in detail difficult to carry out. He could not send troops into Italy, but his financial policy and the new straining of English taxation had given him money in hand. He could secretly hire a Swiss force which Maximilian should lead against Milan to turn the French out. If the secret were kept he could preserve friendship with

Francis the whole time. But the difficulty in carrying out the plan was this, that he could not entrust the money to Maximilian. When Maximilian got money, of which he was always in need, he preferred keeping it for himself, and a sum of £750,000 (as we should call it in modern values) was something worth keeping. Pace was sent off without delay, very soon after the news of Marignano was thoroughly confirmed, in October. Maximilian bargained and obtained. The sums to be paid by England grew larger, more than doubled—still, they must be kept out of Maximilian's hands:—and yet Maximilian was to lead!

The French and Venetians had their suspicions, and the Venetian Ambassador hinted at them, but he got his answer. Wolsey told him that any suspicion that he was subsidising the Emperor was slanderous. He was bold to say "on the honour of his Cardinalate," a phrase of which he had grown fond in the few weeks since he had possessed it, that those who said he was subsidising the Swiss against the French and Venetians lied in their teeth. Pace got to Zurich before the end of November, in time at least to prevent Francis from outbidding him for the use of the Swiss mercenaries.

And then the trouble began with Maximilian; the double trouble of preventing the Emperor from getting the money and yet getting someone to pay the Swiss and someone who had the right to order them. In the dilemma the whole thing was bungled.

Maximilian came down the Brenner in the early spring of 1516, his Swiss grumbling for arrears of pay. He got them to within nine miles of Milan, and he could get them no further. They were on the edge of mutiny, and their pay was not forthcoming. The Emperor went off, the Swiss decamped, and yet another of Wolsey's foreign plans had gone wrong. The French were still solidly anchored in the Milanese.

But Maximilian bethought him of an alternative which might persuade the English king and his friends to come in person. It was a strange alternative, not quite new; there was an echo in it of something he had said three years before, in the campaign of Thérouanne. Let Henry meet him, Maximilian, and march over the Alps into Italy, with forces of his own; the Emperor would invest him with the Duchy of Milan, and, what is more, would declare him heir to the Empire; then they would go on to Rome together to be crowned by the Pope! Pace warned his government against the fantastic scheme, and Wolsey had the sense to reject it. But indeed Maximilian, who had thoughts now of the Papacy, now of canonisation, was of a judgment as fantastic as his tricks for receiving money were ingenious.

His next trick of the kind was the best and the last. To understand it and to see how thoroughly Wolsey's foreign policy had failed, one must go back to the opening of the year.

In the first days of 1516 Ferdinand of Spain died. He left his kingdom to Charles of Austria, his grandson of sixteen. Thenceforward the boy was Lord in right of Spain, South Italy and the New World, the Americas, "The Indies". Well, in half a year Charles had made his peace with Francis. The effect of Marignano was still felt. Such victories do not only excite resistance, they also fascinate—and Charles, his elder advisers warning him what difficulties might await him in Spain, signed the Treaty of Noyon. He promised to give up Navarre (as though the Spaniards would have allowed it) and to

marry the Infant daughter of Francis—that is, to wait
fourteen or fifteen years for his bride. The promises
meant little, the Peace much. It secured Francis in Italy
and it put the seal on Wolsey's unhappy failure to get
back Milan by stealth. Charles' grandfather Maximilian
followed suit. He also made his peace with Francis (but
demanded ready cash for doing it) and in his turn buried
Wolsey's last plan.

It was English money which had provided the pay for
that column of armed men whose march down from the
summits of the Alps in this spring of 1516 had ended so
impotently. For even the English money was insufficient.
The Emperor had taken that money and had now betrayed his paymaster.

Wolsey had rejected Maximilian's offer of the Emperor to Henry. He was right. But that he should even
have deliberated on it is significant. That it could have
been made at all is sufficient proof of the way in which
the Princes, their Ministers and agents, but Wolsey most
of all, were losing foothold in reality and were living in
a world apart, as it were, from the real world through
which were already running the tremors of the coming
earthquake.

Yet they thought themselves in touch with reality, as
men playing the game of high politics always do, they
were convinced, all of them, that the Milanese, the play
and counter-play for predominance in north Italy, the
rival candidatures to the shadowy Empire were the great
impetus of the moment. They so talked, so schemed, so
turned upon themselves continually, not only up to the
very moment when Luther first moved but on through
the whole turmoil, treating the chief event of modern
times, the spiritual disruption of Christendom, as some

though this was the gold purchasing power on the average measured in goods, the number of purchasable things and services was so much less than those of to-day that the social meaning of any sum, but especially of any large sum, was much greater than the mere purchasing value in proportion to the society of the time. In an England and Wales of perhaps four million souls, and a society in the main agricultural and very simple, this annual expenditure by the Government, though not excessive, represented to the full the ordinary functions it had to perform: for those functions were very much less than the great range of activities into which public action developed later on. There was no army. No permanent Navy. No police. No public debt at usury, hardly any civil service. We must have it clear in our minds that this sum of about two millions a year (which could be met out of the Royal income from land dues, wardenships, justice and the rest) was to the England of that time something like what the old Victorian Budgets were to the late 19th century: with this difference of course, that the Victorian Governments had to raise such revenue from taxation, while the early Tudor Government was endowed and normally did not have to ask for taxes, which were regarded as exceptional grants.

Now Wolsey's war policy produced a revolution in this fiscal arrangement. In the first year the amount needed was more than four times the normal, in the second year it was much more than *ten* times. Such immense sums could only be got by pressure such as the past had never known and the fact that the money could be raised at all (it was only raised slowly, imperfectly, and by instalments) is singular evidence of Wolsey's power and of what his rapid concentration of control was doing to England. It is a symptom of a change in the civic mind which permitted the later despotism of Henry, and all the changes built upon that despotism. Wolsey got those extra sums, after the treasure of Henry VII had been exhausted, and the early "10th and 15th" granted by Parliament a ("tenth and fifteenth"[1] meant rather about three-quarters of a million of our money— say less than 55 per cent of the normal annual revenue of the Crown) by a subsidy which he squeezed out of the Parliament of 1514—in which he did not sit. This subsidy was *three* times the "10th and 15th." It came to well over two million pounds and was produced by a 5 per cent income tax and a 5 per cent levy on movable goods. After that came a new and rigorous enquiry into Crown rents and after that forced loans.

Wolsey was emancipated from the old Treasury control. He could spend money without accounting for it. That added to his centralisation of power in execution, as to his powers of raising revenue. It consolidated his strength at home.

Another aspect of this new financial system in England was the economic advantage it gave for the moment to the country among its rivals and allies.

In order to understand this we must be clear upon the way in which a government at the time raised its revenue. When we appreciate the contrast between the fiscal system of those days and our own we have the key to half the problem of Wolsey's real power in Europe.

The original income of any Royal Government in the early Middle Ages was the private income of the King.

---

[1] A "10th and 15th" was a technical term, empty by this time of any literal meaning, levied on a formal assessment long ago fossilised and diminished.

The King was the inheritor of the old Roman Imperial office; as such, he drew without question, without having to ask for it, and without limitation the profits to be had from the courts of justice and from the Imperial land called "forest," that is land outside the ordinary feudal system of the day. He was also a feudal over-lord, drawing death duties on the succession of his greater and lesser vassals. He was also the immediate lord of a great number of villages and towns from which in theory he could demand what he liked, and in practice regular sums which were a sort of customary rent, paid by those who tilled the land or who inhabited urban houses. That was the sort of revenue which gave to William the Conqueror his strength. That was the traditional revenue of an English King, as of a German or French one, or of any monarch in Christendom: the fruit of *endowment*, not of *tax*.

But, as the Middle Ages developed, towards the end of the 12th century on the continent and in England during the 13th, means had to be devised for increasing this revenue. There were two reasons for this. First, the functions of Government were increasing both in amount and in the cost of each item, because the State was growing more complex and more active.

Second, the personal and direct possessions of the monarch, his forests, his towns, his manors, tended to diminish. They were encroached upon when the monarchy was weak through the character of the King or in his minority; they were used to give rewards for services and sometimes directly alienated to pay for some immediate necessity—an early example of the State wasting capital as income.

The consequence of these two factors combined was

that the extra revenue needed in any crisis such as a war
or the provision of a fleet when war did but threaten, had
to be met by *grants* from his subjects, and the necessity
grew not only from the two causes just mentioned but
from the fact that with the process of time feudal payment from villages and under-lords and towns payable
to the King became crystallised; custom set a maximum
which could not be exceeded and that maximum tended
to become lower. The process was hastened by the
growth of commerce and industry in the towns. The
King granted them Charters for ready money and under
those Charters they enjoyed for the future a fairly fixed
assessment, beyond which they could not be drawn upon
without creating a sense of injustice.

All through the later Middle Ages the Crown was
growing more and more to depend upon these occasional
accidental and exceptional offers of money.

For they *were* offers, freely made; not sums taken by
force as our taxes are today. They were not taxes in our
modern sense, and therein lies the heart of the business.

We today inherit a fiscal system long established, which
seems inseparable from a high civilisation and which
was the system of the old Pagan Empire from which we
spring. Under this system the Government having discovered what it needs annually for its activities, orders
the citizens to pay so much and in such and such fashion.
The individuals thus compelled to pay have nothing to
say to the amount, they pay because they must. But
throughout all the later Middle Ages, and, in a lingering
fashion for a long time after, another theory prevailed:
the theory that the Government was endowed, had its
own property and on that property should normally carry
on. If it wanted more under a special strain, it must get

it by negotiation with the Governed, who were indeed under a vague moral duty to support the State but who could not be called upon for precise sums until they had threshed the matter out and decided what they could afford. Hence there was a standing ambiguity out of which arose the whole machinery of representation in Christendom. The King said, "What I am doing I am doing in the public service; the community needs in this exceptional moment of strain a special exceptional sum of money without which I cannot do my business."—as for instance, prosecute a war against a foreign enemy or suppress a rebellion at home.

He would often try to seize the amount needed, or part of it, in an arbitrary manner; but when he did so he always felt that he was in the wrong, that he was acting oddly, and that his only excuse was public necessity. The citizens who had to find these exceptional accidental momentary sums said, "We fully admit that something must be done, but, as it is we who pay, and *as it is not part of your regular revenue*, we must state what we can grant. But we will continue to regard it as a grant. We will never allow it to become taken as a matter of course or see it turned into an annual payment and merged into the regular revenue of the Crown."

This state of mind, this moral theory, which ran through all society was still very strong at the moment when Wolsey gathered the whole executive power of the community into his hands. That is why in countries where no such concentration had taken place the Governments were so often at a loss for money. That is why the Emperor, though at the head of such a vast confederation of States and Cities was over and over again penniless in a crisis. That is why his descendants in

WOLSEY
From the Portrait in the National Portrait Gallery, London

Austria and Spain were dependent upon bankers and perpetually hampered in their operations from lack of gold. But in England, once Wolsey's concentration of power was accomplished, the power of raising revenue was far greater compared with the total income of society than in any of the other states. Taxation was still a grant, but the grant was demanded by one who was master not only (after his chancellorship) of the whole civil system of Courts and the Executive but also (after his legate-ship) of the whole twin Ecclesiastical system which stood side by side with the State. The England of Wolsey had perhaps a quarter, perhaps a fifth, of the arable land of the Kingdom of France; it had far less wealth from commerce than had the cities of the Empire, of France and of Italy, of the now united kingdom of Spain; but the proportion of English wealth obtainable by the man who had all English things in his grasp was far larger than elsewhere.

In the month after Wolsey had received the Cardinal's Hat, old Warham the Archbishop of Canterbury, who had been Lord Chancellor of England since six years before the crowning of Henry, resigned. Some thought Wolsey's ubiquitous energy thrust Warham out; some, more justly, that the old man was weary. Wolsey immediately succeeded. He became Chancellor, thus, in the December of 1515 and remained Chancellor till he fell in 1529.

In reaching that highest of Civil Posts he had still in mind the higher and supplementary one. He was already Chancellor, he was determined after these years of waiting to be Papal Legate.

Wolsey was aiming at the two key points of power.

The Chancellorship was the chief civil post; to be the

Legate of the Pope would give him ecclesiastical supremacy. But the point to notice in Wolsey's effort to attain these two offices, to hold them in one hand, to exercise them for supreme control, is that he had the energy and the tenacity to determine on achieving both and not only one, exercising in each the very plenitude of power.

A Chancellor might be Chancellor as Warham was, and as so many others had been before him. It did not give a complete power, even civilian; it only gave an *opportunity* for complete power.

Wolsey's determination in the matter was not an inclination to hold office; it was a determination to use that office as it had never been used before. It was a determination to be completely master in everything that concerned the state from within.

With the office of Legate (the "Legacy" as the term went at the time in English) this unique and final aim which makes Wolsey different from all others before him is still more apparent; here it was not a question of something elastic as the Chancery was: not a power which might be used less or more, nor one which could be extended almost indefinitely at the will of the holder. It was a more ancient and regular matter, not local but European, not provincial but universal, and, because it was old and because it attached to the highly developed ecclesiastical organisation which had framed Europe for at least 500 years and had grown more and more complex in its organisation—it demanded precise commission. A man might be Legate for a longer or a shorter time; he might be Legate with larger or smaller powers; Wolsey was determined to be Legate after such a fashion that there should be no limit to his powers in ecclesiastical affairs, that he should be very Pope in England. In such a place he could visit and set right the monasteries, he could enforce residency, he could restore the prestige of the clergy, reduce the friction which their enforced payments from the laity had raised, confine to due limits the courts christian and remove the reproach that the Church had grown vile. With the untiring energy and directness of his character, the level violence of his ambition, he achieved his end: yet he did not reform, for he was working for himself alone.

Herein lies the meaning of Wolsey, the explanation of his life with its lack of fruit: that he attained and achieved not for any idea but only as a *person*; that while he fulfilled all *personal* ambition until the very eve of his fall, he used it without a general aim. Therefore the results of his immense labour were utterly different from what he had intended. He it was who created that one machine, spiritual and temporal, under which all men lay subject. The ecclesiastical regimen and the laical regimen had worked uneasily one with the other. They overlapped, causing through the indistinction of their frontiers a thousand daily inconveniences. But they did check the one the other and therefore this age-long dual system had made for a certain freedom and elasticity in life. Even more in the ideal than in the practical world this duality was felt. A man suffering grievance at the hands of the clergy threatened such tyranny with an appeal to the civil laws. A man suffering grievance at the hands of the great of this world could appeal to the general ideals of Christendom and to the Church which was in theory their guardian. But let the two coalesce and all elbow-room was gone, all chance of free play was lost. The coalition of the two was the work of Wolsey. And it was because Wolsey so completely succeeded in welding both powers into one that Henry, the young man whom he had managed, the older man whom he had cajoled, the weak but impulsive will which he had shepherded, somewhat duped, but always led until close upon the end, could take up a machine he himself was incapable of having forged, find it all ready to his hand, and use it or let others use it, for a new purpose.

Never did the powerful short-sighted genius of Wolsey, who forged the united instrument of lay and clerical power combined, intend it for what it became.

He had intended it—would that he had used it!—for the full reformation of the Church within his power and his province; had he achieved the Papacy which he so ardently sought he might perhaps have done in Europe what he failed to do in England. But the machine was abandoned by him when he fell. The control of it passed into the hands of that supplanter who had been his own servant, Thomas Cromwell. In those hands, far more ignoble than Wolsey's, it was used to destroy the continuity of that for which Wolsey had lived. By control over the Church Thomas Cromwell brought the Church down; by his control over the State an irresponsible tyranny was erected.

Wolsey achieved full lay power as Chancellor, with powers the limits of which were set beyond all definition; he had but to thrust ahead and occupy all the field. He could over-ride the Common Law, he could act as minister for any department. He already, before being made vice-regent of the realm (for that was what the word "Chancellor" could then be stretched to mean) could spend national money at will without rendering account: now, as Chancellor he could use the name of the Crown for any purpose that seemed good to him. He could not be theoretically absolute, because, to the conception of the Middle Ages which still survived, the lively idea of Christendom, the theory of absolute power was abhorrent. But in practice he could get nearer and nearer to complete dominance. He even achieved it virtually, though gradually and with difficulty, in that sphere of taxation or rather voluntary grant which remained the most jealously guarded of liberties inherited from the Middle Ages. From being able to spend national revenue at will, he grew to be able, not indeed to raise such revenue at will, but to raise it more arbitrarily and in far greater amount than had ever been known in the past. All lay England was at his feet. Ecclesiastical England was still free.

Where the Legateship was concerned he had to wait wearily enough for opportunity. He was demanding it four years before he obtained it; two and a half years after his Chancellorship. He had to pass successively from a limited to a larger power, from one restricted to a short time, then to a longer time, to one at last granted for life.

The Chancellorship he obtained as a matter of course, because he was morally master of the King. The Legateship in its amplest power he obtained only slowly and ponderously by the steady pressure of a foreign policy in which each new Papal concession was wrung by a promise of support to the Papacy in distress.

He snatched that prize at last, the way in which he passed from the first to the second phase of his domination was by a stroke all of a piece with what Wolsey was; fruitful of glory within, barren of result without, based on intrigue.

Leo's noble project of a crusade was matured in the bill of 1517.

The time was propitious. The Christian Princes were at peace. Old Ferdinand, the most crafty and incessant of the ambitious, was dead. Spain and Italy were in the hands of his daughter's son Charles V, a boy in his eighteenth year, cautious and staid. The French seemed solidly confirmed in the results of Marignano and Leo's concordat with Francis left him in quiet. Maximilian was past fighting, and, like Charles his grandson, had made his treaty with France. It seemed a moment when Europe might be united; it was certainly the moment when the Mohammedan danger was rising with new menace.

Selim I, the new master of the Turks, had conquered and consolidated an Empire that could summon new hosts, far more numerous than of old. He had conquered Egypt and Syria and the Arabs, and now directed one great Moslem mass united against us. He was preparing all that strength which his greater son, Soliman the Magnificent, was to array against the Christian name, seizing Rhodes and all the Levantine Sea, crushing Hungary, besieging Vienna.

In such a day Leo could believe that the eternal talk of united Christian armies might turn to action and a last crusade could be launched.

The Legates who were to come from his side to the great Princes of Christendom were nominated and were on their way. By April 1518 Campeggio, who was to be Legate for England, had started on his way. He reached Calais, and there he found suddenly applied to him the leverage which was to compel his sovereign, Pope Leo, to yield on the essential point. Ancient precedent was claimed, brazenly enough but successfully (for

England is separated by the sea and entry can be watched) that no Legate of foreign birth might be received in an English port till proof would be advanced that he brought no Papal mandate with him which might lessen the power of the throne. For three months Leo's Legate was compelled to wait, looking at the salt water. Dispatches were sent to Rome. It was what the slang of our days calls a "hold-up," it was a pistol put at Leo's head. No one cared a straw about the imaginary constitutional point, least of all Wolsey. What the protest really meant was, and Leo knew it well enough, that unless Wolsey also, Wolsey permanently resident in England, an Englishman, and now already the controller of England on its civil side, was to be made Legate the whole of his plan for the Crusade would be blocked. For until Campeggio landed in England and carried out his mission with the King unanimity was not secured and there could be no common action of Christendom. Therefore was a hurried message sent to Rome, and Rome yielded. It meant something which the Pope had put off year after year, the establishment of a power in England, the delegation of his own power, the setting up of a local Island Pope with full rein over the exempt monasteries, and of opportunity to act in all Church matters with complete authority.

Rome yielded, I say; and on May 17 the Bulls were issued nominating Wolsey *Legate a Latere*;—and still further delay was imposed. Campeggio might not cross the Straits until Wolsey's old enemy Hadrian had been deprived of the revenues of Bath and Wells: Wolsey desired those revenues for himself. Again the Pope yielded, and at long last Campeggio landed on Deal beach: but it was already the 23rd of July (1518) and that year there could be no crusading.

The thing was staged—for Wolsey's benefit—with a pomp that recalled The Hat. The Bishop of Chichester and the Lords of Kent met the Papal envoy at his landing. The Archbishop met him at Canterbury and the Bishop of Rochester with him, and that same day they were all at the High Mass in the Cathedral together. On Monday, in a violent storm of thunder, Campeggio set out with a great train of horsemen for the Rood of Boxley. On the 6th day, the Thursday, he was outside London, where the Duke of Norfolk met him with 2,000 horse on Blackheath, while, within, the City Livery had turned out to greet him and the Prelates in their pontificals; a splendid procession.

The Tuesday following, August 3rd, in the Palace at Greenwich and in the great hall thereof the Legacy was inaugurated with all imaginable display, Wolsey, the head thereof, sitting on a throne above his colleagues and at last unchecked controller of the English Church and of the English State.

. . . . . .

But something less apparent than all this great affair was already born: something that would grow.

In that same lull of 1517, when peace was apparently assured, when no great wind stirred the surface of Christendom, after the rivalries were appeased, the fruits of Marignano apparently secure, and the Holy See at liberty to plan at length an alliance against the Turk which might at last leave Europe free; there fell among the Germans an incident destined later to very great fame, but in the eyes of contemporaries ephemeral.

That summer, and for some time past there had been

WOLSEY
From the Painting in Hampton Court Palace

preached in the Dioceses of Mayence and Magdeburg, which covered the wealthiest part of the Germanies, a certain indulgence originally issued by Julius II and continued by Leo X. Its terms had given scandal everywhere. The Primate of Spain had forbidden to have it preached in that country; it was kept out of most of the French dioceses. Its promulgation on the Rhine and beyond was due to a bargain between the Pope and the young, very corrupt, Hohenzollern who had purchased the Archbishopric on borrowed money, and was promised a share in the proceeds of the indulgence if he would allow it in the lands under his jurisdiction.

The conditions of an indulgence are (or should be) well known. The temporal punishment due to sin, the guilt of which has been forgiven through the contrition of the sinner, is remitted by the power of the Church as against some pious act; the giving of alms or the visiting of a shrine or what-not. The reason this particular indulgence was scandalous in the eyes of Europe, like so many of the acts of the Church of the time, was twofold. First, it was everywhere a mere money transaction; and though in strict definition the money was alms and not given as purchase, the terms in which the preaching of the indulgence was made, the obvious motive of it, the commissions on it made it indistinguishable from purchase in the eyes of the many. Next, half the money so collected was to be devoted to the advancement of the building of the new St. Peter's. This last was a perfectly legitimate object, but, at a moment when there was such necessity for meeting the Mohammedan, when the magnificence of Papal Rome and its worldliness were in everyone's mouth, money from a scheme which was more than half of it motived by a desire for mere splendour and magnificence, the external adornment of the ecclesiastical power at Rome, was ill-gotten. Lastly, the other half of the money received had to go to the young Archbishop of Magdeburg to repay the money lenders the sums with which he had, by simony, obtained his place: and that was by far the worst matter of all.

But I repeat, the thing did not take any very great place in the thoughts of the time. If you had been alive then, travelling in Europe and staying with the people who counted, hearing discussions on the policy of France and England, the chances of the Milanese, the new reign in Spain and Naples, the arts and letters of that great day, it is a hundred to one that you would not have heard of the indulgence.

But when things below the surface are unstable the first shock which leads at last to ruin may be upon quite a small scale, and is nearly always accidental. The preaching of the indulgence (and sundry benefits connected with it) had been given to the Dominicans; the rival order of Augustinians were disappointed.

A prominent youngish Augustinian professor in the Elector of Saxony's new University of Wittenburg, called Martin Luther, pushed on (it was said) by the Superior of his monastery, proposed for discussion in the University a number of points hostile to the use, or at least the current interpretation, of the system of indulgences. He affixed this list of moot questions suitable to academic debate on the usual notice board of the University, the door of a Chapel therein, on the eve of All Souls, 1517. Probably no one was more surprised than the gloomy, fiery, but rather popular University theologian and lecturer when he found, almost immediately after, that he had set the heather on fire.

He had known what universal murmurs the preaching of the indulgence had aroused, he shared with all Europe the knowledge that reform was abominably overdue, he shared with all Germans an irritated racial feeling against the Papacy being turned into an Italian Principate. But the way in which this simple act of his turned into a nucleus round which so many and such various grievances would crystallise no one could have expected. Yet the fame of the thing began immediately. It grew, not with that prodigious rapidity which we who know the consequences to-day ascribe to it, but at any rate quickly enough to be of public consequence on and beyond the Rhine within a few months. It was not more than that— as yet. It took up very little of men's thoughts in Europe during those days of the expected crusade. It excited hardly any notice in England, which, until a common religious movement arose to bind the two races together, took very little interest in German affairs. It was as yet a seed only. But it had sprouted and was to increase.

VII

THE THIRD ACT

"MY TRIUMPHANT GLORY"
1518-1527

WITH the summer of 1518 Wolsey is Papal Legate in England and has achieved all the functions of power which it was possible to exercise within the country. Short of the Papacy itself—to which also he aspired—he was now supreme.

In the April of 1527 Henry King of England first openly spoke of his intentions to obtain that divorce which was the rock upon which Wolsey foundered.

The nine years between those two dates are those in which the Cardinal shone before all Europe and still more radiantly in the eyes of his countrymen; but there are two distinct divisions in this period of his exaltation. There come first the great seven years in which he was completely secure, during which he had no doubts in his own mind that he would be to his death what he then was and that whatever he had established would last indefinitely, moulding all English history after he should be gone. Those great seven years were the years of which he spoke in a proud pathetic phrase to his confidant and near servant Cavendish after his fall. He called them *"My triumphant glory."* They end with the first slight but troubling indications of a new influence growing over Henry's mind. Those slight but public indications are first seen in the midsummer of 1525.

The next two years, up to the April of 1527, are still full of his splendour; he is building his great colleges, he is conducting alone the foreign policy of England, he reaches—always in his mind an essential thing—the

THE BANQUET GIVEN TO THE FRENCH AMBASSADORS BY WOLSEY IN THE PRESENCE CHAMBER OF
HAMPTON COURT PALACE

From the Water-color Drawing by Joseph Nash in the Victoria and Albert Museum, London

highest level of income. Europe thinks him more powerful than ever; he himself acts as though he were at least as powerful as ever. But in the minds of observers close at home, in the mind of Henry himself, much more in the minds of those who were beginning their new domination over the King to the ultimate ousting of Wolsey, things had changed: Anne Boleyn was ascendant. And Wolsey himself was beginning to fall more and more into a new mood, a mood of watching and of anxiety.

The great seven years are marked throughout by that double process we have already noted as the characteristic of the famous story: failure abroad but failure with noise and fame, and, in spite of such failure, the confirmation of strength at home—and, all the while, a blaze of magnificence.

Everywhere he goes he passes in procession and in train. His great double maces and his great Cross are borne before him: his hundreds of men, in livery of crimson and black: his scores of mounted gentlemen flaming in the same colour, with their gold chains about their necks: his Cardinal's Hat borne also before him by two tall men of his Guard: his palaces numerous and increasing in number, their shelves and tables loaded with the high Renaissance work in silver and in gold, their walls hung with such a wealth of worked stuffs that the tapestries were changed weekly—all this was the furniture and clothing of his life. He had a household of eight hundred, nearly five hundred of them at a wage high enough to be assessed for a tax.[1]

[1] At the end of the great seven years there are 429 thus assessed, and though the number is nearly halved a little later when Hampton Court is nominally passed over to the King the change is more apparent than real. The establishment of Hampton Court being nominally the King's is no longer assessed for taxation, but it is still in Wolsey's service all the same. He lives there and works from there and entertains there.

He had in his Chapel the best trained, the most exquisite, the most costly music and musicians of his time, eclipsing those of the Chapels Royal. The expenses of his household alone are on the scale of 60 to 80 thousand pounds a year, and that in an England where all the normal revenue of Government was not much more than 20 times as large. He carried on his prodigious business of dispatches, of advice, of accounts and subsidies, of Chancery work and of arms in the midst of pageant after pageant, of great banquets and masques which astonished even those envoys from the Continent who had seen the riot of Renaissance Rome. It was "The Magnificence." And what he did within such a setting was still the same: stroke after stroke, every one of which emphasized his personal mastery over England; plan after plan for this and that effect upon Europe outside, every one of which was either futile or miscarried.

At the inception of his high new power of the Legateship you get the first example. The Legateship had been granted for two years only; he was determined that it should last his lifetime and, what is more, to have such a Legacy for life officially confirmed. He sets to work by proving to Leo what instruments he has in hand for ultimately forcing such concessions. He had already compelled the dismissal of his enemy Hadrian and kept Campeggio waiting at Calais those three months; he now, throughout the remainder of the year 1518, shows the Court of Rome what further pressure he can bring to bear.

Leo X, intent on the crusade, his Legates in every court, had proclaimed of his own authority a truce between all Christian princes to last five years. Wolsey would make Leo X understand that his own plan should supersede the Pope's. He would make a general political peace confirming officially the actual peace of the last two years. He would have it made, and in London. *His* should be the glory of it. And in doing so he could make manifest to the Pope what he was and what he intended to be. It was a full personal triumph, but as for practical effect upon the life of Europe it was null. The delay had rendered a crusade impossible. The peace was almost immediately succeeded by the violent outbreak of new rivalries and by the set and growing opposition between Francis and Charles. When Erasmus wrote that the settlement finally confirmed in London on that last day of 1518 was the Cardinal's own peace he wrote truth, but there was another truth, which Erasmus did not tell— that of outward and permanent effect there was nothing. And there was a third truth: for now more than a year that religious revolution which was to break Europe asunder at last had been spreading in the Germanies like a rising tide, and yet to Wolsey it had meant nothing at all.

The next action, that of the following year 1519, shows the same qualities but upon a larger scale. The election to the Empire gives you Wolsey still misunderstanding Europe and still failing therein, yet in his failure making his name most loudly heard.

On the 12th of January 1519 Maximilian the old Emperor died at Welz. Seven electors were to determine who should succeed him to the shadowy but still awful office. Of these seven Maximilian had made certain of four for his grandson Charles, already King of Spain and of the New World and of South Italy, of the Netherlands, of the Jura country and now of the Hapsburg domain in South and East Germany as well. The old Emperor, desperately pinched for money as he always was, had spent a fortune in purchasing the promise of those votes, yet three were still doubtful: the Saxon, Treves and the Palatine.

When the succession was open the King of France put forward his candidature, and he and Charles of Austria stood opposed in that contest as they would stand opposed throughout all the life of Francis, and of the heirs of Francis.

Whether, had Francis been chosen, he could have held the office without a foot of land in Germany is doubtful enough; but his candidature was not fantastic. The Pope secretly favoured it in his dread of the Empire's falling into the same hands as already held all Italy to the south of him; and the valley of the Rhine was doubtful.

What *was* fantastic was that Henry should propose himself as candidate. Yet that fantasy Wolsey perhaps initiated and certainly thrust forward. Campeggio, who was still in England, would help—so Wolsey himself tells us in a letter to Giglis at Rome written as early as March. And in May Pace was sent out to attempt the impossible thing. Wolsey infected Pace with his own delusion, the dream of Henry as Emperor; himself, after the sickly Leo X had died, as Pope—and all Europe at his disposal.

Even as Pace was preparing to set out on his impossible mission Wolsey was still overtly supporting the candidature of Francis and there was a little scene in Paris worthy to be remembered. Francis, taking Thomas Boleyn, who had been sent out in embassy, to the embrasure of a window in the Louvre, told him there, leaning out from the casement, how confidently he relied on the aid of the English government.

It was on the 14th of May that Pace, after a dreadful crossing of 10 hours, reached Calais. He guessed that Francis knew of the betrayal and feared for his life. He hastened to the Rhine. And in his letters thence shows himself still full of the absurd hope, though he has hardly any money with which to bribe, while Henry's rivals are pouring it out by the bushel. Moreover, Pace finds himself, as Francis had begun to find himself, at issue with the strong racial feeling of the Germans. Yet he still maintains that there will be a sort of deadlock in which Henry, the third candidate, will get his chance.

"He that shall come last after the great practices . . . shall be in better case than they that came long afore."

He was quite wrong. Sickingen stood with an army at Höchst a few miles from Frankfort. Nassau was paying furiously;—"No Frenchman should enter the country save on a sword or a spear's point"; and as for Henry's candidature even Pace was convinced at last that it was not worth pursuing. On the 28th of June young Charles of Austria was elected by a unanimous vote and the affair was ended. Charles was in his 19th year, Francis in his 26th, Henry was 30 when the new arrangement of Europe began.

What followed was the Field of the Cloth of Gold: and the Field of the Cloth of Gold was yet another instance of the unbroken chain—display, splendour, all the externals—but at the core a double policy which came to nothing.

The Empire had fallen to Charles; Charles' power was thus for the future too great for Francis to meet. Wolsey would show Francis what a support England would be against Charles, and meanwhile he would make all sure by privately supporting Charles against Francis; he had the delight of double-dealing—but with nothing to show for it at the end.

The whole point of the Cloth of Gold was to advertise the close alliance of the English and French crowns. The immense expenditure, the outrageous "publicity" had that for the political object. There was also of course the fun, it was an opportunity for playing a game of ducks and drakes which every man with the power to play at it indulged in in those days. But its central political motive was what I have said; the motive of impressing Francis with the depth and sincerity of Henry's and Wolsey's friendship; Francis, who had to consider the new imperial power of the sallow awkward lad who controlled as best he could Spain, the Netherlands, the inheritance of Burgundy, the Hapsburg dominions, all South Italy and Sicily and Sardinia, and the wealth which had begun to pour in from the Indies—and while so impressing Francis to betray him and follow the stronger power.

While therefore the preparations were being made, while the old gentlemen who could remember Edward IV's wars and Richard's, and who were being called in to advise on the complicated fossil of heraldry and the exact precedents of tourneys; while Richard Wingfield was suavely and brilliantly replacing Boleyn in Paris and preparing the embrace of Henry and Francis, a secret intrigue was being actively carried forward for arranging an embrace even more important between Henry and Charles. It was being arranged that Charles should touch at an English port on his way back from Spain to the Netherlands. He was to come with the nominal ob-

ject of seeing his aunt, the Queen, and secretly he was to
discuss very private European affairs with his uncle, the
King.

It is amusing to see how more candid minds misunderstood Wolsey's passion for false dealing. The Spanish
envoys are sure that he is recalcitrant and difficult to
persuade. (In the same way the French envoys are being
told that he had "no great liking" for the coming Cloth
of Gold.) The Spanish envoys dare put nothing in writing publicly. Catherine the Queen, favouring her nephew
Charles and an Imperial alliance, takes up the very simple attitude of trying to stop the Cloth of Gold altogether. Wolsey, though suffering from a brief illness,
plays the two parties one against the other after the
fashion in which his heart delighted and attributed his
deception of both (though it can hardly be said that he
deceived Francis) to the special patronage of his name-
sake, St. Thomas of Canterbury. The Spanish envoys
arranging for the private meeting between Charles and
Henry are always in terror lest the Cardinal should
break off. They repeat how whenever they object to
some small point Wolsey would jovially reply—*"Bien!
Ne le faictes point!"*—*"Allez-vous en!"* And so kept
them in perpetual subjection. De la Sauche, writing to
Charles's minister Chevres, begs him to ply Wolsey with
money (for Wolsey never lost an opportunity for getting
that!). "Do not merely promise," he says, "or the Cardinal will take us for fools. Do not sing the refrain of the
old song which says 'I will put up a candle for you after
you are dead.'" Ready money, Charles's government is
assured, ready money is needed. Wolsey must have some
Church benefit in Charles's gift worth, say, £20,000
a year.

It was on Monday, May 21, that the King of England
and Queen Catherine started out for the coast. They were
on their way to the Cloth of Gold; but before they
came to that pageant, there was that something singular,
private, unadvertised and important to be done.

All had been well timed. They were at Canterbury
awaiting their guest by Friday, 25th. On the Saturday
the ships that bore from his new southern realm the
young King of Spain and Emperor, the solemn 20-year-
old from whom such wide dominions depended from
the borders of the Mediterranean to the Pacific, were
sighted, and he was ready to land at Lympne. From his
yards blew the great standard, the black double-eagle,
standing out against a golden ground.

Very early on the morning of the morrow, which was
Whit Sunday, Henry had ridden down the 13 miles to
meet the Emperor. They rode up to Canterbury again,
in time for High Mass, side by side, but what was said
upon the journey no man knows, and that is why it is
difficult to write history. Did Henry promise the boy
very solemnly that he would aid him in taking revenge
for Marignano? That he would be at his side when the
dominions of Francis were partitioned? Only two things
are certain. One, that whatever Henry said, he had been
crammed by Wolsey; that whatever Henry said, Charles
replied with nothing very fixed; for he was not only
taciturn nor only cautious, nor only immature with that
grey immaturity of the precocious, but he was also frightened of himself already in the business of intrigue. He
knew already that men were not to be trusted, but he
did not yet know how they should be duped or cajoled.
Perhaps there is a third thing of which we may be certain, that however general was the promise given by

Henry that Francis should be betrayed, some such promise was given.

So the stout, well-mounted and well-riding, falsely
jovial red-bearded man of thirty rode on to Canterbury
beside the pale face of the Hapsburg with its projecting
under-jaw, with its long, curved nose, small irregular
teeth and downcast eyes, and in Canterbury Queen
Catherine greeted her nephew with the simple joy of her
kind. It was too rarely that any memory of her family
could be restored to her, and here was the grandson of
her father Ferdinand speaking face to face with her in
the flesh. They all heard the High Mass of the Holy
Ghost together in Canterbury Cathedral, they passed
three days in company, and upon the Thursday the
young Emperor got into his boat at Sandwich, joined
his convoy, and sailed for his province of the Netherlands. And on the same morning the King of England
crossed the straits from Dover to Calais, landing before
noon.

On that same day the King of France set out from
his strong town of Montreuil in his fine black cloak;
two long marches, three easy days ride, from the place of
meeting. He, or rather his advisers, had met Henry's
vanity on every point. The meeting was to be on Henry's
territory within the pale of Calais, and at Henry's date,
save that it would not be possible to postpone it beyond a
certain moment lest the pregnancy of the French Queen
should prevent her presence.

Both parties to that riot of colour and expense and
pageantry were rivals, but the English show was the
greater, for Wolsey had designed it. There were nearly
3,000 tents upon the plain beyond Guisnes; the moat of
the little place was all weeds, the walls in ruins. The

castle, out of repair, was supplemented by a fantastic
glazed palace of a day, more than 100 yards on each of
its square sides, and all its walls and ceiling hung in
white silk, with a mass of gilding everywhere: a splendid Chapel, twelve golden Apostles a yard high each, a
company of 35 priests, and a kitchen of 200 servitors,
and wine flowing from the fountain in the court. The
great display was Wolsey's through and through; and
he it was who opened the ball with the first visit, an act
typical of him, and carried out as only he would have
done it. He rode out towards the quarters of Francis at
Ardres, towards that great statue of St. Michael in the
much lesser camp of the French (not the half of the
English town of canvas), that statue of St. Michael in
blue mantle studded with fleurs-de-lis: and perhaps in
all his pageantries, which were more than half his life,
which filled his soul, he never surpassed the intoxication
of that day. He used the resources of the state at will, for
indeed he was its master more than any man had been
before. Before him rode the 50 gentlemen of his household in their crimson velvet and black bands with chains
of gold about them, 50 of his gentlemen ushers bare-
headed, the golden maces of the Legateship with knobs
as big as a man's head, the great crucifix ablaze with
jewels. Next before him went 100 archers of the guard,
bows bent, marching with that precision which the men
of the continent and particularly the French have always
noted curiously in Englishmen trained for war. Wolsey
rode in such guard, upon a mule jangling with golden
plates upon its harness, and with his crimson boots beneath his crimson robe thrust into stirrups also of gold,
while the great company was rounded off with fifty
more archers of the guard, in as precise a step as the rest,

bows bent and quivers at their sides. And as he came the great bronze guns from the ridge of Ardres (had not some of them already spoken at Marignano, and had they not seen the Argentière?) fired their salute: and the greatness of his pride went forward to the noise of trumpets and of drums.

It was the greatest day in all those twenty days for him, and perhaps the most vivid display of all, carefully staged and framed, with crowds of the populace watching from the French slope.

The Kings met upon June 7, Corpus Christi; Henry in silver damask with Buckingham Grand Constable of England[1] at his side, Francis coming forward at the head of his long line of men to meet him in the valley between the two declivities; and by the side of Francis rode Bourbon, *his* Grand Constable, bearing the naked sword. Upon all of which great crowds again watched, cheering from the higher land above.

Of those kingly companions, within a year Buckingham's headless trunk was to be carried from the bloody scaffold on Tower Hill; in little more than three Bourbon was to betray his master and fly from his country.

The feasts and tourneys followed day upon day, in a riot of waste and high colour, until on June 24 ended *"Le très désire et plus que triomphant recontre, entrevue, assemble et visitation des très haultz et très excellens Princes les rois de France et de Angleterre."*

And all the while nobody was really taken in. Wolsey was insisting that no French ship should leave any port in Brittany or Normandy till everyone was safely back. King Henry's companions were noting anxiously that the company of the King of France came formed

---

[1] The title signified command of the land forces.

with more armed men than theirs; and Francis, when the last interview was over, set about refurbishing the fortifications of Ardres till Wolsey's government begged him (successfully) to postpone such intempestive precautions.

But before the show was over all men had noted one thing. Wolsey (in his hands was every detail, the lists for the tourneys and all) had not allowed Buckingham to ride and break a lance. It was Wolsey's doing, not the King's.

Henry, immediately after, with Buckingham still by his side, rode over to Gravelines, and on July 10 met the Emperor again, and very earnestly proposed to Charles war against Francis, as Wolsey had designed. Francis heard of the thing, and Henry was eager to tell him that he had rejected the proposal with horror!

In all this welter of falsehood there was one piece of solidity. Charles was to be affianced to the little Princess Mary, a child of four, and to abandon the marriage with the daughter of Francis: of the two, Francis and Charles, it was Francis whom Wolsey had decided to betray, because he thought Charles the stronger.

After the Field of the Cloth of Gold, with its futilities of foreign policy, the execution of Buckingham (who had there ridden so proudly as Constable of England) stands out in violent contrast: it is the prime exemplar of Wolsey's iron grasp over the realm and all that was highest therein. It comes as a sort of culmination to all this active power exercised by the man who was now the unquestioned and sole master in England.

The deed stands out strongly in the very heart of those great seven years which are the summit of Wolsey's career; for it falls in 1521, in the third of them.

And if nothing else remained to us to show what the Cardinal could do in England that one instance alone would suffice to illustrate his story.

Edward Stafford, third Duke of Buckingham, had been of high influence with the King and with his father. He was the very symbol of the Lancastrian connection. Like Henry VII himself, it was through his mother, a Beaufort, that he was Lancastrian. The usurping King and Buckingham descended directly from, were great-grandsons of, those two brothers the Dukes of Somerset who each in turn had represented the Lancastrian claim through the legitimised Swynford branch.[1]

Buckingham had been born before Bosworth, his father, had been put to death by the arch-enemy of the Tudor house, Richard III; he had been restored to the vast wealth of that father and to his honours as a result of the victory, and Henry VII on his accession gave the guardianship of the orphan boy to his own mother, the old Countess of Richmond. The Tudor loaded him with honours. He was specially chosen to meet Catherine of of Aragon in November, 1501, for the marriage with Prince Arthur. Henry VIII, coming to the throne as a boy, took him over as a loved and respected inheritance from his father's reign, a brave, brilliant, immensely wealthy royal elder brother of a sort, eleven years senior to the young King. Henry VIII had further made him High Constable within a few weeks of his accession and had given him the special honour of being the High Steward at his coronation. All noticed thenceforward how high he stood in the King's esteem and affection, and so he might have continued: till Wolsey had reason to strike him down.

[1] See Note C at the end of the book.

Wolsey's reason was this: that Buckingham, so near
to the King and so possible a rival to himself (not in
ability, but in influence over a mind like Henry's) was
the very type of that old nobility to whom Wolsey's
rise and power were abominable. He bore, being royal
in blood, the royal title of Duke; one daughter was married to the son of Thomas Howard; and others into the
Nevilles and the Percies.

Wolsey could afford to bide his time. The man was
open, generous and choleric, strongly religious as such
characters often are, quite unguarded. He had insulted
the Cardinal, and the Cardinal remembered the insult,
but Wolsey was not the man to act immediately against
insult in hot reaction. He would strike at the right moment, and he must use Henry as he knew how, for it
was only by his control of Henry that Wolsey himself
ruled.

There was a manifold basis for the action which he
was planning. The strongest ground was Henry's nervousness about his throne: for Buckingham's claim was
strong and perhaps superior to the reigning King's own
title. As for opposition from the great Lords of Buckingham's own class, Wolsey could deal with that. The proposed victim against whom he was now to move was of
colossal wealth, his establishment was that of a petty
king, with a court and chancellor of his own. His lands
spread through six counties and over whole districts of
the Marches of Wales. Apart from Thornbury and
Bletchingly he had Brecknock Castle, the town jurisdiction and dues of Newport, its castle and haven in
South Wales, where he ruled unquestioned. He held also
Stafford town, and the castle on the hill a mile outside;
another castle in Warwickshire and another, Kimbolton,

in Huntingdon, and another in Essex, and everywhere
he built and planted curious gardens. Such a man fallen
through treason would leave spoils on which all would
wish to batten, and Wolsey could reckon upon the
stupidity of those very men who, in their long-estab-
lished lineage, hated his new power; who saw in Buckingham their representative; but who, when Buckingham had fallen, would batten at once upon the dead
man's confiscated revenue; and Wolsey would have most
to say as to where those revenues should go.

On some day, the exact date of which we do not possess, but which must have been late in 1520 or quite early
in 1521, Wolsey received a long unsigned letter in a stiff
and formal hand. Whether he himself prompted the
writing of that letter we cannot tell; he may have known
the author of it—we can only guess. The most probable
name is that of Gilbert, whom Hall accuses, the Chaplain and Chancellor of the Duke, and the principal witness against him at his trial: the man who betrayed him.
In this letter Buckingham was denounced for words he
may well have used and which would be of the fullest
influence upon Henry. He had fumed against the King
and the Cardinal, he had hinted that he himself had the
best title to the throne; in the accusations the letter contained there was all that character which came out again
at his trial when the witnesses swore to his saying that
what Henry VII had done (the usurpation) was ill done.
With such an instrument the management of Henry for
Wolsey's purpose was secure.

Characteristically, impulsively, Henry having been
shepherded into such suspicion and terror, took the matter in hand himself; and by the spring of the next year
(Wolsey had taken his time) he was examining secretly

into the Duke's affairs. From Buckingham everything was kept; he was wholly ignorant of what was toward until, on April 8, 1521, there reached him a summons which he took for no more than the King's courtesy and invitation to Court. It came to him where he was at Thornbury, building magnificently, surveying the planning out of his new gardens, glorying in his three great parks with their 1,500 head of deer. He set out for the Court.

As he passed through Reading and at Eton he gave largess to the Church; then as he neared London suspicion grew in his mind. He had noticed three knights following him at a distance. He noticed them again. There were archers upon the roads, too many of them, who seemed to watch him. He felt that he was secretly guarded.

By the time he had reached town on April 15 he had the cloud of imprisonment over his mind. He took his barge at Tothill Fields by the river side (where the Tate Gallery stands now) and rowed down Thames on the ebb with his retinue about him till he came to the steps of York House in Westminster: the town house of the Cardinal. He had a mind to call upon the man whom he knew was marking him for death. But the Cardinal sent word that he was ill. Buckingham would drink a glass of wine none the less, and was given it by one of the Legate's gentlemen with great gravity, and the Duke left £25 for the servants. Then he went off and on towards London Bridge.

But there at the water steps stood Marny, the Captain of the Guard, who went on board. There was a company of 100 armed yeomen behind him. So was Buckingham disembarked and taken along Thames Street to the Tower. On the Monday after the Ascension, May 13, 1521, in the great hall of Westminster, with old white-headed Norfolk, victor of Flodden, presiding, and the seventeen peers of the Court to try their fellow peer, the last proceedings began.

They may have taken three days or four: by Thursday at latest they were concluded. The depositions on what this quick-tempered generous Plantagenet had said were heard, his own household (whom some say his careless tongue had offended) bearing witness against him: that he had said he was next in succession; that he had said it would be well if Henry cut off Wolsey's head—all likely enough.

They brought him in to hear his sentence at the bar, and for all his courage he was sweating and he trembled.

One by one old Norfolk asked each peer his verdict, each answered: "Guilty!" "*Dicit quod est culpabilis.*" To Suffolk in especial Norfolk turned and his answer is recorded, "What say you of Sir Edward, Duke of Buckingham, touching this high treason?" Suffolk put his hand upon his heart and, bowing, answered "I say that he is guilty."

There was too long a silence, at the end of which Norfolk, with the tears streaming down his face, turning to the Prisoner said: "Sir Edward, you put yourself on the judgment of your peers, the which have found you guilty." He pronounced the full sentence of hanging, drawing and quartering after the accustomed form. Buckingham recovered himself, strongly denied all treason and ended with pride: he told them he would never sue for mercy.

On Friday, May 17, a little before noon, they brought him out on Tower Green to die as his father had died.

The people lamented, but none rose or moved. The Cardinal had conquered.[1]

At home I say the Cardinal and the King were secure, but the thing was of violent effect abroad. Remember that everywhere in Europe the Tudors were still thought of as upstarts; the traditions of the Wars of the Roses were very strong in men's minds; it was of high import that foreign courts should not think Henry's throne insecure or believe that there was any wide conspiracy against him. Wolsey was busy to prevent it. To Charles the thing was explained as best it could be, the greater difficulty was with Francis. To the French Ambassador Wolsey lied superbly. It was a dreadful thing, no doubt, this execution, but Buckingham had brought it on himself. Can you guess why? Because he had opposed the French alliance. As to his treason there could be no doubt of it; he had himself confessed it before his death—and so forth.

On the Sunday before the trial of Edward Stafford, Duke of Buckingham, had opened there had been played at Paul's Cross, the preaching place outside the Cathedral of London, a scene which was the opening of Wolsey's slight attention to the tremendous things which were beginning overseas in the matter of the faith of Europe. He himself and the Bishops about him, the Envoy of the Emperor and of the Pope, came solemnly to that place and there, after the Bishop of Rochester had preached, Luther's books and pamphlets were burnt before the eyes of a great crowd.

It was the prelude to something which seemed more really important in the eyes of the Cardinal Legate than any religious squabble among the Germans, something

[1] See Note D at the end of the book.

which, with Hampton Court and the unfinished cloisters at Christ Church at Oxford, is still a monument of his passage through this world. For you may see that something in abbreviated form upon the copper coins of England to this day. It is the Latin title granted to Henry by the Pope: *"Fidei Defensor"*—Defender of the Faith. The disturbance in Germany was only one of many such which had broken out in the past elsewhere throughout Christendom; it was not a matter of high policy. But the pleasing of the court of Rome on which those high politics really depended and the gaining of a title really prized by his master were matters of more moment.

Henry needed no urging; his music and his theology were, after his fine calf (or perhaps before it) strong points of pride. He had already written to the Emperor exhorting him to withstand the new Lutheran movement. He wrote out with care a Latin "Defence of the Seven Sacraments" in contradiction of the Lutheran rebellion, and it is worthy of note that he used rhetoric of an especial zeal in defence of Holy Matrimony: to which sacrament indeed he felt a peculiar attachment and had shown it in his anger with his sister of Scotland when she kicked over the traces. Men said that his Latinity was not all his own and that his old tutor Fisher was more the author than he. Yet there is no reason to doubt either the scholarship or the theological learning of the King; he had been trained in theology and he was a competent writer of Latin. Clarke, the Dean of Windsor, was sent to bear the book in person, and as a sort of ambassador on so solemn occasion to the Court of Rome. And with him he took the humble request that the Head of the Church would approve it,

and the promise that Henry was eager to add deeds to
words and would put the whole power of England in
arms at the service of the Faith and the Vicar of Christ.

In the first Diet of the Empire held by its young
new chief at Worms Luther had been sent for to defend himself. He had been saved by the patronage of his
direct sovereign the Elector of Saxony, who had been so
useful in helping the election of Charles. He was to be
saved further in the future by the ever present political
idea that the new movement could be used by the Emperor in bargaining with the Pope. Luther and his fac-
tion had grown prodigiously in those four years, till a
Papal Envoy could say that of a thousand men in Germany one at most might be unaffected by the revolution
in progress. Luther himself had passed to open war.
The Pope was now "Anti-Christ," his Bull was burnt,
Luther himself was "The Holy of the Lord." And when
he appeared at the Diet he rode upon the crest of a wave
impelled by a whole race.

Surely such things were portentous? But their fruit
in Wolsey's policy was no more than this book and the
title that was to follow it.

Leo's pleasure was sincere and deep. His weak eyes
had difficulty in reading the small print, he peered at
it through his glass. He was more than satisfied; and
when he was asked to reward, to give the signal distinction for which Wolsey pressed, he agreed.

It would be a great error to belittle the value of the
title. We must always look at history with the eyes of
the time, and to the men of the time these honours were
very important indeed. If I contrast their emptiness with
the magnitude of the great spiritual war already engaged, it is not to decry Wolsey's sense of actuality as it

seemed to him and to nearly all his contemporaries; it is only to illustrate that with him only the near things counted.

Beside the Emperor, whose title was supreme, there were but two great kingships, those of France and Spain; to these England, though lesser, stood third. Spain had its Papal title "The Most Catholic King," France its Papal title "The Most Christian King." England had none.

When Louis XII had stood against the Papacy of Julius II and had summoned against the Pope the schismatical Council of Pisa, his title of "Most Christian King" had been taken from him. Leo was urged to give it to Henry instead. Surely Henry had deserved it by joining the Holy League! But Leo was all for peace. Louis XII was beaten and reconciled with the new Pope. His title was restored to him. Eight years had passed since then without further recognition for the King of England. Surely such recognition was overdue!

Therefore in this high matter Wolsey easily had his will. His envoy pleaded for the title and the title was granted. Lest it should lapse it was renewed by Clement VII.

When, many years after Wolsey's death, Henry feared to lose it through his quarrel with Rome, he had it turned into an English title by Act of Parliament and made heritable to his heirs. The Act was repealed by Henry's Catholic daughter Mary, but she retained the title and it still stands. Not all of Wolsey's actions perished.

This important thing having been accomplished and set going over the centuries, the menace of war throughout Europe came to drown all in its clamour. The chance

of common action against the Mohammedan menace
had passed. The long peace was ended. Belgrade, the
bastion of Christendom on the Danube, had fallen—yet
the West paid no heed.

The clash between the new Emperor and Francis I,
in expectation of which Wolsey had played his double
game after the Cloth of Gold, came in that same summer of 1521 which saw the execution of Buckingham
and Henry's book against Luther.

Charles, in the treaty of Noyon long before, had
promised to hand back to its native line (vassals of
France) Navarre, with its capital of Pampeluna, beyond
the Pyrenees. But Charles had good reason for not fulfilling his promise. He had already found himself in
grave difficulties with his subjects in Spain because he
was a French-speaking Fleming and because he had
brought in, to govern Spain, French-speaking Flemings
like himself. There had been insurrection and high peril.
He could not surrender Navarre against the Spanish national feeling. Francis abetted the native house in their
attempt to regain it single-handed, and the men of Béarn
went across the mountains and took Pampeluna (it was
the occasion when Ignatius Loyola was wounded). They
could not hold it for long but it meant war between the
main antagonists. The Pope was determined to get rid
of the French grip on North Italy. Charles made a secret
alliance with him. The Papal and Imperial forces combined succeeded, the French under Lautrec were driven
out of the town of Milan before the end of 1521 and
had lost all save a few garrisons in North Italy. Wolsey,
still protesting warm friendship to Francis, joined the
Emperor openly.

There followed that accident whereby Wolsey could make his first bid for the Papacy:—

. . . .

The news that Milan had been taken so moved Pope Leo that Rome was illuminated, to signify that Italy was free. The joy might have killed him, but he did not suspect how near he was to death. He was still in early middle age, younger by three years than Wolsey. He had no suspicion that his time was so near. He had been well enough hunting in the woods round Corneto of the Tarquins, that mysterious town of ancient graves and gods, statues of majestic antiquity, earlier than the birth of Rome. He had snared birds in Viterbo, he had fished in the wide lake of Bolsena, he had gone down to the sea at Ostia as autumn closed in, giving largess to the peasants, enjoying his popularity to the full. Then came that happy news of Milan, and it invigorated him—but also it enfevered him. He was awake all night. The next day, fatigued by that vigil, he made for the city, and there he suddenly felt weakness come upon him and in four days he was dead. It was the midnight between the 1st and the 2nd of December, 1521.

Now struck that hour when the fate of Europe might have been changed. If Wolsey's determination to be Pope had by some impossible chance been fulfilled, see what would have followed! A man in the full vigour of life, determined to rule, England linked firmly to the Holy See, the disruption avoided by something stronger than the French concordat, and the Papacy at length something more than an Italian Principate, something nearer to its former international self.

Wolsey was to fail, of course, and while he failed he was to show once more that central defect in him, that blind spot in the eye of his judgment, the inability to pierce men's inmost motives. He who could so well choose a servant could not discover the real hidden intention of an equal.

He had great reserves of money wherewith to bribe. He was prepared to pay half a million pounds of our money today, and that was a great deal for the turning of key votes in a small electorate of some forty men. He had the open support of the Emperor for whom he had just declared, he even had the open promise of Francis, who hoped to regain English assistance. Neither the Emperor nor Francis intended to other than deceive him: please him with words and despise his ambition—in their eyes ridiculous. Within a fortnight after Leo's death and even before the embalmed body was buried, Charles V had written to his agent in England to tell Wolsey publicly that he should have the Emperor's interest, and had determined to oppose him in private.

The strongest candidate among those Cardinals was of course the Medicean cousin of the dead man, of whose promotion to the Sacred College Henry had heard during the campaign before Tournai eight years before; the man who was later to be Clement VII. But though he was the strongest he could not command a decisive vote. For two-thirds of the votes cast were necessary to an election. But he was strong enough to prevent any compatriot from proving a successful rival.

The Cardinal-Legate of York set about the task with all his energies at full drive. He promised English subsidies for an army wherewith Charles V might march on Rome; he sent an envoy to remind Charles of his promise, he dispatched Pace to Rome to report for

him; he urged Campeggio, his informant from within
the conclave, to put forth every effort. The Pope had
been buried a week before Christmas. Two days after
Christmas, on December 27, the election began. There
were thirty-nine Cardinals in the conclave, each in one
of those little cubicles of sixteen feet by twelve feet which
stand round the Sistine Chapel. Each would be so confined until a result was arrived at. What with secretaries
and servants there were locked into that assembly two
hundred souls.

What passed in the conclave so far as Wolsey was
concerned it is difficult to determine.[1] There were eleven
scrutinies. All that is certain is that at none of them
did Wolsey receive one-third of the votes cast, probably
he never received one-fifth of them. He had misjudged
his security with the French as with Charles. The fourteen votes which Francis had promised him were a blind.
The active support which Charles had promised him was
a deceit. The Emperor wrote to his Ambassador openly
urging him to support Wolsey, but meanwhile his agent
in Rome proposed in the deadlock the name of Charles's
own tutor, the Dutchman, Adrian, Cardinal Archbishop
of Tortosa. It was Giulio Medici, himself the leading
candidate, the man at once too strong and too weak at
the moment to command a sufficient majority, who decided the issue, and Adrian was elected at the 11th scrutiny, on January 9, 1522. The Romans, who for all those
days had been laying odds outside could now settle their
accounts, with the book heavy against the favourite.

From the balcony Cornaro's weak voice announcing
the issue to the crowd below was not heard. The stronger
tones of Campeggio roaring out the name were caught

[1] See Note E at the end of the book.

by everyone, and the noisy crowd dispersed, marvelling and jeering that one not Italian should sit in the chair of Peter.

To Wolsey, when the news reached him in his disappointment, Charles profusely lied. He could not understand the result, it bewildered him; he had given no instructions in support of any other man. But Wolsey was not daunted. We shall see him again within two years attempting the assault, on Adrian's death. We shall see him almost grasping the reality, though not the name, of the Papal power four years later, in 1527, during the captivity of Adrian's successor, and even as late as 1529 on the eve of his own fall eagerly putting forth his claim on the false news of that successor's death. The dream never left him, nor could he imagine a Europe in which the Catholic Church should not remain all powerful, continuing in its existing organisation and the Papacy at the head of our unity.

But the most important thing which appeared in that year, 1522, for Wolsey, for England, and, in the long run, for the world, was not Adrian VI's election but, again, an incident which passed with very slight notice at the time. It followed on the return of Thomas Boleyn's daughter, Anne, from her long residence in France. She was in her 21st year[1] or perhaps a little over, perhaps 22, and ready for adventures. Discreet, reserved, sharptongued and watchful. Wyatt was one of her lovers, though whether she went so far with him as he later told the King after her death, when it flattered the King to hear it, was doubtful, for Wyatt was both a poet and a liar. But it is certain that without paying much regard to him she flew at once for higher game.

[1] See Note F at the end of this book.

The greatest name in England after that of Howard was the name of Percy. They were the Lords of the North, for the Percy was Northumberland. That great Norman family which lived on into the 18th century until it died out in heiresses. The name is carried on by the family of Smithson.

But in those early years of the 16th century the name Northumberland, the name Percy, were not merely decorative as they are today; they meant real power: the control of landscape and of men; possibly of armies. They were little kings under the main King of England and, I say again, after the Howards the greatest name in the Kingdom and rich enormously.

It was in this year 1522, when Anne was well grown, that she determined upon bearing the name of Northumberland.

The lord Northumberland of that day, the Earl of North England, had a son and heir bearing his name of Percy; destined to die very young, perhaps sickly, certainly sentimental, an easy prey. He was set to service in Wolsey's household, so important was it for the greatest to do homage to the Cardinal. He would wander in his leisure to the room where the Queen was with her maids of honour, and among these was Anne. She made sure of him soon enough. And we must admit, perhaps with regret, that she could inspire passion, for at least two men fell wholly into her hands, this young fellow and later the unfortunate King. It seems that the young man had less discretion than she—as might be expected in such relations.

Now in the year before, Henry had already married off Anne's younger sister Mary. But she had probably remained his mistress. He designed a marriage between

Anne and the heir of the Ormondes so as to settle a quarrel upon that heirship, for her father had a claim to it. But that did not prevent his noting the family type. Mary had been his, and Anne was of the same mould. That she could or would resist could not yet have entered his head, nor can we say at what precise moment the first glance was given which was to lead to such lasting consequences. But at any rate Henry would put an end to this business with Percy.

Such was the small beginning, the first moment of caprice—which turned next to habit: then into a vice.

Henry learnt early in the affair of these tender exchanges with Percy. The news inflamed him. He bade Wolsey to break the thing at once. Wolsey executed that order with thoroughness.

It was in the great gallery of York House that he summoned the young man into his presence, though all his household was about him, and publicly rated and browbeat him—"Marvelling not a little at his folly, that he should thus entangle and ensnare himself with a foolish girl, even there in the court—Anne Bollen." He scolded the wretched lad in his domineering manner, asking him if he remembered to what he was born, and why he had dared so to act without speaking even to his father, or to the King.

At this violent public admonition the poor boy, though in tears, answered from his heart. He said, truly enough, that the woman who had mastered him was of good blood, "near to the Norfolk Blood," in estate and descent equal to his own, and he ended despairingly by telling the overwhelming master of England that he begged the King's favour in the matter "which I cannot forsake."

That cry was true enough, poor beast! So it was to be

with Henry Tudor in a very short time. "I cannot forsake." That is the universal plea of the victim. "It is
stronger than I." Then did Wolsey in that long gallery of
his great house, York House, that house which he was
pitifully to lose, to be made over to the King's theft, and
to be turned into Whitehall—break out into the anger
that always appeared at such rare oppositions as he en-
countered.

"Did Percy imagine that they" (Wolsey and the
King) "knew not better than such a stripling as he? I
will send for your father out of the north parts, and in
the mean season I charge that thou resort no more into
her company, as thou wilt abide the King's indignation."

With that the Cardinal, in his great Cardinal's cassock,
sailed away, like a red galleon, I suppose, before the
wind, to his private room.

He was as good as his word. Northumberland, that
very great Earl, that second name in England of the laity
and of the traditional noble blood, trembled and obeyed.
He came before the Cardinal; they talked together in
private, drinking wine. The father was sent off to rate
the son again in the great gallery. A second scene took
place. Northumberland sat on the common bench where
the servitors would repose and scolded his lad for a
wastrel—"a proud, licentious, disdainful and very un-
thrifty waster." "What joy, what comfort, what pleasure, what solace, should he have of such a waster?" And
Lord! How obstinate he had been against his natural
sovereign, the King! He threatened to disinherit the
young man. There was no doubt at all of the gravity
of the affair.

So was first known to the world, in the year 1522, this
truth: that Henry Tudor, somewhat over thirty years

of age, being now for three years well weary of his wife
and within a very short time to deal with her no more,
had thought, among we know not how many others, of
a third principal mistress, successor to her own sister
Mary, who had in turn succeeded Elizabeth Blunt.

But Henry Tudor was wrong. He had discovered no
mistress, he had stumbled upon a master. To that mastery of Anne's he was to become, with all England dependent upon him, a slave . . .

Yet did poor Percy still weep. He wrote piteously
to a private friend, miserable that Anne seemed to be
changed to him—(this friend had known them at the
moment when she had entrapped him)—imploring that
she should never in his absence be married to another
man. "Bid her remember her promise, which none can
loose but God only, to whom I shall daily during my
life with many prayers commend."

Later, under terror of the King, when Henry was so
far fallen that he would even sink to marriage with
Anne rather than to do without her, and when (under
the Catholic sense of the time, a former engagement
to another would have prevented such a marriage, Percy
gave way.

He took a solemn oath, confirming it with Communion, and praying it might be to his damnation if
there ever had been a contract or promise of marriage
between Anne and himself. He might have spared himself the humiliation;—within six weeks he was dead.

.   .   .   .

So much for the little incident, which, at the time, half
a dozen noticed and which was forgotten even by these
in a day or two. Much greater seemed the prospect of yet
another alliance, yet another war, in that interminable

series of shift and wrangle which introduced so meanly the august, approaching tragedies of European religion.

The next year, 1523, was filled with the greatest of Wolsey's mistakes upon the continental field: of Wolsey's standing the more thereby in Europe's public eye, with a sort of impotent renown: of Wolsey's audacity in going to any lengths at home in the raising of revenue for his fruitless adventures abroad.

It was the time at home when—after an interval of nine years—the Commons were summoned to grant new levies on a scale as yet unheard of. It was the time of their despairing resistance.

It was the time abroad when Wolsey made his second effort to attain the Papacy—more completely rejected even than had been the first. It was the time when he launched his last war—which came to nothing, as did all his wars.

He imagined that, in alliance with the Emperor, he could overset the French throne and give Henry all the old Plantagenet inheritance—half France: Normandy, Brittany, Anjou, Gascony, Aquitaine—while the Emperor should seize Burgundy and the northeast. It was a scheme quite irrational and it broke down absurdly.

Bourbon, Constable of France and cousin to the French King, rebelled against Francis on a grievance, joined the Emperor and, in attempting to push war into his own country, failed.

Suffolk, at the head of a large English army, ravaged a belt leading from the sea towards Paris. He, too, broke down and was beaten back beyond the frontiers.

Yet all the while the splendour of Wolsey in England shone undiminished and he once more—in that same year of 1523—made a bid for the Papal throne.

Adrian VI died on the 14th of September, leaving Christendom in chaos, with the Turk at the gate. Rhodes fallen and all the eastern sea in the hands of the enemy: with the religious revolt in the Germanics exalting and moving to victory: with the short peace which might have united Europe against the Moslem torn to shreds and all the west at war.

The Apostolic See lay vacant and what Wolsey—untaught by experience—believed to be his second opportunity, had come.

In a former page upon this great Pope I have written *Utinam*. Would that Adrian of Utrecht had lived! *Utinam*! Would that! . . . It is one of the innumerable "Would that's" which crowd so thick in the disastrous shipwreck of Christendom.

Had Adrian lived we Christians still might be one united people. The two-fold vice which had fastened upon the Papacy just when it most needed to be free from such degradation, returned with violence upon Adrian's death: the general vice of worldly motive and the particular vice of motive Medicean. All during the outbreak of the storm it was a Medicis (concerned with the Medicean grasp on Florence) who had ruled in Rome; now after those few brief months of real attempted reform it was to be a Medicis again, Giulio, that cousin who had been as it were Viceroy to the Papacy for so long and who even, because he was the outstanding figure of the conclave, might for that very reason have been rejected.

For the second time Wolsey throws his whole weight into the great ambition, and for the second time we may say with justice that the ambition seemed far less futile than it seems to us today. Not a single vote did he receive in that long conclave, yet there were moments when the deadlock might possibly have been solved by his sudden election—for his flamboyant figure was in all men's minds.

There was spoken, in the worst of the dispute, when none of the three parties would give way to the other and when Rome outside was getting so angry that it passed from murmuring to threats, a phrase which throws a most vivid light upon his chances.

A week had passed since the conclave had met, the thirty-five Cardinals had gathered while it thundered overhead and rain fell in torrents, on the 1st of October, 1523. On the 6th, just as the first scrutiny was about to be taken, the French Cardinals, who it was hoped would be delayed, rode in; their haste had put them into laymen's clothes, they appeared with the mud of their ride upon them, booted and spurred. Upon the 8th the solemn count was taken. The Emperor urging for Giulio commanded 11 votes, 11 followed the French party, 11 formed a third. This deadlock was the cause of Roman anger; and then it was that Armellino cried out to cow the crowd: "If you complain too much with your clamour for an Italian we will give you quite another—one who lives in England." But the Romans still clamoured for their Italian Pope, they remembered too well that Adrian had been not only a foreigner but a reformer, and they said: "It must be one of those present, though he be but a log."

Still the deadlock continued. All pretence at secrecy broke down, one may almost say that the conclave mixed with the crowd when for nearly three weeks the halt was still continuing: the Mantuan Ambassador wrote "They look as though they want to pass the winter thus."

At the end of the 4th week the Cardinal Farnese and the Medicean were still equal; the Romans were fuming. With the end of the 6th a little company of new French Cardinals raised the total to thirty-nine, and then it was that against all calculation the King of France, the supposed necessary enemy of the Emperor, interfered for Giulio, the Emperor's choice: why, we shall never know. It has been suggested that the candidate gave a secret promise of neutrality between Francis and Charles were he elected.

On the 17th November twenty-seven votes were given for the Medicis and the opposition had failed. On the 18th the voting was verified. Giulio de Medicis was declared Pope and took the name of Clement VII. For the second time Wolsey's attempt had failed. He had been in suspense for fifty days.

For the second time Wolsey had had Charles' public support; this time even more strongly expressed than during that first election of two years before. He trusted twice the man who had once betrayed him. Charles had actually written an open letter demanding Wolsey's election, he had caused copies of the letter to be sent to England and presented. Nothing could seem sounder. What Wolsey did not know was that the writer had given orders typical of the time. The bearer of the letter was to be detained in Barcelona till the voting was over, and it was never presented in Rome!

During these last years of such foreign war, Papal effort, glamour and personal expenditure at home, Wolsey's power over the kingdom remained such that he would drain money from it after a fashion hitherto quite unheard of. He pushed things so far that even his omnipotence was checked—and the main cause of all that extortion was the fever for playing so great a part abroad, which part he played so ill.

Because in 1522 the Papacy was at war with Francis, because Francis was threatened by the superior force of Charles, because Wolsey's own double intrigue in the time of the Cloth of Gold the year before demanded some outlet, therefore had he made war again, with wild proposals to set Henry back as master in the old provinces of the Plantagenets. He began by borrowing half a million from London in the next year; he went on to raise a forced loan equivalent to more than four years of the normal revenue of the country, eight millions. In order to squeeze out that sum he made an assessment of goods held by all but the smaller people and demanded as a loan a quarter of that assessment to be spread over five yearly installments. That was a capital levy on goods to the value of 1/- in the £ each year. And yet in the first year of the war the expenses of it were still owing. Already his assessment had been so rigorous that it more than doubled the old yield of eight years before, when also he had asked for 1/- in the £ of men's goods in a capital levy. For the absurd campaign of 1523 he was compelled to call a Parliament, and therein it was that he came against the limits of his power. He wanted more than sixteen millions, not far short of twenty. He could only get it by a capital levy of one-fifth, and this time not on goods only but on land. There was universal protest and the Commons, who had little to do in those days with legislation but whose very object of existence it was to discuss grants, refused the extravagant and ruinous demand. They offered half, to be spread over a number of years, and in the main Wolsey gave way. He had no choice to do otherwise. With the clergy he could be more authoritative. He took the value of half the benefices, spread over five years. But I say that he had reached the limit, and there was a temper abroad closely approaching rebellion. Insurrections had already begun.

For all this wild fiscal excess, quite abnormal, danger-ous and grievous in the extreme, there was nothing to show save a few burnt villages in the north of France and a treaty of peace which left things as they were. The lesson had been learnt. Though Wolsey was yet to prom-ise, more than once, support to policies abroad which, had they been realised, would have meant renewed pres-sure for money, that pressure was in fact not renewed; and a few years later the memory of the last extortions was sufficient to prevent a renewal of war. The hatred aroused against the man who had hitherto done what he would with the country did not die down. The contrast between the strain upon the average citizen and the flam-boyant luxury of the Legate's establishment and train had bred an intensity of personal feeling which added popular momentum to the envy of the greater men— and all this was on the eve of Wolsey's first doubts and anxieties, all this culminated with the end of the great seven years. Moreover in that time came the first hint that Henry might later change, might feel less strongly the pressure of Wolsey's will—and might therefore re-ceive that of another. The King had criticised the plan of campaign for France, and the event had proved him right.

But as yet there was no lessening of the Cardinal at all. He continued to extend the powers of Chancery, of which he made a new thing; he had gained extension of the Legateship and the right to use it for the reformation

WOLSEY WITH A COAT-OF-ARMS

By Courtesy of the London Library, St James' Square

of the clergy and the visiting of monasteries exempt from Episcopal control and subject only to the Pope. He planned to use his powers: to use them—as he did in time use them—for suppressing small monastic houses by Papal licence and using their revenues for new colleges—notably his great foundation at Oxford which was to be called "Cardinal's College" but which was later, and is still, known as Christ Church. In that work of suppression he was to use a man whose intelligence he had appreciated, whose power of organisation and whose capacity for work he discovered to be exceptional, Thomas Cromwell.

The wild anarchy into which the Germans next plunged in 1524 and on through 1525, the rising and suppression by massacre of the peasants, seems to have impressed him somewhat—as certainly no other effect of the Reformation did. On the eve of death he warned his friends against heresy, not for itself but because it had bred in his day, as it had bred in the Wyclifite and Hussite troubles of a century and more before, a popular rising and attacks upon wealth.

For the rest, the war—in which he might no longer join, because the country had been drained dry—continued. Bourbon, for the Emperor, besieged Marseilles and was driven off. Francis, in the same year, 1524, crossed once more into Italy by the Mont Cenis to recover Milan.

He seemed successful: he laid siege to Pavia all that winter: on his own birthday, the 24th day of February, 1525, he blundered in the use of his magnificent artillery, was caught, his great army wiped out and all his guns captured.

Charles stood in that hour of Pavia the victor of

Europe: for the moment there was no other force to withstand his own.

In the shock of Pavia (the reversal of all Wolsey had dealt with abroad since Marignano) his bewilderment was greater than ever. Francis was a prisoner in the hands of the Emperor. There was for the moment no French army to reckon with. His first impulse was to fall on the conquered. But the country was on the brink of insurrection against existing money levies—it refused to pay; and the example of the peasants' revolt at full spate in Germany was a warning. His second impulse, therefore, was a sudden veering around to support the captive Francis—and this course Pope Clement, in his dread of Charles' new power, also leaned to.

So the next few years might have seen nothing but a further extension of alliance and counter-alliance after the pattern which had been woven and unwoven ceaselessly since Henry's first wars as a boy and the advent of Wolsey: they were in fact so filled—but not wholly. A thing greater in the fate of Europe, and in the fate of Wolsey decisive, had already appeared within six months of Charles' victory and the capture of Francis. Henry was moving—in profound secrecy—for the annulment of his marriage. Some faint rumour of it was abroad by the summer of 1525. By the spring of 1527 it was public.

All that time between Pavia and the first open business of the divorce was filled for Wolsey with the sense of coming change.

The great seven years were over. The water was no longer smooth. Wolsey had felt the swell of the open sea, and there was weather ahead.

But the main blast that was to come, the thing that

was to overthrow him and to bring his tragedy to its
climax was not suspected by him. It was not suspected
perhaps by more than half a dozen men in Europe, and
those half dozen were not in touch one with the other.
The gradual entrapment of the King by Anne, the slow,
hidden, unwitnessed process by which from a caprice
he had been subjected to a vice, and from a vice to a
mania; the parallel process whereby the woman behind
the scenes was taking greater and greater advantage of
each step in the degradation of the unfortunate man—
all this was hidden below the surface, hardly known.
Henry himself could not have recognised his condition
fully, for men never do understand in time the pursuit
of that which is to destroy them. Even Anne herself can
only have slowly formed her plan, and Wolsey was
ignorant of it altogether. And yet, holding, as he still
did, all the avenues of information, being, for all his
lack of sympathy with other minds, a man accustomed
to probe hidden action, he should have had a better
knowledge of what was going on. That Henry intended
an annulment of his marriage with Catherine he certainly knew within the course of the year 1526, for in the
early summer of that year he talked of the good progress
which certain affairs of the King had been making at
Rome for some time past, and those affairs at this moment could only have been the divorce. He probably
guessed something in 1525, when Charles the Emperor
had dropped a hint. He was then well awake to, and, as
we shall see, supported the Divorce. Yet it did not enter
his mind that a marriage with Anne was the object, still
less that Anne was directing the whole affair.

As early as September, 1526, the annulment of the
marriage was officially afoot—and almost certainly

earlier. There is on that date a letter to Wolsey from the Bishop of Bath and Wells, Clerk, in which he talks of the Bulls which are coming for Wolsey's College, and alludes to all things going well "save in the matter of this accursed divorce."[1]

It is probable that Wolsey had guessed long before even this Autumn of 1526 that Henry had cast an eye upon Anne. He could not have misunderstood any more than we do the sudden honours heaped upon her father the year before, and what could not have been hidden from the Court must have been familiar to him, who knew Henry's temperament—who knew of the connection with Anne Boleyn and all the rest of it. Further, he knew that there had been some talk on the Continent of an annulment of Henry's marriage as early as 1526, for in that year the Emperor had remarked a possibility that the Princess Mary might be bastardised.

In that same year, 1525, on the 30th of October, the French Ambassador wrote to the Queen Mother in France the significant words—that he had a very private communication to make to her, on an exceedingly important matter, which he dared not put on paper. So it was all round: a mystery was in the air during 1525-26 and early 1527, and that mystery was Henry's growing

[1] The letter is cryptic, of course, it cannot be anything else. Some have thought that it might allude to the breaking off of the Princess of France's engagement, and Friedmann thinks that it "clearly" refers to the pending divorce between Margaret of Scotland and Angus. But, learned man though he is, he gives no good reason for that "clearly." Professor Pollard, by far the greatest modern scholar on the subject, inclines to the view that this sentence refers to Henry's project. I do not see how it can well be interpreted otherwise, for what other of the innumerable annulments and counter-annulments of which that time was full can have been of such import in the eyes of the English Minister and his servants?

intention to procure a sentence of annulment against his wife.

Wolsey then knew that there was talk of divorce for during all that turning point of 1525-26 there was distant faint talk. He knew that Henry was stirred by Anne, as he had been stirred by others. But what he quite failed to do was to connect the two things. The annulment, if it was to come to anything, was a piece of high politics: the other was a piece of private and passing appetite.

What he did not know, what was to come to him with violence and suddenly, a discovery which imperilled his whole position and his future, was that the affair was not on the ordinary lines of a royal amour, but was being shepherded by this secret and determined woman towards a marriage. What he did not conceive and what no one, save Anne and her prey, conceived as yet, was that there could be a connection between Anne's attraction for the King, and the proposal to repudiate Catherine. No one as yet had thought it possible that they would see Anne Boleyn crowned Queen of England.

VIII

INTERLUDE

INTRODUCTION TO THE DIVORCE

THE divorce of Henry VIII was not only of capital importance to the history of England, and therefore of Europe, but in particular the immediate cause of Wolsey's tragedy. It was the mainspring of his fall. He had accumulated enemies even more than do most men in the exercise of so much power. He was hated almost as much as he was dreaded. He was surrounded by a ring of angry jealousies and indignations working in the midst of all the most influential men of his time. Nevertheless would he have maintained himself upon the throne he had mounted; he would perhaps have died there, still supreme, certainly would he have ended in honour, had it not been for the thrusting in of an alien factor which he had not understood, for which he had not calculated and which more directly imperilled the King than could Wolsey's own experience, energy and habit. It threw him off the rails. This alien factor was the inflexible will of Anne Boleyn. And the outward manifestation of that will was the divorce.[1]

There are three things which we must understand clearly about the divorce before we proceed to follow the successive stages of the affair. These three things are, its character, its motive, and its date of origin.

It is essential to understand the nature of the demand made by Henry and the nature of the opposition he had to meet; it is difficult because we live in a time where for the mass of men not only the institution of marriage

[1] See Note G at the end of the book.

itself, but all legal forms surrounding it belong to another world than that of the 16th century. Our modern
terms mislead us altogether.

It is of equal importance, though in another fashion,
to grasp the motive at work; for upon that motive depends the whole story. Had that motive been what some
still pretend it to be, anxiety for the succession, all would
have been different. The King's first wife might have
admitted the plea of necessity, and have consented to
Henry's making a new, rational, marriage consonant
with the dignity of the Crown. But the main motive
being what it was, to wit, the compulsion under which
Henry was to satisfy the iron resolve of the woman who
had seized him, upon that main motive all turned. Catherine might have admitted a Royal Alliance. She would
never admit a Court prostitute.

The importance of fixing a date of origin may seem
less clear, for it may be argued that one date of origin or
another is indifferent to the result; once the project was
started the curtain rises, the drama is opened, and we
have but to follow it; this date or that can make no
difference to its character any more than the hour at
which the curtain rises makes a difference to the play.

But it is not so. To establish as far as may be within
certain limits the probable or certain origins of the project
helps us to comprehend its motive and to understand the
stages through which it passed. Had it begun as late as
some suppose, had it first entered Henry's mind at the
beginning of 1527, we should have to judge differently
of that mind and therefore of the process and the consequences of the business. Had it been present in that mind
much earlier, say as early as 1514,[1] as some assert, we

[1] See Note H at the end of the book.

should have again to revise our judgment of its main character. That it began as a fact in 1525 conditions the whole affair.

First then, as to the nature of what Henry proposed, or rather what was imposed upon Henry by the persistent will of another.

The word "Divorce" is used today to mean what it meant in the old Pagan world from which we spring and to the morals of which we are rapidly returning. It means the ending of an existing marriage *admitted to be a marriage*, and the leaving of the parties who were formerly married free to marry again.

Divorce thus interpreted depends upon the doctrine that marriage is only a contract which may, like any other contract, be terminated. Because society reposes upon the institution of marriage, as it does upon the institutions of property and of inheritance, the contract has never been treated as one to be made and unmade at will. The marriage bond must have some durable element about it if society is to endure. Still, so long as the bond is regarded as resulting from contract only, it can be severed under conditions laid down by the law for that particular contract. Under this conception (which is that of all human society outside the Catholic Church, which is that of the Mohammedan as well as of the Pagan) a man and a woman continue validly married up to the moment of divorce, after which they cease to be man and wife; a new second marriage can be undertaken by either without affecting the validity of the first, and third or fourth or fifth, sixth, seventh marriages after successive divorces will be equally recognised.

In the society of Western Europe at this date (1525) such a conception was unknown. The conception of marriage in the mind of that society was that it was a contract indeed, but a contract which produced in both parties to it a permanent condition, terminable only by death. That conception is still the fundamental conception of those in communion with the See of Rome. To it is added the conception that marriage is a sacrament, and that its permanent quality is confirmed by all the sanctions of a sacrament; in other words it has binding it all the forces of religion and of Divine institution.

Divorce, then, in the modern, the ancient, the non-Catholic sense, did not exist for the Christendom of 1525. A man and a woman validly married had entered into a condition which neither could change. The husband was the husband of the wife and the wife was the wife of the husband until the death of either party. No other idea of marriage existed in the general mind of the time. And the fundamental idea that marriage was of its nature permanent, and its permanence of a Divine character, lingered long after the break-up of the united religious scheme under which it had arisen.

A full 115 years after the outbreak of the Reformation the dissolution of a marriage by process of law seemed so shocking a thing that it could only be carried out even in Protestant England by a special and solemn act of the legislature. The Statute which permitted it was only passed in the second half of the 17th century and even then against the protests of the Anglican Bishops. Such a novelty remained exceedingly rare, it did not become common until our own time, and the long delay in the establishment of the modern conception is proof of the strength, of the deeply rooted character, of the older one. Within living memory a divorced person in Europe was one to be avoided, to be held in marked disfavour, and the remarriage of one so divorced was felt shocking even in countries where divorce was permissible by law. In some, in Italy and Ireland for instance, marriage has remained indissoluble to our own day. In France the new idea of it was only introduced after a fierce struggle towards the end of the 19th century.

But to return to 1525. How at that date did those who desired to put an end to what all had regarded as an existing marriage, and who were sufficiently powerful to attain their object, proceed? They proceeded by application to the Pope as Head of Christendom for a declaration in his supreme court, and by his authority, *that the supposed original marriage had been no marriage at all.* A man or woman desiring to put an end to the existing relationship and to establish a new one did not say "I am married and I want my marriage dissolved." They said: "I maintain that I have never been married; I maintain that my so-called marriage was no marriage at all and should be declared null and void." Only after it had so been declared null and void by the ecclesiastical courts and, in the last appeal by the Papal courts, could another marriage take place; and this second ceremony was, in the theory of the time, the *first* true marriage, for the first one had never existed.

Now all this, of course, in the case of the powerful people who so acted, was, in the great majority of cases, a piece of hypocrisy. And, in the great majority of them, the ecclesiastical courts (and in particular the Papal court) which decided in favour of nullity were equally guilty of hypocrisy. It was a subterfuge and a sham. But it remains true that there is all the difference in the world between a trick played to avoid the consequences of an admitted law and the bold denial of that law. There is all the difference in the world between hiring a lawyer to trick your neighbour out of his property and denying the right to property. The powerful men and women of the 16th century who thus evaded the obligations of marriage did not deny the law of permanency.

A decree of nullity could be recorded on many pleas. The principal of which (and the only ones we have to consider in connection with the case of Henry) were that the marriage had taken place within the prohibited degrees of relationship or that the marriage had never been consummated.

The degrees of relationship within which marriage could not lawfully be contracted in the eyes of the Church were widely extended during the Dark and Middle Ages. They came to include even a distant cousinship. But there had also arisen a system whereby ecclesiastical authority could grant *dispensations* allowing people to be married in spite of such relationship, and at the time of which we speak, such dispensations, duly and officially issued from the Court of Rome, rendered the marriage based upon them valid beyond question.

But there was necessarily considerable doubt and corresponding debate upon the limit beyond which this power of dispensation could not go, and as we shall see, the whole of Henry's case turned upon a debate of this kind. The Pope could grant a dispensation for, say, the marriage of second cousins; it entered no one's head to doubt that, although without such dispensation nullity could be claimed. But could the Pope grant a dispensation for the marriage of a man with his sister-in-law, his dead brother's wife? He could issue the document of course, but was the action of any effect? The theory of the Papal power of dispensation reposed upon the idea that though there is a law of Divine institution from which no one can dispense, not even the Vicar of Christ, there are also other laws of human ecclesiastical institution from which ecclesiastical authority and especially the Vicar of Christ can dispense. To give an example, no one would admit that an ecclesiastical dispensation could leave you morally free to poison an enemy. But everyone would admit that an ecclesiastical dispensation could leave you morally free not to fast in lent. Some maintained that the prohibition of marriage with a sister-in-law was of divine institution and could therefore never be valid. Others said it was only an ecclesiastical prohibition which a dispensation could overcome.

The nature then of the demand made by Henry was that his marriage with Catherine of Aragon, contracted so many years ago and for so long undisputed, was null and void from the outset. He might plead that there had been no proper dispensation allowing him to marry his brother's widow; or he might plead that even if the dispensation was in due form it was beyond the Pope's power to grant it, because the prohibition in the case of so close a relationship was a divine law in the case of which no dispensation was of effect. On the other hand Catherine could plead that the dispensation was in due form, was valid, and (an absolutely invincible contention if proved) that she had never really been married to Henry's elder brother, Prince Arthur, at all, because that boy who died at fifteen had never consummated the marriage.

So much for the nature of the action, now for its motive. The ostensible motive set forth by Henry was a conscientious objection that had arisen in his mind through the tragic experience of child after child still-born or dying immediately after birth, of the lack of male issue, of having only one sickly daughter remaining precariously alive out of seven such frustrated hopes. A real political motive which might have been sufficient to account for what he did had he done it in a different fashion and at a different time was the fear of a disputed succession. It was known from about 1519 onwards that Catherine could have no more children. Should Henry not re-marry (through her death) or not be permitted to do so earlier through a declaration of nullity, there was no chance of a legitimate male heir. There was no active precedent for a woman reigning over England, at least none since the disastrous experiment of Matilda, hundreds of years before—an experiment which had failed—which had been made in a totally different kind of society and which no one regarded as of political application. For the matter of that, if women had the right to reign, Henry's grandmother, the Lady Margaret, who outlived his coronation, should have been on the throne of England in place of his father and himself. The point must not be too much emphasized, for the sanctity of Kingship was so great at this moment that when the only heir was a woman public opinion in Europe accepted a reigning Queen. Catherine's own mother is an example in point.

But there was one last consideration which did count strongly and that was the instability of the Tudor tradition; it was only forty years since Henry VII took the throne, without any defined title. He and his son between them were always in terror of possible claimants, and to have only a woman for the Tudor successor was a peril. Moreover that woman would presumably marry; a marriage with a native would introduce the claims of royal rivals at home, while a marriage with a foreigner might introduce foreign influence upon the throne.

For all these reasons it would have been comprehensible that Henry should, from somewhere about the date 1519, have the succession as his motive for dissolving his original marriage and contracting a new one, and indeed some have tentatively advanced arguments to prove that this was his motive.

The contention will not hold water for a moment. That Henry desired a male heir is obvious, but had that desire impelled him to what he did he would have done it earlier and he would have done it differently. He was but thirty when he knew that his prematurely elderly wife could give him no more children. Why should he wait eight years before moving? We know from his own admission how soon he ceased to live with Catherine after he found that all hope of male issue had ceased, but, so far from seeking a new alliance, he took up at once with a mistress, Mountjoy's sister, Elizabeth Blunt, who had been about the Court from childhood, who was healthy, robust and beautiful, a full contrast with the unfortunate woman whom he had discarded. She bore him an illegitimate son in that same year. There is no trace of any effort to procure legitimate male succession. That effort, at a new marriage, only begins after long delays; it does not begin in connection with a woman who he could be sure would have issue, it does not begin in connection with a woman whose issue would be accepted by the nation, by competitors, and by foreign rivals, without demur. It is carried on obstinately, when once it has been begun (so late in his life!) and is carried on in the teeth of every consideration of dynastic stability, of popularity, and even of decency. Moreover Henry is clearly

impelled by a motive so strong that not only does he
begin thus late and throw everything to the winds in the
progress of his belated effort but is compelled, driven, to
a religious revolution, and ends exhausted at fifty-six before the thing is accomplished. What all contemporaries
have taken for granted, what all posterity has taken for
granted, what, under the plainest considerations of common sense all must take for granted, is that the motive
was Anne Boleyn. And what is more, as we shall see, the
directing mind throughout the matter was not the King's
but Anne's.

Such turpitude on the part of the great, such an
example set by them to the rest of Christendom, was a
commonplace of that corrupt time. It was as much a
commonplace as simony or the open keeping of mis-
tresses by Prelates, it was as much a commonplace as the
giving of great sees and abbacies to children, it was as
much a commonplace as the betrayal and counter-be-
trayal of Emperor, French King and English Chancellor
in the ceaseless cat's-cradle of their alliances and secret
clauses. Henry had lived in the thick of such things, the
cases of his two sisters were notorious. He did but follow
their example. Margaret was the heroine of a double
divorce. She obtained one against her second husband,
her paramour Stuart obtained one from his legitimate
wife in order to marry the Princess after openly living
with her. His sister Mary had compelled Brandon to
marry her, nor could Brandon do so until he had obtained a similar release from his wife. Henry was indeed
moving in a family group. But all Europe was full of
the thing, and although when Henry began to act the
thing came like a thunderbolt, we must not think of it as
a piece of work unusual; it was in the very air of those

days. All the rich world was full of it, the unusual element was Catherine's invincible dignity and refusal to yield.

And now as to the date of origin. I have given elsewhere (in my History of England, Vol. III, page 366 in the English edition published by Methuen, page 423 in the American edition published by Putnam) my reasons for fixing this in the summer of 1525. These reasons I will now capitulate.

(1) It was almost certainly in 1522, but certainly not later than 1524, that the King ordered Wolsey to interfere with a project for Anne's marriage to the heir of the Percies.

(2) It is in 1524 that Anne is sent off to Hever in disgrace.

(3) After some hidden negotiations she is recalled.

(4) Early in 1525 the Emperor Charles V hears of, and alludes to, a vague rumour of divorce.

(5) In June of 1525 Anne Boleyn's father is raised to the peerage.

These indications are of very different values. The interference with Anne's marriage is highly significant; it indicates that Henry intended to make her his mistress, as he had already made her sister his mistress. Anne married to the great Percy family would not have been an easy prey. The exile of the girl to her father's house in Kent is also significant. In the light of what follows we can explain it by her refusal to yield to Henry. There is an interval of a whole year. Then comes the first vague rumour of divorce which has reached Charles abroad. Lastly the family of Anne is ennobled, and apparently some plan is beginning to be arranged.

On the last indication, the raising of Boleyn to the

peerage, it would be unwise to lay too much stress. He had been employed in important public business, he was closely related to the great Irish families, he had married into the highest English one, the Howards, and the peerage had already been talked of for two years. But all the points together and their sequence, the convergence of the whole, is fairly convincing.

There is indeed one argument against this conjecture, and it must be given its full weight. If it was as early as the summer of 1525 that Henry, perceiving Anne to be obdurate, thinking that she would never receive him except as his Queen, began to entertain the idea of divorcing Catherine, why did 18 months go by before any action was taken of which record remains? It was not till the end of 1526 that Henry's tender conscience pretended to have scruples about the marriage with his brother's widow. He put it down later to the Embassy of the Bishop of Tarbes. It was not till early in 1527 that he initiated the first steps for actively questioning in a court of inquiry the validity of his marriage.

The delay is lengthy but it is explained by Henry's character, and by the nature of the struggle through which he was passing. The capture of a man of Henry's temperament by a woman of Anne's is not immediate. Action which, at the beginning of the process, rightly seems monstrous to him, only gradually begins to seem first conceivable, then convenient, and at last necessary. Henry passed through various stages of recalcitrancy, drawing back, returning to the attraction, and did not finally fall completely victim to it, bound hand and foot and driven by the mastery of this single violent passion, until the years had done their work. Even as late as the summer of 1528 he was capable of panic and momentary resistance, when the plague in that year put him in fear of his life. He sent the woman away, he joined Catherine in her prayers, he took frequent communion. But, as might have been predicted, the flesh, or rather the mania, conquered. The peril passed, he summoned her back, and such a hold had she on him that she could make her own terms and take her own time, disdainfully.

Not only does the nature of this obsession, and what we know of the growth of such obsessions in any man, explain Henry's delay, but his especial character explains it further still. He was always hesitant, halting between any one of those considerable and at last revolutionary decisions to which his fate drove him. It is the same story with his appeal to the Universities of Europe: not undertaken until two years after it had been presented to his mind. Cranmer gave the last push in 1529 and decided him, but he had already had the idea put before him very fully as early as 1527. It is the same story with his gradual and reluctant abandonment of Wolsey, his secret presents to his old friend, his long gaps of inaction, his sudden violent jerks of decision which he owed to another will. It is the same story with the long, long spinning out of the breach with Rome only finally resolved by Anne's pregnancy. It is the same story at the very end when he is tossed to and fro between the Seymour and the Howard influences, and only on his deathbed signs the death-warrant of the Duke of Norfolk.

In the light of what he was and all that he did after the change had begun in his character, the delay is understandable enough, and the summer of 1525 stands as the origin of that momentous business out of which at last after more than a century a new and utterly transformed England arose.

IX

THE FOURTH ACT

THE DIVORCE: 23 April, 1527—28 July, 1529

THE 23rd. April, St. George's Day, was always kept by the Court of Henry with special pomp and pageantry.

It was during the come and go of that great Feast, as it was held in the year 1527, that King Henry VIII spoke the words which launched the overt and public business of a divorce.[1] We find them in the narrative of the Clerk to the French Parliament.

The French Ambassador had suggested that on a number of points he would consult the Cardinal, when Henry said to him privately this:—

"I have certain things to communicate to your master, of which Wolsey knows nothing."

There you have the line of cleavage. There you have the moment after which Wolsey is no longer in control. Hitherto the loss of hold has threatened. Now it has come about. That thing "of which Wolsey knows nothing," and which it was so urgent to communicate to the King of France was the proposal which would make Henry of necessity take the side of France against the Emperor: it was the now accepted, and soon to be acknowledged, policy of divorcing the Emperor's aunt. They had known the subject of the thing months before in Paris. Now it was directly communicated.

Three weeks passed and more. During those weeks it was agreed that the first step should be taken, and in the taking of that step not only did Wolsey concur (he may

[1] See Note H at the end of the book.

even have planned it; it is quite agreeable to his character
to have done so) but Warham concurred. The step so
planned was the setting up of a private court in which
Wolsey and Warham should sit as ecclesiastical judges
and try a case which was to be put before them collu-
sively by the King, the case being whether he were not
living unlawfully with his brother's wife. The proceedings were to be kept dead secret like everything else
connected with the affair. The plan was this:—to hear
pleadings and put them on record, to put up in defence
of the legality of the marriage an advocate hired by the
King himself to make out the worst case possible, but to
have the strongest case possible put forward in favour of
the theory that the marriage was unlawful; to issue a
summons to Catherine to appear (which she would never
receive but which would appear upon the record); to
declare her contumacious because she failed to come;
then the two ecclesiastical judges, Wolsey and Warham,
to declare the marriage unlawful on the evidence they
had heard. When all this had been accomplished without a word leaking out, the sentence could be published.
The Queen, having been declared contumacious, would
be debarred from appeal; the sentence would be sent to
Rome as a matter decided in the highest ecclesiastical
court of England, in which the Legate and the Primate
had sat side by side. Henry might marry again and seek,
if necessary, confirmation of the sentence from Rome
after he had contracted the second marriage; or he
might wait to get confirmation first. But in any case the
thing would have been settled in England rapidly and
apparently finally.

That Wolsey, I say, should have lent himself to such a
plan or even should have arranged it, one can under-

stand; that Warham should have done so is another matter. He had a great soul; a high character, unblemished; he had no love for political intrigue; he had always said what he thought on the great matters to which his office called him. We can excuse him, or at least account for what he did, on two grounds. First, that in those days it was hardly conceivable that even a high official should stand openly out against the interests of the King. Secondly, that Warham had been from the beginning doubtful of the legality of the marriage.

This very secret court met on May 17. It was not so secret but that the Emperor's representative in London, Mendoza, heard of it: he told Catherine. The court sat again on the 20th and again on the 31st. Then suddenly the thing was dropped and the whole plan abandoned. Every conjecture may be made as to why the policy was thus abruptly given up; the most probable explanation is that Wolsey got to know of Catherine's having heard of it, which would expose the plot. At any rate, dropped it was.

Meanwhile, during the proceedings of this closely hushed-up tribunal, tremendous news had come to England. Twelve days before Wolsey and Warham had held their first hidden session, an army of Imperial mercenaries had carried Rome by storm, had sacked the city for days with fearful cruelties, and were closely besieging the Pope himself in the castle of St. Angelo.

This was what had happened: a mixed body of armed men many thousands strong, under the Constable of Bourbon, were loose in Italy with no definite strategic aim. They were Imperial troops, part of them levied in Spain, principally from the renegade Moors of the south, destitute and easy material for the making of mercenaries; partly from the German freebooters who hired themselves out for such work and who were at this date mainly Lutheran. This army, badly disciplined, as much marauders as soldiers, under the insufficient command of a man outlawed in his own country, was in theory working for the Emperor. The troops were Imperial troops, levied to fight against the French and their allies. Though their actions when they had broken loose were no longer controlled by the Emperor, that must be remembered. Charles was finally responsible for whatever they did, though he had given no orders for it. The Spanish and Germans of the mixed force, with Italians also among them, were not properly paid—that eternal trouble of the Empire, lack of pence, was at the root of the matter. Less and less did they aim at any political object, and more and more with getting by loot what those who had hired them could not give them. They swarmed down towards Florence, with the idea of gutting the riches of the Medicean town, but the allies were too strong for them. They swarmed down southwards towards Rome, the richest prize of all.

It had entered no one's mind that they would dare such a thing, no sufficient precautions had been taken, the defences were ill-kept. On May 5 Bourbon had led the assault upon the walls of the city; he was killed as he did so, but his hungry and maddened troops poured in; and there followed that catastrophe under the shock and horror of which the whole Christian world reeled. What the consequences of the Pope's imprisonment were, and the effect of the whole new situation upon the plans of the divorce we shall see.

The secret court having been abandoned without appointing a judicial court to annul Henry's marriage,

Wolsey turned to a new plan. The Bishops were to be summoned, in the hope that they might give a unanimous opinion against the validity of the marriage. The solemnity of such a sentence would suffice. The culprits, Henry and Catherine, would be enjoined to do some penance, and the King would be free to marry again.

This plan also miscarried. The Bishops were not unanimous. Even the most subservient seem to have hesitated, and the venerable Fisher, Bishop of Rochester, Henry's own tutor, and a man whose moral stature gave him weight beyond all others, especially insisted on the full doctrine of the Church. A Papal dispensation such as had been granted for the marriage of Henry and Catherine was sufficient and rendered that marriage lawful.

A third step followed. On June 22 the King put the matter to his wife herself. He begged her to agree, to admit the illegality of the marriage which had been maintained all these 18 years, and to leave the Court as a sign that she had made the admission. Then did he discover that invincible obstacle which henceforward was to wreck all he did. She wept bitterly, she protested, but she resolutely refused.

A violent scene between Henry and Wolsey followed. It was the first tentative revolt of the mastered man against his master, the first sign that a new hand had got hold of the reins and was beginning to drive, where Wolsey had driven so long. But whose that hand was Wolsey did not yet dream.

All he thought was needed was time to allow Henry's anger to cool. He was certain of getting full control again as a matter of course. He would have preferred to keep in touch continually, and when he was asked to

France as Ambassador to the French Court he hesitated. But he made the best of it. He would go off in person, making a splendid embassy of it, to negotiate the final alliance with the King of France, returning with all the prestige of that action and the public repute of it throughout Europe, returning with far greater international power than he had yet possessed; and he would be more necessary than ever.

For the Cardinal believed that he had, in the misfortunes of the Pope after the sack of Rome and his imprisonment, an opportunity for far larger things than any that had yet fallen into his grasp.

He was Chancellor; he was Legate; during all the great years of his triumph he might seem to have reached the summit of his desires. He had been uncontrolled arbiter of his own country. But he had failed in his ambition for the Papacy. Now he might play the Pope in practice and be the ecclesiastical master not only of England but of the West.

It could be pleaded that, with the Pope a prisoner of Charles, Christendom needed some free Prelate of the highest standing to take on the duties of the unfree Pope. Wolsey was such a Prelate, and Francis and Henry would support him. He said that Charles meant to send Clement as a prisoner to Madrid and transfer the Papacy to Spain. The liberties of Europe needed a free-acting Head of the Church and Wolsey could be that Head.

He might occupy a position whence he could himself decide in the King's favour, playing the part which Clement in the thrall of the Emperor could not play. With his prestige, and with France behind him—for he was secure of his power over anyone in whose presence he stood and who could hear his voice—he would be in action and in fact the ruler of the Church in the West; nothing that Clement did could be accepted, for the Pope was no longer a free agent. He could work upon the indignation all men felt at the pitiful subjection of the head of Christendom and of the outrages he had suffered. He could pose as Clement's protector, and be virtually at the same time Clement's supplanter.

With all this in mind he set out within a fortnight of the King's outburst for the adventure, and, as he hoped, the triumph. It was as yet but early in July; in a few weeks he could be back, far greater even than he had been before.

But in all this he miscalculated atrociously. It was a blunder from which he never recovered. He knew that Henry was the tool of whoever could overbear him by physical presence and a permanently stronger will, daily mastering his own; what he did not know was the strength of a woman and how it could be used.

He went off with all his usual pomp, passed by the regular route through Abbeville to Amiens and there met Francis: an Italian who was present has recorded for us the impression he made. Time had worked its common effect; what had been thought pride and especial display had now become in the eyes of others the natural surroundings of a great man in a great office.

Very much more than the actual treaty was in Wolsey's mind, indeed all that plan of hierarchic primacy over the West which, since he had failed twice in his attempt at the Papacy by direct means might, it seemed, now be obtained by the happy chance of Clement VII's imprisonment. He proposed that the Papal functions might be undertaken by the now natural enemies of the Emperor who was the Pope's jailor, Henry and Francis. The

Crowns of England and France were of sufficient guarantee. He went so far as to invest one nominated Cardinal with the insignia of his office. He caused a protest to be issued that, with the Pope enslaved, someone must speak and act for him in Europe—and that someone he meant to be himself. He drafted a form of vice-regency, a delegation of Papal power to himself.

But the irritant thing which thrust its side issue into every plan was here to disturb him again. He had to consider not only the large lines of Europe and the Papacy, but this business of the divorce.

To be sure he was in favour of it; indeed he saw how it could be turned to the profit of high policy. Since Henry was tired of Catherine and had no male heir, let him, when he was rid of Catherine, marry the French Princess, the daughter of the late King and the sister-in-law of Francis. So would the bond between the two western crowns against the Emperor be riveted; so would he, Wolsey, have his final and permanent revenge against Charles for defeating him at the last Papal election by a trick.

He suggested that the Cardinals, at any rate those of them who were within the orbit of the French crown, should meet at Avignon—Papal territory—and in a sort of council over which Wolsey would preside they should declare the nullity of Henry's marriage. The Pope being unfree, Wolsey having with the more or less open support of the French and English the power of acting for the Pope, the sentence would stand and be on record. He wrote home of this plan from Abbeville at the very end of July. He had miscalculated again, the Cardinals would not act.

The plan was fantastic no doubt, and there was in it

no small element of Wolsey's habitual exaggeration of his real position. He was very great in Europe, but not as great as that. Men would not follow him in the part he had assumed.

But though this misjudgment on his part was serious, a far worse one, a disastrous one, had been the misjudgment of leaving Henry to the private influence of Anne. Had he known what Anne intended he could not have done so. He thought of her only—as indeed did all others—as Henry's mistress, which *we* know that as yet she was not—for her refusal of Henry till he could make her secure of the crown was (unknown to all Europe and especially unknown to Wolsey) the very core of the position.[1] He thought that Henry would soon tire of a mistress once fully enjoyed. He knew his Henry and there he was right. What he did not know was the abnormal strain under which Henry was living, and that Anne was not yet fully the King's.

In his absence the woman, completely sure of her captured man, had arranged a scheme of her own and was going to act behind Wolsey's back.

There was in those days an elderly gentleman called William Knight. I call him elderly because though he was a year or two younger than Wolsey he had gone to pieces much quicker. He was already going to pieces while Wolsey was full of vigour. He was one of the few who did minor work for the King without being of Wolsey's choice. He was of Henry's, and Henry's choice was not good. He was in orders, from Oxford like Wolsey himself (from New College, of which he had been a Fellow in his eighteenth year). He had been sent on missions to Spain and the Low Countries, granted a coat-of-

[1] See Note J at the end of the book.

arms for his services, made Chaplain to the King, granted as usual a good income out of benefices, but nothing very enormous. He had even been sent over on a mission to the Emperor eleven years before, but his incompetence or lack of address had told against him, and when he was to have returned to the same court five years later, after Charles' accession, they begged that he might not come: complaining of his manners under the style of his birth. The most important of the secondary things on which he had been engaged was the negotiation of the treaty with Bourbon against France during the ridiculous adventure of 1523. Now, four years later, in 1527, though his age was telling upon him badly and he was beginning to go blind, Henry could suggest to Anne no better medium for her design of acting independently of the Cardinal.

Some years before, when the short-sighted and ailing Leo X was failing to support the coalition against Louis XII and urging peace, Wolsey had laughed at him, calling him "The Blind Man." Fate saw to it that the joke should now turn against himself. A blind man was to upset his own plans.

Knight was given a secret commission to obtain from the Pope some instrument whereby Anne could get her will at once. He was to demand a dispensation for marriage in spite of any defect of consanguinity (this was with an eye to Henry's previous connection with Anne's sister) and he was to demand a Bull giving Wolsey full Papal powers to act in this matter during the Pope's captivity. Not that Wolsey was not to be told of the demand, but it was to be held in reserve, so that Wolsey on his return might dissolve the marriage. Then the dispensation would take effect and Anne's plot would bear fruit. Meanwhile, to dupe the Cardinal, Knight, besides these secret instructions, was given open ones which he was to show to Wolsey, and these open instructions only bade him act with Wolsey's agency, so that Wolsey might be deceived into thinking that there was no secret mission at all.

Knight went off and on September 12th he met Wolsey at Compiègne. Wolsey rightly judged him incompetent. Even though he was ignorant of the much larger matters Knight was to arrange, he thought he would be incapable of smaller ones, or even to act as Wolsey's own agent. His criticism was not admitted and Knight went on his way. The treaty with Francis was signed; that much of prestige (and it was easily earned) the Cardinal brought back with him to England. He had failed to get the meeting of Cardinals at Avignon and the sentence in favour of Henry there; he had failed to become the Vice-regent of the imprisoned Pope; but he was still quite confident of his position. He was to learn almost at once what he had sacrificed by his absence.

He came, on the last day of September, to the court at Richmond. He sent in to ask a private audience of the King: he, who at such audiences had done his will for fourteen years at least, unquestioned. His messenger was astonished to be told that instead of a private audience the Cardinal was asked to come to the general presence among the courtiers, in the great room where Anne was standing by Henry's side. Wolsey on receiving that message was more than astonished, he was alarmed; his power was rocking. It was Anne herself who had said loudly, "Where should he see the King save here, where he is?" And Wolsey had to present his obedience, watch-

ing the mockery on faces not too friendly and unable
to speak a word of state matters, where all could hear.

Immediately afterwards he must have learned at last
what was the true object of the policy for divorce. He
had supported and furthered it for now perhaps a year
past. It had been in his eyes no more than an instrument
for strengthening his own international policy by marrying Henry to the house of France. Now he knew that all
must be sacrificed to Anne.

He was granted his private audience in due time, and
then it must have been (though we have no exact record
of the date) that the scene to which he himself alluded
later on in his misery took place. He implored the master
of the kingdom not to make havoc of all high affairs of
state, and to be rid of so insane a project as this marriage.
After the custom of the time he went upon his knees,
and used all those hitherto undefeated powers of per-
suasion—what had been so lately undefeated powers of
mastery—but the King had now long stood between two
masteries, and the second one, that of the woman, was
already the stronger.

There is one moment in every life when a man takes
his decision between the courses of calculation and of
simple heroic resolve. It had come now for Wolsey. But
heroism does not live with love of power. All his character, all his habit forbade heroism in him. Even now
where heroism and simplicity would have coincided with
his own large plans for the state and for the future he
was incapable of it. At this cross roads he took the wrong
turning with his eyes open. He made his alliance with
the woman who had been rival to him. In a brief delay he had chosen. He determined to continue his support of the divorce and to continue it with the new

shameful object which all the Court had guessed weeks
before, which to him in his absence in France had not
been whispered.

Note that he was not even now free from ambiguity.
To the very end he kept several strings in his hands,
hoping against hope that Henry might yet tire, that
something would save him. But his main object still
remained; the maintenance of his own position and the
recovery—which, as he thought, might well be—of all
that he had once been with the King.

He was wrong again. This time Divine judgment was
at work, falling, as it commonly does, in one critical and
revealing moment. He had tempted justice too far, and
from that moment, step by step, he went down to the
loss of all things and the tomb.

Wolsey having now made up his mind to direct the
divorce to this new and base end, would at least do with
all his might the unpleasing task which he had assumed.
It was his very nature thus to put the whole of his
energies into all that he did. He surveyed the field, with
a grasp infinitely superior to that of his master, or his
master's mistress. He persuaded the King easily enough
that it was folly to continue the simple plan of bigamy
which had seemed sufficient to him. To ask the Pope for
so astonishing a thing would endanger the undoing of all
that had already been done. Henry agreed that new instructions should be sent, and that the Pope should be
asked to constitute a full Legatine Court to sit in England, before which court the issue should be tried and
decided without revocation to Rome.

Even so the King could not combine his old subservience to Wolsey with his new subservience to Anne. There
exists, preserved in an Oxford College (Corpus Christi)

a letter which Henry wrote secretly with his own hand to Knight in November. It is puerile in its dread lest the Cardinal should learn that he was playing truant. He still clings to the idea that, possibly, the dispensation to marry within the degrees of consanguinity would suffice, though he says that it would only be used after the dispensation to marry at all had been obtained; but the significant thing in the letter is the phrase, "the Lord Cardinal will not hear of this, for all his craft." He is still afraid of the old control and faces a fearful daring.

Knight reached Italy, Parma in October, Foligno in early November; and the chaplain of the Boleyns, Barlow, joined him there, forcing him on to Rome. The journey was perilous. He could not get into the castle of St. Angelo. But the Pope escaped to freedom, and Knight saw him at Orvieto on December 18.

The old man made a fool of himself. He presented the documents for signature. Pucci, the Cardinal of Santi Quattro, excellent at his trade of canonist, went over them, rectifying them solemnly with his pen, and with a few touches destroying their value by leaving all conditional on the annulment. He handed them back thus rendered innocuous, was thanked profusely, and was offered an excellent present of £10,000—which he refused. His secretary was gratified with £200. Knight was overjoyed. He sent the papers back by special messenger. Hardly had Wolsey seen them when he discovered that they were merely conditional through the changes made, not even permissive, and therefore of no service to him. There was indeed the dispensation for Henry to marry again, but *only if and after the original marriage should be declared null.*

By the end of February Knight was back in England,

to receive, as he supposed, triumphant thanks. He rather deserved curses. But after all he was Anne's and Henry's envoy; they did what they could for him. They had already made him a Canon of Westminster, and before he died the King was to make him a Bishop. He concerns us no longer, for the real conduct of the affair now passes into other hands.

At the very end of the year, while Knight was negotiating at Orvieto, Wolsey had drafted a Bull for the constitution of the Legatine Court. He proposed that the Pope should sign this draft *as it stood*, without alteration, and send it back, so that he might have full powers. To that draft he attached an accompanying letter. This letter is most instructive. It is the document of a man in extremities, fighting hard, but no longer master of what he tries to control. It is full of emphasis and repetitions. It perpetually insists on the necessity for haste. The King will not wait! (One may be certain that Anne was pushing.) Spend money freely! If the Pope says that he ought to examine the matter himself, tell him that it has already been fully examined. The King will not assent to further delay. Let the envoys follow out their instructions strictly, and again (for the third time) let them hasten. And (again) let them have no fear for money. There should be no excuse for poor speed. He will send all the money required —— But get the thing signed! Get it signed! He is in such excitement that he does not remember till the end a necessary postscript giving the names of Cardinals Trano and Farnese, who might be favourable if Campeggio, whom the King would prefer, will not serve.

The draft of this Bull which Wolsey so desired to have signed without alteration and sent back to him with all speed, we possess. Unfortunately we do not know what changes were made in it before it was returned from the Papal court. But the essential point in it is this. It declares the dispensation granted to Henry for his marriage to Catherine, the dispensation issued by Julius II, to appear invalid, having been granted upon false pretences. The Pope therefore appointed Cardinal Wolsey with Cardinal...... (a blank follows) to proceed conjointly in this cause, and if one cannot the other may. The two Legates are to proceed summarily, and if either or both is satisfied that Julius' Bull of dispensation was invalid they are to declare the marriage void, and the parties shall be free to marry again. Against this sentence to be delivered by the Legatine Court in England there shall be no appeal, and whatever it does the Pope promises to ratify and never to infringe.

The Cardinal sent out his chief secretary, Stephen Gardiner, the man whose talents he had recognised and whose career he was making. He, and Foxe of the Royal Chapel, were so to shake and bully and threaten that they should gain their ends and that this Legatine Court, which might decide the matter without appeal, should be ordered. Wolsey bids them insist on the danger to the succession if Henry's marriage is not dissolved, and also bids them dilate on the virtues of Anne, whom (he says) has been maligned. On the contrary, she is of regal descent, chaste, pure, maidenly—and he, Wolsey, thoroughly approves of his master's marriage with anything so immaculate.

The struggle was long and violent. The threat of schism was heard. It was not till April 8, 1528, that the joint commission was issued to Wolsey and Campeggio to hear the case. Foxe returned with the precious document to England. It is significant that he took it straight to Anne in the palace at Greenwich before anyone else should see it. She was delighted. Henry came in, and *he* was delighted. They both felt the marriage with Catherine as good as dissolved. They saw no obstacle remaining.

But late that night Foxe went on with it to the palace of the See of Durham in the Strand, one of Wolsey's great houses. There he saw the Cardinal, and once more did the Cardinal discover that the Pope's diplomats had duped his envoys. The new commission did not make the decision of the Legatine Court final, therefore for his purpose it was worthless. It left to the Pope the right of making the last decision.

What was he to do? He dared not tell the duped pair. His now shaky hold on power was not strong enough to resist a second disappointment of them. That night (it was the short night of the 3rd of May) he must have turned over many things in his mind. Before day he had resolved. He would keep to himself his discovery that the Pope had reserved Catherine's right to appeal to Rome. He would try and turn the difficulty by a ruse of his own. But he knew that if this ruse failed he was lost.

The next morning Anne's father came to him from Greenwich, and the Cardinal set him at ease. All was well (he assured him) and he, Wolsey, was perfectly satisfied. With this falsehood Anne's father was satisfied too.

Wolsey knew that he must act very quickly to ward off the peril. He sent Gardiner instructions to obtain from Clement a Decretal Bull. He could not ask for a re-draft of the Commission. He could not start a new argument with the Pope upon a document which had been signed and sealed after such delays. It would be risking everything. But he could, by the side move of this "Decretal Bull" get all he wanted. I will show why this "Decretal Bull"—if he could have got it published —would have solved all Wolsey's trouble.

The Decretal Bull was this: a document issued by the Pope and giving a *Decree* on the point of law: the Legatine Court would thus have to decide on the facts only, i.e. to decide only the point whether Catherine had really been married to Arthur or not. As to the main point in canon law, whether the case of such a marriage dispensation were possible, or that other main point of whether the actual dispensation given were in due form the Pope was asked to decree once for all (hence the term "decretal") that the law forbade such a marriage. The Pope was asked to say that if the marriage could be proved to have taken place, then the latter marriage with Henry was *ipso facto* null. In other words, the Pope was asked to create a situation in canon law such that, upon Wolsey's declaring the first marriage with Arthur to be proved, the King should as a necessary consequence be declared not married to Arthur's wife and therefore free to marry again.

The attitude of Clement VII towards these demands was weak and tortuous in such a degree that history has never forgiven him. He ought to have refused point blank. It was clear that such a Decretal Bull as he had been asked for (under the threat that he might lose the allegiance of England) undid all the reservations he had hitherto made, made a mockery of the supreme court at Rome and destroyed the essential right of appeal to it from a lower court. It prejudged the whole case of whether Julius' dispensations were valid. What he decided to do was this: to sign the Bull; also, it would seem, to sign a promise that he would not revoke the case to Rome, *but to give careful orders that neither Henry nor Wolsey, let alone any lesser man at the English court, should have possession of the documents, and that they should be destroyed at once after the King had seen them.* To put it in plain English, Clement made a solemn promise which he intended to break; he made it in order to preserve relations with Henry: and to prevent his being compelled to keep his promise he ordered that no record of it should fall into Henry's hands.

There is one excuse for him, and though it is insufficient it is powerful. The Germanies were breaking away; already great districts had declared that they would establish their own religion, and the destruction of the Catholic faith might spread to the whole country. France had recently threatened schism. If England went, all was lost. That was the reason Clement acted in such a fashion— the more daring methods of the greater Popes would have served him better. He should have remembered that causes have been saved a score of times by one man standing out against the world.

Campeggio embarked on July 24 for England, by way of France. He was to make all possible delays to postpone the actual meeting of the Court. For by delay the situation might be saved. He had the excuse of a man elderly and certainly ill, yet it was not till after mid September that he left Paris; he was not in London till October.

With Campeggio returned, the Legatine Court to be held in England already in sight, and Wolsey prepared to take the final steps, there is one last point to be remembered and insisted upon. It is delicate, but it must be understood lest all the rest should be meaningless.

Henry's courtiers, as we have seen, had tardily understood a year before that Henry was only being pushed to the divorce because Anne was determined to be his wife and Queen. Wolsey, having committed the blunder of going over to France and leaving Henry wholly under Anne's influence, had come back to learn too late, as we have also seen, what the courtiers had guessed for some weeks past. So far so good. But what nobody had guessed and what is the capital affair was this: Anne was not yet living in full relations with Henry.

Wolsey of course, the corrupt courtiers about the King, the Pope himself and all his advisers and informers— one might almost say all Europe—took it for granted that Henry was living with Anne as with a wife. *None of them had the key to the problem*, which was, that whatever else Anne might have admitted in the way of familiarities, she was as yet giving her unfortunate victim *no full satisfaction and no chance of an heir*. I will not insist further, but the matter must be made clear, for, disgusting as it is, all turns on it. The future was to make it abundantly apparent that things stood thus. The King was not fully satisfied: he was still caught and held expectant.[1]

We must remember that his disease was now at last producing its worst effects upon his hitherto robust body. He was growing irritable; his caprice increased; with it went a nervous violence, and with that nervous violence what was not at all incompatible with it, but rather a consequence of it, namely his offering even greater opportunity than of old to be influenced by whoever was

[1] See Note J at the end of this book.

for the moment his director; and his director now was Anne. It is difficult not to admire the secrecy and tenacity with which this woman pursued her end. All the world outside the privacy of these two took it for granted that Henry, now fully satisfied, would soon tire as he had tired of others. What no one knew save he and herself was that of which she was the authoress, his continued and unsatisfied subservience.

Campeggio followed his instructions exactly. First, he delayed as long as he could; next, he must attempt to reason Henry out of his mania. Failing in that, he must try to persuade Catherine to enter a convent; failing in that, he must still delay as long as possible in the hope that some accident might yet save the situation, and only open the Legatine Court at the last moment.

Henry of course was far too far gone to listen to argument. Catherine was, as ever, superbly simple and superbly strong: too simple perhaps, but as strong as adamant. She was Queen and she would remain Queen. She was Henry's wife and nothing should deprive her of the title.

Campeggio followed his last instructions. He only *read* the Decretal Bull to Henry and to Wolsey. When they asked to hold it and to read it for themselves he refused. Wolsey's agent at the Papal Court urged the Pope in November that the Decretal should at least be lent to show to the King's Council. Had it ever left Campeggio's hands it would never have returned to them. It would have been kept in triumphant proof and record of Wolsey's power to declare Henry's marriage with Catherine null and void. The Pope, on being thus pressed to lend the Decretal to the King's Council, said that he would rather have lost a finger than have signed it (he should not have signed it!) and on December 15th, Clement sent his most confidential secretary Campana with plain but secret orders, Campeggio was to destroy the Decretal at once. We know from Campeggio's letter to Salviati that he did so. And at the same time Campana was to present the Pope's excuses and to say that he much regretted his inability to allow Henry's Council to see that essential document. Henry and Wolsey knew nothing of its destruction.

Now before Campana reached London a new element had entered into the problem. Hitherto, whether he could have the Decretal Bull made public or not, Wolsey had decided to fight the case on one main point—"The dispensation given by Julius II for the marriage of Henry and Catherine all those years ago was invalid through irregularities of form." The Pope's power to dispense in the case of a man marrying his brother's wife was to be admitted. The issue upon which Wolsey had advised the legal battle to be joined was a defect in the original instrument. In other words, Henry's case, on the advice of Wolsey, admitted that Pope Julius *might* have given a sufficient dispensation, but through bad drafting and mal-information *did* not do so.

Well, at this point, where Campeggio is still spinning out things as much as possible in England, there came in a thunderclap a new piece of evidence put in by the Emperor, Catherine's nephew, and the heir and guardian of the archives of his grandfather, King Ferdinand of Spain. He told the Pope that he held a brief issued by Pope Julius with the dispensation. This brief was especially designed to cover every possible flaw or lapse in the original dispensation; it was drafted in the widest terms, and if it were genuine the case which Wolsey had advised the King to argue fell to the ground; this supplementary brief covered all.[1]

This crushing blow was met by a reply that the brief was a forgery and Catherine, poor soul, was persuaded to ask for it to be sent to England that it might be tested! She believed in it well enough; but certainly had it ever come over to England Charles would never have seen it again. The Pope, as in duty bound, said that the weight of proof lay with those who called this official document a forgery, and that till it was proved a forgery he must admit it.

Immediately after this, in early 1529, Clement VII fell so ill that his death was reported throughout Europe. Had he died his commission for a Legatine Court would have lost its value, all would have had to begin again. For Wolsey this presumed certitude of the Pope's death provided the last chance of that to which all his energies had been directed for now nearly ten years. Again, doubtful as his position was, and shaken, lacking as he now did his old instruments of international power, he still clutched with energetic pride at some last chance of nomination to the Holy See. Clement recovered, and the proceedings went forward.

The cause of delay now was on Wolsey's side, not Clement's. Every effort had to be made (and communication with Italy was a lengthy business) to get the Pope to declare the brief false. Failing that, the Legates sent to Clement begging him to revoke the cause to Rome, but to give a secret promise to Henry that he would decide in the King's favour. The Pope was still but convalescent when March, 1529, was passed in that negotiation. During April the King's agents urged on the same lines.

[1] See Note I at the end of this book.

They admitted that it would be breaking the forms of law to promise a verdict before hearing a case, but they depended on renewed threats of schism. Henry's temper went from bad to worse; he dismissed his wife finally from the court, put Anne Boleyn at his side, complained (or she complained) that their cause had been betrayed. Gardiner was recalled from Rome (in May) to plead the King's cause before the Legatine court in England. Wolsey, less certain than ever, begged to be sent out of the country as Ambassador, was refused, and at last, on June 18, the Legatine court was formally opened in the great hall of Blackfriars.

Because it is the best known and the most vivid, the most dramatic episode in the long story of the divorce, the day when the Trial really opened on the morning of June 21, has been given too great importance in history, and the Trial, which stretched over some five weeks, has been thrown under a fierce light which exaggerates its significance.

Whatever happened, the Pope had determined—indeed had made it clear to the Emperor—that ultimately he would have to decide; for it was certain that Catherine would appeal.

In the interpretation of Wolsey's disaster it is equally secondary; for though it shows him deeper and deeper in the toils, approaching the final misfortune and struggling in vain against his fate, yet that fate had really been decided when the Pope's determination to hear an appeal had been made.

In that very first active session, on June 21, the Queen, appearing in person, refused to accept the Court at all. Its judges were both of them Prelates of her husband's, it was sitting in England, a venue which forbade impartial trial, and she appealed to the supreme authority of Christendom, the final court wherein all appeals on marriage must terminate at last—the Pope.

The five weeks dragged on. Campeggio spun out the proceedings as much as he could; Wolsey kept himself in the background as much as he could. Who knows but that even now he might be saved? Only a year ago Henry, in terror of death during a violent epidemic, had parted from Anne and appeared continually in public with his wife, had confessed daily, frequently communicated, and in general showed signs of release. Moreover time is always fruitful of accident. . . . But in his heart he could not but have already begun to despair.

Anne saw clearly. She had made certain by this time that Campeggio was not working for her. She believed—rightly enough—that Wolsey, for all his protestations and his alliance with her of the last few months, was envisaging alternatives. She had had news, not perhaps of the Pope's negotiations with the Emperor, but at least of the intentions to which he had turned. She had already decided that this pompous show of a trial was a façade, and she had begun to frame her new policy.

On the very day after Catherine had made her famous appeal and had withdrawn from the Court, Stephen Gardiner, the man whom Wolsey had made his secretary for his ability and vehemence in negotiation, landed in England from his long mission with Clement. Anne Boleyn had appreciated how that lever might be used. She had, before his departure, begun to draw him to her side, and he being now returned was frequently with the King.

The trial still dragged on. The evidence put before it may be read by anyone who wills. It turns mainly upon

the consummation of the marriage between Prince Arthur and Catherine, and is quite inconclusive. While
opposite to such evidence there stands the solemn declaration of Catherine herself, a woman whose word is not
lightly to be doubted, and the fact that she appealed to
Henry's conscience in the matter, an appeal that would
not have been made without her own certitude of the
testimony that conscience gave.[1] In any case that evidence was not strictly relevant to the issue, for the power
of the Papal dispensation was not denied even though
the original marriage with Arthur had been a real marriage instead of a simulacrum. The true issue was
whether the dispensation were valid or not. Doubtless it
would make a moral difference to prove that the marriage was a real one. It would have weight with opinion.
But in strict legality it was not the issue before the court.

However, in the eyes of the public, and especially of
those not in the very inner circle of all, in the eyes of
such men as the Dukes of Norfolk and Suffolk, even of
Boleyn, Anne's father, and of all the world which surrounded her and the King, it was thought as the month
of July proceeded that the end was approaching and
sentence would be delivered at last.

However doubtful Anne herself might have been she
took care not to spoil her chances by betraying her
doubts, even to Henry. But before the month was half
run, on July 13, far off in Rome, Clement had revoked
the Commission of the Legates and recalled the case to
his own court. He could plead to his conscience that the
secret promise he had so weakly given a year before was
conditional. Its terms we do not know, but we do know

[1] See Note K at the end of the book.

that Wolsey at the time had discovered both it and the
commission to be conditional and to leave a loophole
for appeal. He could plead to the same tribunal of his
conscience with far more justice that a spiritual subject
having appealed to him he could not in justice or honour
refuse to hear her. That she was the aunt of the Emperor, Queen of a great Christian realm and daughter
to the mighty power of Spain may indeed have added
to her strict right, and gave her appeal a moral weight
which was irresistible.

The news of the Pope's action could not reach England for some weeks, but already, only 10 days later, on
July 23, long before that news could be heard in London,
Campeggio prorogued the court, postponing its next
session to the next term in the autumn.

The disappointment, expected by Anne, and therefore
by Henry, astonished the outer ring of those who were
expecting a favourable sentence.

There were violent scenes, of which the most famous
is that of Suffolk striking the table and shouting how no
Cardinal brought good to England, with Wolsey's re-
puted retort that, but for a Cardinal, Suffolk would not
have his head today upon his shoulders; to which if they
had continued the quarrel, Suffolk might have answered
that, but for the Cardinal, he would never have been
lured into that marriage whereby he risked his head.

Manifestly the policy upon which Wolsey had staked
all, the appointment of a Legatine Court sitting in England, with power to annul the marriage, had broken
down.

Five days later, on July 28, 1529, Stephen Gardiner
was nominated chief secretary to the King, and that sign

was unmistakable: it was for Wolsey the beginning of the end.

. . . .

If the nominal master, Henry, had been more balanced and of stronger foundation, if the minister had been of wider vision, or of a more subtle appreciation in the depths of human motive, or better still, of nobler ideals, what followed need never have followed. But the combination of Henry's weakness and Wolsey's was fatal to the continuity of England. The chain of national history was snapped: a new era opened; and, in the slow process of a hundred and fifty years the nation was utterly transformed.

It is from the beginning of this dramatic action in 1529 that there comes right out into the open the tyranny of the woman who had struck her talons into Henry's soul and body. It was four years since he had first begun to experience her obstinacy and since there had first been planted into his very flesh the seed which had grown up into such a torturing bramble. It was somewhat more than two years since he had been goaded into blurting the whole thing out and talking openly of repudiating his wife. The fever had grown prodigiously; negotiation, disappointment, delay, the manœuvres of opponents, but, much more than all else, the steady pressure of the woman, fed that uneasy flame. Now he could no longer escape. His whole mind was enwrapped by the affair. He had entered through the gate which allowed of no returning.

But, for all that, the past persisted in the man. There were two natures in him for still some months to come: one, still sane, though dwindling, still capable of human affections though these were paling out, still possessed of its own soul, though that soul was grown thin and anæmic. This old self of Henry may be said to have sickened in his reluctant abandonment of Wolsey, to have taken to its bed after Wolsey's death, and its last poor breath to have been drawn when Catherine went out of this abominable world: unless some spark of it remained to shed tears when poor silly little Jane Seymour perished in giving him an heir. He did then, at least, shed tears for another. Thenceforward his self-pity shed them only for himself.

.   .   .   .

The Court opened its first active session in the Great Hall, once of the Dominicans (the popular name for which order was "Black Friars"), on the site still called by that name in the south-west of London City; near the Thames, just where the Fleet ditch runs into it, on Midsummer's Day, 1529.

It is essential to the significance of all that followed that we should grasp exactly the issues before that Court, for the larger considerations involved turn to the confusion of the reader unless he sees the precise legal point. We have here a Court of Law which has to decide specific points in accordance with a code of law (to wit the Canon law). It was not a court of last instance but subject to appeal, the court of last instance being that of the Pope in Rome. The Court had to decide upon three charges in descending order, which were as follows:—

(1) Was Catherine's original marriage with Arthur real, or a mere form?

(2) If it was real, was the Pope's dispensation given after Arthur's death given in sufficient technical form?

(3) If it were not, did there exist authentic documents (a *Breve*) issued by the same Pope providing against his

irregularities of dispensation and so rendering the second marriage unassailable?

(1)—Was the marriage with Arthur a real marriage, i.e., consummated, or was it only one of form? If it had only been one of form and had never been consummated, the issue apparently fell. No dispensation would have been needed and the validity of such dispensation ceased to be material. It is true that Wolsey, in his efforts to serve the King, suffered an alternative issue to be put forward, to wit, that even if the marriage had been only one of form, it had been publicly accepted as a true marriage and should therefore in the interests of general morals be so accepted; but this attempt to divert the discussion from its true end proceeded no further.

(2)—If the marriage with Prince Arthur had been a real marriage and duly consummated, then there arose a second issue:—Was Julius II's dispensation technically regular and sufficient to cover all possible points of objection?

This point, apparently trivial in morals, was very important in law; and indeed upon it, as we shall see, the heat of the discussion turned. It is of crucial importance to remember again that Wolsey had decided not to fight upon the ground of contesting the Pope's power to dispense in the case of deceased brother's wife. That point was put forward much later after Wolsey had fallen. It was a second thought and a second best policy, to which Henry and Anne were driven by the exasperation of delay after the whole cause had been revoked to Rome. The ground on which Wolsey chose to fight in this Legatine court, a Papal court created by and dependent upon Papal authority wholly, and accepted by Henry as such, was not the Papal right to dispense (which no suitor in such a court could deny), but whether the dispensation had been sufficient and regular. It was for Henry's counsel to prove that it was not. If the original dispensation were regular, again the issue fell and was automatically decided; for even if the first marriage had been consummated, due dispensation permitted the second marriage.

But if the first dispensation, the terms of which were of common knowledge and in the possession of the English crown, were irregular, it did not follow that the second marriage was void, for a third issue had arisen.

(3)—This third issue was raised by the alleged existence of the Brief issued by Julius II to cover all defects in the original dispensation and to make it valid against any objections which might be raised to the regularity or sufficiency of that dispensation.

Now this brief was not to be found in the English records; the officials said it was not to be found, nor any copy of it. The original, which Catherine's party claimed to be authentic, was in the possession of the Emperor. Was it authentic or no? On that, in the last resort, all the case depended.

In other words, allowing Henry's case every advantage —that the marriage had been consummated and that the original dispensation by Julius II was insufficient in form —the authenticity of the brief would still be sufficient to render Henry's marriage with Catherine lawful and binding.

X

THE FIFTH ACT

WEDNESDAY, the 28th of July, 1529: from that day we may date the last act in the tragedy of Wolsey.

All through the summer date after date marks the progress of something which is felt rather than seen; long before overt action appears the signs of its coming are apparent. It was on the first of August, 1529, that Thomas Boleyn, Anne's father, who had for some months held the King's order to receive the revenues of the Bishopric of Durham but who had not yet dared disturb those who were collecting them for Wolsey, thought the time had come to demand the arrears. In the same month the Abbot of Wigmore, who had humbly bowed to Wolsey's demand for resignation, now refuses the proffered money, trusting in the coming fall of his oppressor. And all the while excuse was found to keep the Cardinal from Court, and all the while what had been whispers against him while he was still omnipotent became open words and, though still secret, written words and perhaps printed words as well.

In the week (July 28-August 4) immediately after the appointment of Gardiner to be the King's chief secretary —the point of departure for all that followed—an epidemic caused the King to move from place to place, going at last as far off as Woodstock near Oxford, where he stayed till well into September. He had always shown an exaggerated fear of death: something which accounts, perhaps, for his careful avoidance of all risk to himself in his wars. All this while Gardiner was with him, but the two Dukes of Norfolk and Suffolk also joined him toward the end. It is remarkable that so far no decision had been taken. Wolsey had fallen, that is, he had ceased forever to be the chief councillor of the King, but what would happen to him still remained in suspense. There was evidently some sort of struggle going on. Henry, as always, was reluctant, uncertain, waiting for suggestion from others.

While the King was at Woodstock, Wolsey, who still hoped quite unduly, begged the King to receive him. He had that to say which could not be written. He knew, or thought he knew, that if only they could get face to face something of the old ascendancy would return. He got his answer not from Henry himself but from Gardiner; it was not exactly a refusal but an awkward putting-off. Evidently it was still in the balance whether Henry could be persuaded to deal the Cardinal the final blow.

Why had the thing been so gradual? What is the explanation of that apparent hesitancy in Henry, those half returns and all that long postponement. If we depend on documents alone we cannot reply, it is a riddle without an answer. If we consider the probable motives, the nature of the wills at work, Henry's old friendship and new passion, the answer should be clear enough. Anne was the factor which, unseen and in the background, like a dark planetary body which cannot be seen among the general stars but whose influence can be calculated by the movements of others, determined the hesitating attack on the man to whom Henry still felt some subjection.

Indeed, the stricken man achieved something in his own favour at last by demanding to come as Legate when the other Legate, Campeggio, came to take his official leave of the King; he was admitted, but it was only through Campeggio that he got leave, and it was against a good deal of friction that he got it at all. They were to come without any ceremony, and reception was cold.

Henry was of course in two minds—rare were the occasions of his life in which he was not, save under the sudden impulse of a fit of passion. The influences making for Wolsey's future disgrace and ruin he could not face, so he shirked having the Cardinal lodged at the Court on that Sunday, September 19th. On the other hand he kept Wolsey to dinner, and talked with him privately long after, well into the evening, for it was dark when they parted. Yet at that dinner there was something said that might have troubled him; it was said by the man who was the least able but the most pertinacious of his enemies, Anne Boleyn's uncle, the Duke of Norfolk. Wolsey had been speaking at table in favour of the Prelates going back into residence in their Sees; for himself he would go to Winchester: but Norfolk caught him up and said "rather to York." Norfolk's excuse in that suggestion was that York was the Archbishopric and the principal of the two Sees; but what he meant was much graver, he meant that York was two hundred miles away —and Wolsey knew that he meant it.

The incident is most significant; coupled with so many other indications it shows whence the principal pressure upon Henry was being brought, the only source from which it could be brought, Anne. Only a few days before, the French Ambassador, Wolsey's chief confidant, had warned his master that the influence lay now with three names, Norfolk, Suffolk and Rochford. The mercurial Suffolk does not count in our calculation, but while Norfolk was Anne's uncle, Rochford was her father.

Some have thought that Gardiner also played the traitor in this crisis. Against that supposition may I think be quoted Gardiner's character. Certainly he had left his old master and become to the King what he had formerly been to the Cardinal, principal secretary. Certainly he was in many things the King's new adviser; certainly, also, to lean to the King's side in all things was not only his duty and his necessity but his choice: yet personal treason against a man who had made him and always befriended him is not answerable to what we know of Gardiner's open and vigorous life over so many years. No, what is driving the hesitating Tudor is still the woman.

Wolsey attended the Council on the morrow after that dinner; he continued to attend it one day and another for more than a fortnight longer. But shortly after, at long last, Henry was pushed into action.

The action came coincidentally with the certitude that the Decretal Bull had disappeared and that Wolsey's last use to Anne was gone.

Campeggio left London on Tuesday, October 5. Historians love to tell us that he went with slow dignity to Dover, but he was not so slow for a man in great physical pain and already advanced in life; he covered his twenty-five miles a day and slept between each stage. He was prepared to leave the port on Friday the 8th.

Then it was that something happened which is of manifold interest. It throws light upon the power the Princes of the day could exercise against that still supreme power in Rome to which they all deferred: it shows the close organisation of that central monarchy,

lacking though it did an army or system of police: it
shows the considerable spy system which was at work:
it shows the hesitation Henry always felt at doing something decisive on the spot and at once which would have
involved his own responsibility. The thing might have
been done in London, it might have been done at any
time during all these months, it was only done now when
he was about to sail; his luggage was searched for the
Decretal Bull.

Was it indeed the work of Henry? Was it perhaps
suggested by the much more decisive will of Wolsey,
working through some agent by way of suggestion to
his former master? If the Decretal Bull could be found,
Wolsey might yet be saved. The Decretal Bull was not
found. There was no hope for Wolsey remaining.

The rummaged clothes and papers and furniture were
put back into their packages, the courier went off at once,
galloping up the London road. Early next morning (or
perhaps that very night)—with relays the distance could
be done in seven hours, easily in ten—the news was delivered. The Decretal Bull was missing. No wonder!
It had been destroyed months before. On that same day
—October 9th—the morrow of Campeggio's sailing
from Dover, Christopher Hales, Attorney to the King,
preferred a Bill of Indictment for Praemunire against
the Cardinal in King's Bench.

It was quick work. All had clearly depended upon
the news that might be had of that search of luggage; on
the preceding days Wolsey's chances had been still in
the balance. Forty-eight hours before Campeggio had left
London the Council had met in his own house to discuss
with the French Ambassador. On the Wednesday of that
week, on October 6th, while Campeggio was on his way

down to the coast, Wolsey was again in council to meet the Ambassador of the Emperor, and that same day the man whom he had made and who was now working in his place, Gardiner, wrote to him for certain writs which he, as Chancellor, had to issue. On the very day when the luggage was due to be searched the King was passing back through London, and there must he have received the news; at one blow the hopes of Wolsey were over.[1]

This fatal Saturday, October 9th, was the first day of the Michaelmas Term, when the Courts of Law opened, the Chancery among them, with Wolsey as Chancellor presiding. Even as he sat in Chancery, Anne Boleyn's spokesmen in the Council were at Windsor with the King; and the Law Officer of the Crown was preparing his indictment of the Cardinal in the Court of King's Bench (that is, at the Common Law), under the Statute of Praemunire.

It was a solemn hour in the history of England, and of Christendom. A Papal Legate, the man who represented the highest authority of the autonomous Church, was challenged by the civil power. If that man gave way the independence of the Church for which Beckett had

[1] It is well known that some few of Henry VIII's letters to Anne Boleyn, which are among the most vivid proofs we have of his abjection, were conveyed to Rome and are to be found in the Papal archives. They have been published, they have been commented upon a thousand times. Parts of them are dirty, parts maudlin, the rest so-so. It has been suggested that they were carried off in Campeggio's luggage. If that were so, why were they missed during the hunt for the Decretal Bull? How they reached Rome and through whom cannot, I suppose, be known; at any rate it is a mercy to history that they have survived. Would that they had been dated! They are in French, of course, the grandest court language, the one in which Surrey addresses the King after Flodden, and the one with which Anne was certainly most familiar, for she had lived as a French girl throughout her teens.

died, the whole principle that the Church was free from the jurisdiction of laymen, was so violently shaken that it must fall. If he resisted he might not avert the disaster but he would have left a record forever, a precedent and possibly a later chance of restoration of the Church's power.

For the moment Wolsey acted neither way. Upon the morrow, the Sunday, he wrote a tearful, humble letter begging for mercy, he expatiated to his friend, the French Ambassador, upon the misery of his plight and begged for the support of the French King. But meanwhile, all those following days, Anne Boleyn's spokesmen and particularly Norfolk, the head of the anti-clerical clique, already hungry for the loot of the Church, were in perpetual movement between the capital and the Court at Windsor. Eleven days passed. Upon Wednesday, October 20th, the indictment under Praemunire was pressed. But Henry even at this moment was so far wavering that he gave the fallen man an opportunity to appeal to the Parliament that was even now being summoned, if he would prefer that to trial in a court of law. In his heart Wolsey must have known that he had no friends: that Parliament (which meant of course the Lords) was but the organised body of his enemies: the Prelates whom he had offended, for he had bullied them all; the Bishops, the lay Lords, the great Abbots who had trembled before his power and had secretly so much resented it.

From not a few of these he had wrung payments.

Wolsey capitulated. He accepted the jurisdiction of the Lay Courts; on Friday, the 22nd, the great surrender was made, and by the pen in Wolsey's hand that which Beckett had done in England was now, in a far different day, undone. He pleaded guilty, and on the eighth day, Thursday, the 30th, submitted to the King at his mercy.

.   .   .   .

A suggestion may be made—it cannot be affirmed—that Wolsey's health had already begun to break down in the course of that summer of 1429. There were certainly signs of decline by the autumn. In his passionate complaints privately made to the French Ambassador, he wept and was incoherent; he seemed to be losing grip, and it is possible, to me it seems probable, that the physical break-up had begun earlier. If that be so it would explain (though it is not necessary for the explanation) why the Cardinal failed to resist.

The problem of that failure is not so simple as it seems. Henry ruled by terror during all the latter part of his life but he had not yet begun to rule by terror. Men yielded to new and dreadful powers abominably exercised for coercion, and very nearly all—all save a handful of heroic monks and the two shining examples of Fisher and More—became abject. Cranmer's complete abandonment of all morals and dignity under the effect of the terror is so extreme as to be grimly comic. Cromwell's is pitiful, falling at last to a whining letter squealing for life and begging to kiss once more the royal hand and smell its heavenly savour. But there was nothing of all that as yet; the faint beginnings of insane excess only appeared in the clutch which Anne had fastened upon the man; for the rest he was still for the most part the Prince whose youth lingered with him in spite of his disease and whose memories of affection, whether for the wife who had so nobly supported and served him, or for the great minister upon whom he had so thoroughly relied, were still strong, active and of some linger-

ing effect. Wolsey could have reacted. He did not. There
was a field for action, as the whole colour of Henry's
treatment of him shows. Almost to the last he was secretly favouring his victim, but in that field Wolsey did
nothing. And I suggest that had his powers been what
they were a decade before in the fullness of his strong
body and clear mind, during the vigorous forties of his
life, he would not have thus yielded without a struggle.

But whether his physical weakness had now reached
a point which can explain the affair or whether it was
calculation which made him yield, yield he did, and
completely. And in so yielding marked that date the
significance of which Henry himself certainly did not
understand, the permanent character of which for all
future history Wolsey himself did not understand, though
he appreciated the revolutionary character of the moment—I mean the plea of guilty which Wolsey stooped
to pleading in the King's secular court. Here was, for the
first time since the last centuries of the Roman Empire,
the submission of a Prelate of the first rank, for the first
time since the Papacy had acted in Britain, the submission of one who represented the Pope himself, for the
first time since the College of Cardinals had existed as
Princes of the Church, a Cardinal admitting that the
Church was not self-governing: that its highest authori-
ties were subject like the meanest layman to the civil
power. That is the meaning of Friday, the 22nd of
October, 1529.

. . . .

Here we must clearly understand what Henry had
been persuaded to do; for modern conditions are so different that the vileness of the action may seem to those
who think of it in modern terms less vile than it was.

Recall that dual jurisdiction of Church and State which none then questioned and upon which only the limits, not the essence, were debated. Remember that there was a universal clerical jurisdiction applying to the whole of Christendom and a particular local civil jurisdiction exercised by the Prince of a particular district—England—Aragon—Saxony—or what not. The two overlapped, the boundaries were not clearly defined, there was ample room for a quarrel, innumerable cases where the one would complain of encroachment by the other, and innumerable examples of violent rhetoric, in which the one would affirm its supremacy over the other or even deny all rights to the other. But universally and in the general mind of Christendom the two co-existed and the mass of men could no more have thought of life without a clerical organisation common to all Europe and culminating in the Pope than the mass of modern men could think of life without the action of private property.

Now Henry had deliberately, of set purpose and with full open initiative of his own, agreed to Wolsey's receiving Bulls from the Pope making him a Legate with gradually increasing powers. He had for now eleven years supported and identified himself with Wolsey's Legatine powers. Those powers had been used to gather all possible authority into the hands of the central Government. And now Henry, in the hands of Anne, forswears himself. It was relying upon his good faith that, of the two overlapping jurisdictions, the ecclesiastical had been so suddenly and greatly strengthened. It was relying upon his kingly word and signed and sealed writing that Wolsey in person had exercised the enhanced clerical power; and now the very man who had passed his word and signed and caused to be sealed the document confirming the Legacy repudiated his own pledge.

Wolsey was indicted under *præmunire*, a statute of 1392 enacted to provide a weapon for the Crown against the fiscal or other encroachments of the Papacy upon its rights. It forbade, under penalty of loss of goods and outlawry, the paying for or receiving of Bulls *detrimental to the King*. But it was a permissive statute; not one of universal and permanent application, but one which could be invoked by the Crown when it desired to restrict encroachments of Papal power in England. When the Crown did *not* desire to restrict this power in a particular case it gave a license to exercise it and in point of fact the reception of Bulls was continual and a matter of course. In the same way the Statute of Provisors (on which *præmunire* was modelled) forbade the King's subjects to accept the Pope's forestalling the rights of patrons and his reserving a living or a see in England for one of his nominees; but when the King wanted him to exercise the power the King would actually ask the Pope so to act; and if, after so acting, the King had pretended that the nominee could be ejected under the Statute of Provisors and attempted to eject him, then the King would have obviously been acting with gross injustice.

The indictment of Wolsey is on all fours with this. Henry had solemnly licensed the Cardinal to accept full Legatine authority, which Legatine authority he and everybody knew was to be used as an instrument for centralising power. In that capacity Wolsey had done a great number of things necessarily irritant to individuals who suffered from it. He had provided livings, he had coerced Abbots, he had undertaken the rights of visitation over English Bishops who, but for his Legatine authority, would have been his equals and not amenable to his authority. He had also of course in this exercise of universal power admitted the abuses which were the commonplaces of his time. A sum of money had been presumably paid on the reception of the Bull, but that was only in the general course of things. Sums of money which were equally customary had passed from the administered to the administrator for licenses and privileges. That also was of course in the time and by the customs of the day. When Wolsey pleaded with indignation, though in private, that the King was party to his actions, having deliberately admitted and sustained his Legatine authority and having confirmed this by a document, when Wolsey said that he held the King's license under his own hand and seal, he was not only telling the truth but the most pertinent truth that could be told.

That document was stolen, and obviously it must have been stolen by and for Henry. Henry must have badly wanted to get rid of so damning a piece of documentary evidence against his good faith. Men living at the time, and hearing all that was said and thought at the time, later accused the traitor Cromwell of having committed the theft. They were presumably telling the truth.

There is still a stronger evidence of Henry's nervousness in this matter. When Wolsey was later impeached the Lords vaguely allude to the fact that the King had licensed him, and this was clearly put in with the object of forestalling a reply.

There was no question of Wolsey's having exceeded his Legatine authority, there is nothing equivalent to "I gave you leave to do this and that, but you did a great deal more than I gave you leave to do." There is not a shadow of such a moral position. No, the whole thing is a piece of arbitrary falsehood, whereby the man who has actively pursued a particular policy and wants to rid himself of the responsibility of it, takes refuge in the pretence that his accredited agent had no right to do what he had been told to do. It is an immorality which is still going on all round us continually, when men desire to go back upon their most solemn pledges, but Henry's is the most flagrant case in our history. There was no precedent for such an outrage. It is unique, even in the long tale of State-Lawyer enormities.

Wolsey, then, capitulated to the monstrous demand on Friday, October 22, 1529. Already on the Sunday before, October 17, he had been deprived of his Chancellorship.

That memorable day Cavendish, the eye-witness, has revealed.

For on that day those two men who wished him most ill came from King Henry's side, the King's brother-in-law Suffolk, and Norfolk, Anne Boleyn's uncle, and demanded the Great Seal. Nor was this all their message, for they told him that he must be off in a sort of exile to which they were commanded to bid him depart: to Esher, one of the episcopal houses of his Winchester diocese.

Then Wolsey, remaining seated while they stood before him in their finery (keeping their heads covered), asked them for their commission. What writing could they show? But they only answered roughly that the King's word to them was commission enough. Wolsey would have none of it; though they browbeat him and used him with indignity, he stood firm, saying, "The Great Seal of England was delivered me by the King's own person to enjoy during my life, with administration of the office and high rule of the Chancellorship of England.". . . So at last they went away in a fume.

They came back the next day, and this time brought with them the King's letters signed. These Wolsey took and read with respect and care and then handed over to them that same Great Seal of England and told them that he would obey and be off to Esher.

But before he went away he had all his store of wealth in the great house set out in order, that the King's officers might take it by Royal order, and in the October morning light the mass of gold and the gilt and the silver and the stuffs of all kinds, the hangings and the precious stones stood reflected on the dark tables of his rooms. Then he set out to go up river in his own barge, and from his own steps, for the tide served.

But when he came out from the end of the gardens to the steps and saw his barge lying there he saw also the body of the water almost hidden by a mass of boats, hundreds upon hundreds, which were those of the populace who had crowded thus to see the fall of him whom they also hated, and they backed their oars against the flood to keep in place lest they should miss the grand sight of greatness humbled. They had come up from the City downstream to feast their eyes on him, and they thought that at the turn of the tide he also would go down whence they had come and that his lodging was to be the Tower. It was a disappointment to them when they saw the barge cast off immediately before the end of the flood and steer up as though for Lambeth and beyond. So he left that luxury behind and with all his gentlemen was borne upstream by his rowers.

When he came to Putney Staith and they had moored, and the gentlemen about him had landed, all the horses were there waiting for them and the Cardinal's mule also. But hardly had the cavalcade started when a young man came riding hard down the hill through the main street of the little town to meet them; it was Norris, so coming from the King with the message that he must not think he had lost the King's favour, nor that the King had any indignation against him, but had in a way been compelled to act as he had done for the pleasure of others, and in proof of this he held out a ring—Henry was apologizing for Anne.

Now this ring was the ring which Henry had always sent privately to Wolsey when there was some business urgent and private between them.

When Wolsey saw the ring and heard those words, he was so moved that he leapt to the ground from his mule and knelt in the mud of the roadway to receive the gift, holding his hands up like a man overjoyed, and when Norris, seeing this, at once dismounted himself, Wolsey said to him that he had been so overwhelmed with the good news that he must needs give thanks to God in that very place and moment—"And to the King, my Sovereign Lord and Master"; and as he said it he would have pulled off his velvet cap in reverence; but, because the knot was too securely fastened upon his chin, he tore the laces apart in his eagerness.

Then he would have mounted again; but this excitement had weakened him and they had to help him to the stirrup and up into the saddle. Yet he talked eagerly with Norris all the way up the hill till they came to the heath at the summit, and when he reached the place where the road to London branches off eastward by Wandsworth, Norris had to be off back again; but before he went Wolsey took that chain of gold, that little chain which he had always worn round his neck and against his skin with the golden cross hanging on it wherein the piece of the True Cross was, and for the last time he held it in his hand. Then he pulled it off and gave it to Norris, saying:

"When I was in prosperity I would not have parted with this for a thousand pounds, but now I beseech you take it and wear it about your neck for my sake."

Then he took Norris' hands and said goodbye. Yet he called back Norris again to complain that he had no token to send the King, being despoiled. Yet he had something to send (he bethought him) and that was his Fool, Master Patch. He was a very good Fool, he said, for whom a rich man would willingly have paid a thousand pounds, so admirable was his folly. But the Fool loved his master, and so raged and tore, rather than be separated from him, that it took six strong servants to hold him and bear him away, which they did.

So Norris went off to take that counter-gift and pledge of the Cardinal's to his master. But as for Wolsey, he set his face westward and made off to Esher.

The raid upon his property and income was at first ruthless. They took away St. Albans; they took away the huge temporal revenues of Winchester; they seized his gold and his silver, his jewels and his cloths and his tapestry, his coffers, the beasts in his stable—all that he had. They left him the income of York alone on which to live.[1]

But the most startling act in that confiscation was the seizure of York House. It was a forerunner to that loot of the Church which hung as a threat over all Europe,

[1] He also retained the *spiritual* revenues of Winchester and was given a yearly pension.

which had already begun in the German anarchy and was to reach high-water mark here in England. For York House was the property, not of Wolsey, but of the See of York. Wolsey was but the life-tenant of it, and never before had it been dreamed of that the civil power could rob the Church of her wealth. Always in the past Church land or buildings needed or desired by the Crown had been exchanged. This time sacred land was taken bodily without why or wherefore.

Wolsey protested, but gave away in this as in every other matter, and as a monument to that firstfruit of the spoils of religion Whitehall stands today. For if Whitehall was a Royal Palace all those years of the 16th and 17th centuries it was only so because it stood on the land which Henry had snatched from the Church, and it was from a window in Whitehall that the monarchy went to its death and fell beneath the axe which beheaded Charles I of England.

In Esher during those dark winter days there were strange signs that the King, however subject he might be to Anne Boleyn, could not bear wholly to abandon the man under whose influence he had lain unquestioning for so many years.

During a tempest of rain and wind, the vilest weather any man could remember, on the Eve of the Day of the Dead, All Souls, John Russell came at midnight, cursing the weather. Henry had chosen this one of his hangers-on, a man not too important to be given such uncomfortable orders, and yet of enough station as to show that the King still cared. He came dripping to Esher with his many horsemen about him, bearing yet another ring, and repeating the good will which Norris had so lately given. They made a great fire to warm and dry him; they woke the Cardinal, and Russell gave him that ring with its engraved turquoise and bade him good cheer from the King. Wolsey rejoiced, and hoped against hope once more.

Norfolk was sent to him also, whom he received in some state. Norfolk also had orders to treat him with respect, and reiterated the King's good will. The traitorous Cromwell had already passed to Wolsey the lie that Norfolk had become his friend, for Cromwell would have a foot in both camps, though he was striding already from one to the other. And Norfolk in this visit played the traitor in his own way, pretending to be all humility before so great a man as the Cardinal; refusing to wash his hands in the same basin as he, sitting opposite at table on a lower seat; flattering him in every way, but urging him to be off to York, to the north. All the courtiers knew well, and Anne best of all, that he would, at York, be removed entirely from Henry, and that thus the King's uncertain will could be the better weaned from him.

For Cromwell's treason had already taken place. One day, a little before Norfolk's visit, Cavendish found, in a bay of one of the windows in the main hall of Esher Palace, Thomas Cromwell, reading the Hours of Our Lady and crying bitterly. Both sights were strange in the eyes of others, for piety was not Cromwell's reputation, nor did he mourn spiritual evils. But it seemed that he was mourning the loss of goods; he complained that his service of his old master impoverished him. He asked leave to go to London, using the famous phrase that he would "make or mar"—and he marred.

He went off in the dark November weather, with one serving man to attend him.

Of what passed there is no record—but he saw the King; and henceforward he begins to surplant his master. Point by point in the succeeding months and years Cromwell advances just as Wolsey had done, though in far less noble fashion, imposing his judgment, his flattery and his will; and point by point Henry follows him. It is Cromwell who suggests the gradual breaking with Rome, Cromwell who first suggests that there is monastic wealth to loot; Cromwell who organises the great spoiling, and in doing so vastly enriches himself and those of his own base blood.

Yet Cromwell was a great artist. He had not read his Machiavelli for nothing, and though it be true that "The Prince" is not a manual of advice but rather a savage observation of men, yet certainly Cromwell conformed to the irony of that famous treatise. He loaded himself with false virtues. He even made the man whom he was betraying grateful to him, making—if we are to believe the comrade who saw most of him—such a speech in Parliament as saved some part of Wolsey's revenue. Certainly if Cromwell did so—if he so spoke to help the Cardinal —it was with orders from Henry. Nothing would have suited Henry better than to have softened the fall of his servant without angering his mistress, and Cromwell could here be useful. For Cromwell might appear to be speaking independently.

At the turn of the year, in Christmas week, in the depth of the cold and darkness, the Cardinal fell ill. Once more did Henry show how much he was moved. He sent Buttes, his own doctor, to him; and when that physician came back with bad news (finding Henry and Anne together, as usual) the King prayed God that the Cardinal should not die, saying that he would not lose

him for £20,000. But Buttes said that if the King would
save him he must send him good news. And for the third
time Henry sent him a ring, with his own portrait cut in
a ruby upon it. It was a ring Wolsey himself had given
him in better days. He even summoned the courage to
get something out of Anne by way of token, and Anne
sent Wolsey a little square of gold from her girdle.

With February the sick man, partly recovered, moved
to Richmond. Even in his illness the habit of his life was
strong upon him, and he was still intriguing to know
if the French could do anything for him. They would
not help. He thought the Emperor might do so, his old
enemy—but he received no aid from him either. They
judged him no longer of use to them.

Cromwell, the traitor, now serving the King but
thought by Wolsey to be serving himself, brought him
the hint that he should take to his spiritual duties. He
meant York; but the word York was not yet pronounced,
though Norfolk in the winter had pronounced it. Wolsey
said, "Well then we will go to Winchester." But Cromwell brought a second message, backed this time by Norfolk with threats. And Wolsey in the Charter House at
Richmond sat all day long alone, or one old Carthusian
with him, beginning, it seems, to think of his soul. Cromwell was told "that he would gladly go northward" but
that he had not the means. The Council advanced him
some thousands of pounds, and Henry, still pitiful in his
heart, more than doubled them. Wolsey searched around
in every direction for aid, even for loans, for when he
had been ruined there were still great sums undischarged.

It was on Tuesday April 5th, the Tuesday after Passion Sunday, that he started forth, still attempting something of his old magnificence, for, after all, could an

Archbishop of York enter his See without some train? He was at Peterborough on the fourth day, and there remained at the great Abbey over Holy Week and Easter.

At Peterborough he kept a great Easter: he bore his palm on Palm Sunday; he washed the feet of fifty-nine poor men on Maundy Thursday, giving each a pound apiece and to one of them two pounds. He adored the Cross on Good Friday; he was up betimes for the ceremony of the Resurrection on the Sunday.

He went on northward, and, that week, walking in the garden of a host of his (Fitzwilliam) and there saying his office, still in grandeur, he made a confidence to his closest and most trusted attendant. He knew how shameful his surrender seemed. He excused it by saying that he must needs save what he could and heroism would have meant martyrdom. But his heart was ill at ease. He knew that he had shamefully surrendered a trust and shamefully subjected his Order to the lay power.

He went on slowly all that summer, visiting church and abbey in his diocese. He won the hearts of the people, who had especially hated him for an absentee. But all the while his old rut of intrigue held him. He had not made a clean decision to retire. His false judgment bore its old fruits. He believed he could return, and he kept in touch—most dangerously!—with the Emperor's ambassador and Queen Catherine's cause: even with Rome, very secretly.

Some of all this his friends at Court knew, the rest they suspected. Agostini the physician whom he used as a go-between was watched by them. Time pressed them, for the King was already feeling the gulf between their incompetence and Wolsey's grasp of negotiation.

The Cardinal had fixed the 7th of November for his enthronement at York with renewed, belated splendour. He had summoned all within his power to meet him at Cawood on the eve and conduct him to the city in solemnity on the morrow, with hundreds of mounted men—then, after his enthronement, he would preside over his Convocation of the Northern Province. The day never came.

On Friday, the 4th of November, Wolsey was at dinner in the hall of Cawood Castle. He had nearly finished his meal and was at dessert. His mind was overcast. Three days before his great silver cross leaning against the wall had been overset by that same physician Agostini, and he had taken it for an evil omen. This day the omen was fulfilled.

Percy, that same Percy whom he had nourished in his household during his "triumphant glory," whom he had separated from Anne in York House all those years ago, Percy, now Northumberland, was at the gate. He had come from the King to arrest the Archbishop for "Hault Treason."

He entered. Wolsey received him kindly. He laid a hand on the Cardinal's arm and his speech failed him. It was in a voice "very faint and pale" that he said: "My Lord, I arrest you."

They brought him south by Sheffield Park—whither Henry in his strange vacillation had sent orders he should be received by Shrewsbury with great honour and comfort, and Shrewsbury assured him, truly, that the King sent word every day protesting his love and favour for the fallen man. But already that man was failing in body. He asked for physic and men noted his change of mien.

More than a fortnight passed. Then came a new en-

voy from the King—and Wolsey learned that it was
Kingston, the Constable of the Tower. He had come
with twenty-four of the guard, men who had once been
in Wolsey's service, and was to take the prisoner to London: Kingston—the name of ill omen! And Wolsey's
malady increased under the shock, and he professed,
rightly, that he could not live.

He was so weak that they dared not move him for
another day, but then they took him by slow stages to
Hardwick, to Nottingham—where he seemed worse than
ever—and so on the third day, Saturday, November the
26th, to the Augustinian Abbey at Leicester, which they
came to after dark, under torchlight. He was now so ill
that he could hardly totter to his bed on Kingston's arm,
and all Sunday and on to Monday, death came nearer.
Yet even then they must harry him, and Kingston
pressed in a matter of money—many thousand pounds, a
treasure of some thirty thousand which they thought he
had concealed. He bade them give him peace.

Before his attendant passed from him on that winter
night of Monday, November 28, the broken man had
said that by the stroke of eight his folk would lose their
master. Men about to die do sometimes so prophesy.

In the full darkness of the winter morning, by five at
latest, the old man began his shriving, making his long
and full confession to the Head of the House. He was
at that business a full hour, and what passed is hidden
from us, only save that his soul was clean at last.

It was still far from dawn when the Constable of the
Tower came in after the absolution was accomplished,
and once more, like a true official indifferent to the
humanities, urged the broken thing before him to give
some last information upon the matter of the missing

THE ARRIVAL OF CARDINAL WOLSEY AT LEICESTER ABBEY, 1530
From the Painting by Sir John Gilbert in the Victoria and Albert Museum, London

money. But the Cardinal still waved him aside and the faltering voice was only heard to say:—"If I had served my God as diligently as I have done the King, He would not have given me over in my grey hairs." Whereupon he continued, with a last rally of his mortal powers, to speak of the things to which he had hitherto been so blind, and which were now falling upon the realm—for with the approach of death he saw them—the King out of hand, the urgent need of defence against the flood of foreign heresies submerging England. The threat of all the society he had known dissolving, the license of the past. He spoke for very long, and, in his exhaustion at the end, sent again for the Abbott.

They stood around. The Head of the House anointed him with the Holy Oils, and with the giving of the Viaticum recited those awful words which summon the going forth of a Christian soul. The clock struck eight, and immediately thereafter he passed. It was the morning of Tuesday, November 29, 1530.

NOTES

NOTE A

ON THE DATE OF WOLSEY'S BIRTH

THE evidence consists in four points:—

(1) *The date of his ordination.* Wolsey was ordained Priest at Marlborough on the 10th March 1498. It is to be presumed that his ordination would not have taken place till after his attainment of the canonical age: he was not in early life of such importance or means as to procure a dispensation forestalling that date (nor was there likely to be any reason for such a dispensation). Now the canonical age is 24. Wolsey therefore must have been born not *later* than early 1474; but may well have been born earlier.

(2) *The ceremony of April 14, 1530.* Maundy Thursday of the year 1530 fell upon April 14. On that day the number of those who benefited from the special alms allotted by Wolsey on the day was 59. Now it was the custom of Kings and other great people who gave such largesse to a number of poor men every Maundy Thursday, to make the number of the beneficiaries correspond to the age of the donor. The year was counted at that time from one Lady Day (25th March) to another, and the years enumerated were charitably estimated at the maximum; that is, not the total amount of completed years the donor had lived but the total number of years *in which* he had lived: Allowing Wolsey to have been born sometime before Lady Day 1473 but after Lady Day 1472 he would thus have lived on April 14, 1530, *in* 59 years, though he had only lived 57 completed years.

(3) Of less value but worth mentioning is a rough estimate written by Giustiniani on October 9th, 1519 which says that Wolsey was then "about" 46 years of age. A man born in late 1472 or early 1473 would in October 1519 have been drawing on to his 46th birthday. This confirms point (2). Giustiniani was in a position to hear precise details and of a character to note them exactly.

(4) There is indeed an indication which would advance the date of his birth by at least a year, but it is too vague to outweigh the more precise evidence I have just given. It is an allusion by the Abbot of Winchcombe on August 6th, 1514, saying that Wolsey at that date was under 40. That would put the birth after August 6th, 1474, but it is not a precise reference.

I conclude, therefore, for some date between 25th March, 1472, and 25th March, 1473, with a probability for an earlier rather than a later date in these twelve months.

PRICES IN WOLSEY'S TIME—1510-1530

To estimate the value of money in a past period is both a task of great difficulty and one in which we can arrive at no exact conclusion; only an approximate result is possible. But it is easy to show that the purchasing value of the pound, the shilling and the penny in the first part of Henry VIII's reign was more than 20 and nearer 24 or 25 times what it is today: that is, one must reckon the penny as at nearly 2/-, the shilling at well over a pound and the pound at certainly not less than £20 to £25 of our present 1930 currency.

In considering the value of money at any past period compared with our own we have three quite separate points to estimate.

The first and the most important point is (in spite of the loss of the old bimetallic standard) what amount of what goods a given unit would purchase.

This is of course the obvious and fundamental matter. If *on the average*, for instance, *one* unit—one penny, shilling or pound—would purchase in sheep, horse-flesh, wheat, leather, wood, iron, wool (and so on through the main categories of ordinary expenditure) *six* times as much under Oliver Cromwell in England and the earlier colonial days in America as it will purchase today, then we have a multiple of *six* by which to judge the mere direct purchasing value of money in goods when we are translating the money statements of those days into modern terms.

But there is a second much vaguer but very important consideration, and that is, the number of things and services purchasable in the past compared with the number of things and services purchasable today. It is clear that an income of £1000 a year in a society such as the Falkland Islands where there is nothing to purchase but a dozen simple commodities is quite a different thing from the same income in New York where a man *may* purchase a thousand more kinds of things and *must* purchase a dozen times as many.

Lastly we come to the third point. In a community small in number and poor, the relative social value of a given sum is much greater than in a society numerous and rich.

Unfortunately, neither of these two last points is capable of even approximate calculation. We must for practical purposes in historical writing confine ourselves to the first one: the actual purchasing value of the unit; its purchasing value measured in goods. On the other two all we can do is to add such a phrase as "seeing the comparative sim-

plicity and poverty of the older society, the real social value" (of such
and such an income) "was much greater than that of the modern income into which we have translated it."

To estimate the purchasing value in goods of a given unit—say, the
pound sterling—in a given period as compared with its purchasing
power today it would seem at first sight that we had only to find out
how much of some main commodity, such as wheat, the unit would
then purchase, then what it will purchase now, note the difference and
establish our multiple accordingly. That is how the too simple academic
method first went to work.

But a little reflection will show that this method is quite inadequate.
We only arrive at the true multiple by considering a great number of
purchasable objects, *giving each their relative importance.* Something
which is largely used by the mass of the community and bought in
great quantities was, say, 20 times cheaper in a given year of the past
than it is today, but something which is very little used was only 10
times cheaper. You cannot strike an average and say that the purchasing value of the monetary unit was "about 15 times greater." The
relative dearness of the article which was little used does not outweigh
the cheapness of an article that was widely used.

To get the true purchasing value you must try to estimate the relative
amounts used of each article in your list. Now considering goods or
commodities as we use them today it is possible to get some rough idea
of this relation. We know more or less about the weekly budget of an
average family, and we say that there is much more wheat purchased
than oats, more iron is used than copper, more wool and cotton than
silk. But when we are dealing with the past we have not only different categories of things but different social habits to judge. For instance
—comparing Henry VIII's time with our own—in England four hundred years ago beer was the universal drink. The average man purchased far less clothing, but required it to be substantial and wore it
much longer. Such articles as tea, coffee, tobacco, potatoes (to talk only
of things largely purchased) were unknown.

It is this element of variation which makes an estimate so difficult.

Nevertheless I think it is possible when we consider early Tudor
prices in detail (of which we have a very considerable record), and
compare them with the prices of 1930, to come to a rough conclusion
and to establish at least a *minimum.*

The first thing we notice is that if we consider cereals of all kinds,
but especially wheat, we are dealing with a particularly high multiple,
that is with a commodity in those days dear. The cost of production of

wheat was from 3/– to 5/– a quarter; that gives you on the average of modern years a multiple of 12. Other grains are cheaper in proportion compared with modern prices but they are all high; and the average was very much higher than the mere cost of production because a wet harvest, common in the peculiar climate of England, could make cereals rise to famine prices. You find a college buying wheat in one year as low as 2/– a quarter, this gives you a multiple as against the price at the moment I write these lines, of nearly 20; yet shortly after the disastrous harvest of 1520 the same college had to pay 5 times as much at the worst moment.

Rye was cheaper than wheat and also more stable, and rye, which now is not used in England for bread, was then largely eaten. The same is true of beans. They are cheaper on the average than wheat but they are at a multiple of much less than 20. A pound never purchased 20 times as many beans, even in the most plentiful years, as it purchases today.

If therefore we had nothing but cereals to guide us we should have to take a low multiple. It is when we come to other articles of general consumption, necessities of life, that we begin to modify our conclusions. Wood for burning, the universal fuel of those days, was 20 times cheaper than it is today. Pig flesh, much the commonest form of meat, gives you a very high multiple. A weight of pig for which you must pay today some 80/– could be bought at an average of rather over 2/– —that is a multiple of 40. Fresh new laid eggs, in the English country side, cost from 4d to 6d for 10 dozen, which gives you an enormous multiple. Today you would pay at least 60 to 80 times as much. The commonest kind of cheese, that which formed and forms a staple with the mass of the people, gives you another very high multiple. You could get 5 lbs. of it for a penny—a multiple of 30 at least. Butter gives you a multiple of nearly 30. Poultry for the table gives you a multiple of 30. Sheep and mutton give you a multiple of nearly 40. Horses of all kinds especially the cheaper serviceable sort (for no rule can be derived from the fancy prices of mounts for the Court) give you a multiple of 20 or more. Hay gives a multiple of 20, so does lead. But quite a number of common manufactured objects, such as boots, spades, saddles, give you multiples of between 30 and 40.

An excellent way of testing our general result is the cost of living of the labourer per day. It is perhaps the most general and certain test and it gives you a multiple of something between 30 and 40. The average rent of land (rent was, however, still largely customary) gives you a multiple of 40.

Take it all round we may say with fair certainty that a multiple of 25 errs if anything on the conservative side and that to talk of "20 to 25" is to keep well within the mark.

Of course when it comes to the *social* values of the higher incomes the multiple is very much lighter. A man with £2,000 a year—10,000 dollars—in Wolsey's day, was a far bigger person socially than a man with £50,000—a quarter of a million dollars—a year today. A great monastery with a revenue of £4,000 did not correspond to a very rich man today with £100,000 a year, it corresponded rather with a great steamship line or railway company of today; for it stood in an England with only a 10th of our modern population and far less than a 10th of our total wealth.

BUCKINGHAM'S CLAIM TO THE THRONE

The claim of Edward Stafford, third Duke of Buckingham, to the crown of England, is not always clearly understood. It is commonly referred to as secondary to that of the Tudors, and the Duke himself as one who, though possibly rival to the reigning kings, had not an equal title with themselves. This is an error. He had a better title by the ideas of the time, and for that matter by the general rules of succession as the following table will show.

John of Gaunt, son of Edward III, Plantagenet, had by his mistress, Catherine Swynford, a bastard son called John. He gave him the title of Beaufort from a Castle of his in France and he was made Earl of Somerset. His descendants which concern us are as follows:—

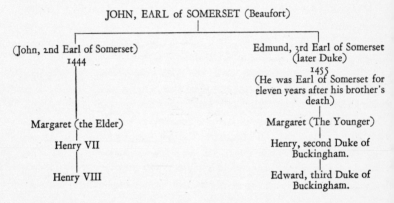

JOHN, EARL of SOMERSET (Beaufort)

(John, 2nd Earl of Somerset) 1444

Margaret (the Elder)

Henry VII

Henry VIII

Edmund, 3rd Earl of Somerset (later Duke) 1455
(He was Earl of Somerset for eleven years after his brother's death)

Margaret (The Younger)

Henry, second Duke of Buckingham.

Edward, third Duke of Buckingham.

Granted that the Beauforts, the bastard branch of the Plantagenets, had any title to the throne at all, Buckingham had a better Lancastrian right than Henry VIII.

Henry VIII was the son of Henry VII, whose only Plantagenet claim was derived from his mother Margaret, Countess of Richmond. Margaret, Countess of Richmond, was the daughter of John, 2nd Earl of Somerset.

Edward Stafford, whose head Wolsey cut off, was the son of Henry Stafford, 2nd Duke of Buckingham, whose mother was the daughter of Edmund, 3rd Earl of Somerset, the younger brother of John. This mother was called Margaret like her cousin, and we will call her Margaret the younger.

At first sight, Margaret the younger, daughter of Edmund seems not to have had the same title to the throne of England as Margaret the elder, daughter of John—for the elder Branch succeeds before the younger. But Margaret the younger was the daughter *of the last reigning Earl of Somerset*; that is the point. The father of Margaret the elder, John, killed himself in 1444, and Edmund succeeded him as Earl of Somerset in that year. He was Earl (afterwards Duke) of Somerset for eleven years; falling at the battle of St. Albans in 1455; and during all those eleven years it was Margaret the younger who counted as the heiress after her own brothers, and those brothers all died before the battle of Bosworth. Though this Margaret the younger was the daughter of the younger brother Edmund, while Margaret the elder was the daughter of the elder brother John, yet Margaret the younger was thus the daughter and heiress of the *reigning* Duke of Somerset during all those years, while Margaret the elder was only the niece.

Take the case of the succession to a private fortune in land. A man dies without male heirs and the estate passes to his younger brother. That younger brother has male heirs. These last have no male heirs. It would be natural that the land should be left, in this default of male heirs to the remaining child of the younger brother. It is true that, according to our *modern* rule of royal succession in England, if John had been King, Margaret the elder, on his death, would have been Queen; but then, Edmund would not have succeeded his brother. John was not King, he was Earl of Somerset; the relationship was to the Earls of Somerset; and Margaret the younger, as heiress of the last reigning Earl of Somerset inherited the stronger Somerset claim. That is why Margaret the younger's son Henry, 2nd Duke of Buckingham, had really a better claim than his second cousin Henry VII. And *his* son Edward, whom Wolsey beheaded, had a better claim than his third cousin Henry VIII. Buckingham had yet another claim through Thomas of Woodstock, Duke of Gloucester, youngest son of Edward III.

NOTE D

ON THE RESPONSIBILITY OF WOLSEY FOR
BUCKINGHAM'S DEATH

Tradition took it for granted that the prime mover in the destruction of the Duke of Buckingham was Wolsey. Tradition in these large matters of motive and character, particularly when it comes from the very source and can be traced to contemporaries, is so generally right that any academic case against it must require heavy positive proof in its favour.

It has been the academic fashion since the last third of the 19th century to exonerate Wolsey. This came in part from the general academic contempt for popular opinion, but also from exaggerating the use of documents against tradition: the great flood of documents on this period having been printed for the first time in the later part of the 19th century.

But when I look at those documents, and consider the academic arguments advanced to exonerate Wolsey I can see nothing to support the new conclusion. All seems to me in favour of the old, and Wolsey remains indubitably the author of Buckingham's tragedy.

What are the arguments in favour of Henry's being the true initiator of the business?

The first argument is that Henry, like all the Tudors (and like James the First, for that matter) was in terror of rival claims to the throne. But if that was Henry's motive why had neither he nor his father been affected by that motive during so many years? On the contrary, he and his father heaped honours on Buckingham. One hears nothing of this sudden dread of a rival till Buckingham is 42 years old, and till he has been the intimate companion and friend of the King for many years.

The suspicions against Buckingham did not begin to arise till Wolsey started them in 1518.

Against this it may be urged that Henry may not have suspected Buckingham of any likelihood to press his claims until news came to him thus late. Well, who put forward that news? Undoubtedly Wolsey. It was the anonymous letter which Wolsey had in his hands, some weeks before Henry could make up his mind to move, which is the starting point of the whole affair.

A second argument continually put forward to show that the initiative cannot have been Wolsey's and must therefore have been Henry's is that Polydore Vergil, the contemporary who specifically accuses

Wolsey, is a tainted witness because Wolsey had put him in prison and he was Wolsey's enemy. The argument is only of value as against a better argument on the other side. Because a man is prejudiced against another it is probable that he will lie in his disfavour; but it is not probable that in repeating a common opinion and a likely one, and one for which there is no contemporary contradiction, he should be lying. French and English propaganda against William II during the Great War gave rise to many lies. But it did not lie when it accused William II of having made warlike and menacing speeches.

General considerations, which are the best of all in such matters, can I think determine us. Put yourself in the place of Wolsey in that year 1521, remember his character, his power of restraint and calculation, the affronts he had suffered, the hatred felt for him by the class of which Buckingham was the best representative, the Cardinal's dread lest anyone should supplant him or weaken him in the ears of the King, the recent conspicuous rôle of Buckingham in the splendid feasts of 1520, the Cloth of Gold; remember also the effort Wolsey was at to exclude Buckingham from shining in the tourneys, and the way in which none the less the King continued to befriend him, and you have before you a situation which makes Wolsey's initiative against him not only reasonable but inevitable.

On the other hand, put yourself in the place of Henry, impulsive, readily influenced, readily taken in, acting suddenly upon suggestion, very much attached to the Court traditions he had inherited from his father, receiving unexpected and terrifying notice that his friend and relative was intriguing against him, receiving after two years of suggestions, that anonymous notice from Wolsey, by whom he was completely dominated. Ask yourself whether Henry's action in early 1521 when he was moved to such wrath and fear in the matter of Buckingham looks like a policy thought out by his own brain.

NOTE E

ON THE PAPAL ELECTION OF 1522

There are three pieces of evidence available for the scrutinies of the Papal election in 1521-1522. Official record is lacking, but such testimony as we have will I think be found to corroborate what I have said in the text.

(1) Clerk, the English observer, speaks of as many as 19 votes having been recorded for Wolsey on one occasion, 9 on another, 12 on another.

(2) We have in the Spanish Calendar[1] Berosa's transcript of the Papal archives made for Philip II, which tells us that Wolsey's name had appeared in only one scrutiny out of 11 and had then received but seven votes.

(3) Campeggio told Wolsey in a letter that his name had appeared in each of the eleven successive scrutinies and that he had on occasions received 8 and on others 9 votes.

Now of these three witnesses the first could only go by hearsay, and many a Cardinal had a motive for telling Clerk, regarding him as the man of the King of England, that he had voted for the King of England's Archbishop—while telling Charles's man that he had voted for Charles's candidate.

The second witness is official but a very late transcript.

The third witness, Campeggio, is a reliable witness, for Campeggio was an honest man and an eye-witness. On the other hand anyone addressing Wolsey directly on the matter would tend to flatter. The 8 or 9 votes of which he speaks may well be an exaggerated number. Berosa's is the best evidence we have.

[1] Spanish Calendar 1509-1525, pages 389-391.

ON THE DATE OF ANNE BOLEYN'S BIRTH

It is important to have a right judgment on the date of Anne Boleyn's birth because at each stage in the divorce our judgment of the motives at work in her, and, in a less degree, our judgment of the attitude others took towards her depend upon her age. But the point has long been disputed.

I have in the text of this essay taken the year 1500 as the most probable date. The latest admitted is the year 1507. But an individual judgment on the matter is worthless to the reader unless he have the elements of the problem put before him.

These are four pieces of direct evidence:—

(1) Camden, the author of the History of Elizabeth, has put, in a marginal note at the beginning of his book the date *"Nata anno MDVII."* (Hearne's edition, p. 2.)

(2) Sanders (De Schis: p. 18 says 1500).

(3) An autograph letter written by Anne Boleyn, which letter can be fixed at latest for early in the year 1514 and more probably late 1513.

(4) The Holbein portrait at Bale which is dated 1530 and has inscribed on it the words *"Aetatis suae 27."*

Of these four pieces of direct evidence the best is the letter (No. 3). It is hardly legible, hardly comprehensible, and very badly written, but it cannot possibly be the letter of a *very* young child. It was written in reply to her father's request that she should write one without help in order to see how she was progressing, as he was thinking of bringing her to Court, and it speaks of her affairs in a fashion possible to a school-girl in her teens but not to an infant of six or seven. It cannot have been written later than early 1514 and that points to the writer's being born either in or shortly after the year 1500.

The next strongest piece of evidence is the Bale portrait (No. 4). That would put the date of her birth in the year 1502-3. It has been well remarked that if the information was given by herself she was more likely to take a year off her age than to put one on.

The next piece of evidence in order of importance is that of Sanders. (No. 2.) It is true that Sanders was a man with strong prejudice and wild in his statements, as also in his failure to appreciate the importance of dates (otherwise he would never have started the absurd story that Henry was Anne's father). But on the other hand he had no motive for giving an earlier or a later date, and he is the nearest personal witness we have. He was a child already able to understand what was being said around him at the time of Anne's death, and who by the time he was twenty must have met plenty of people who were familiar with all the details of the time. Also he made the breach with Rome his special study. His date 1500 therefore has great weight.

Camden's evidence (No. 1) comes last in value. He gives no source for it. He was not born till 15 years after Anne's death. Unlike Sanders, who was more than 20 years his senior, none of the people he met are likely to have been contemporary witnesses with a memory extending to the date of the birth. He does not put the date down till he himself is an elderly man—and even then seems to put it down as a sort of afterthought. Moreover his work did not appear until nearly a century after Henry's first attraction to Anne, and nearly 80 years after her death.

Apart from this direct evidence we have strong indirect evidence. (1) Anne came back from France in early 1522, in that same year her name was certainly coupled with that of the poet Wyatt, a loose fellow at court who was also later one of those who most benefited by the spoils of the Church. Later, after Anne had been executed, he told Henry that *she* had pursued him and made proposals to him which he, in his virtue, had rejected.

Now allowing for all the precocity of the time, it is not likely that a child of 14 and a half should be the subject of these amorous poems, he must at least have intended it to be believed, and Henry would never have believed it of a child of that age.

(2) In the same year 1522 she caught that very valuable *parti* Percy, the heir to the Duchy of Northumberland. A child of fifteen at the most does not lay out and carry to a successful conclusion a plot of that kind. The thing is possible if she were born as late as the year 1503, it is probable if she were born in the year 1500, it is impossible if she were born in the year 1507.

Against all this converging trend of evidence there is the difficulty often brought forward of reconciling so early a date as 1503, let alone 1500, with the dates in the life of her supposedly *elder* sister Mary Boleyn. But this difficulty comes from arguing in a circle. It has been generally believed in modern times (never stated by contemporaries) that Mary was the elder sister, and the high authority of Brewer has been used to confirm it. But there is no real evidence for it. What has led people astray in the matter is the fact that Mary Boleyn was Henry's mistress before Henry was captured by Anne. It seemed natural that the elder sister should be sacrificed before the younger should be attempted. But Anne was not on the scene when Henry's liaison with

Mary was going on. Mary was married off in February 1521 to a Mr. William Carey. The intrigue may have been begun before that date (she was then eighteen) it may have gone on afterwards, for when her son was born after the marriage some thought him Henry's. But at any rate the affair was prior to Anne's return from France in early 1522. The only piece of positive evidence that Mary, who was born in 1503, was the elder sister, is the letter in which Lord Hunsdon, Mary's grandson, nearly eighty years later, asked Burleigh to let him have the Earldom of Ormonde in virtue of his grandmother's right, as being the "eldest daughter" of Thomas Boleyn, who had been the Earl of Ormonde as well as Viscount Rochford and Earl of Wiltshire. But this is a presumption from the fact that Mary was the sole heir; and she was the sole heir *not* because she was the eldest, but because her sister Anne had been executed and *attainted*, i.e., incapable of inheritance, and her brother had also been executed and attainted.

The statement that Mary and not Anne was taken to the Court of France in 1514 rests on nothing but the presumption of her being the elder sister. Thus Dr. Brewer says, quite rightly, it would be ridiculous to expect a child of seven to have been taken over in the train of Henry VIII's sister to the Court of France. But there would be nothing absurd in a girl of 14 being taken over. Moreover we have evidence both direct and indirect that it was Anne and not Mary who was taken to France in the train of Mary Tudor at the time of the French marriage in 1514. A French poem of the date 1536 (the year of Anne's death) and full of detail, called "Histoire de la Royne etc." states it, so does Bourgueville, writing somewhat later. Further all the facts of her life in this connection point indirectly to having been taken to France with Mary Tudor in 1514 and remaining at the French Court during the years of her adolescence. Her familiar language was French, the King writes to her in French, the translation of certain phrases of hers is clearly the translation of a French idiom, Henry after the tragedy deplores the corruption which she owed to her French upbringing, Frenchmen allude to her as being so French that no one would take her for an Englishwoman—and so forth.

The conclusion seems to be inevitable in the absence of further evidence, that Anne was born at the latest in 1502 and more probably in 1500, that she went to France in the train of Mary Tudor in 1514 and remained there till 1521; that Mary Boleyn (born in 1503) was the younger sister, seduced by Henry before the King had seen Anne at all, and supplanted by her elder sister after Anne's return from France; that Anne was 20 to 22 when the King began to consider her,

NOTE G

ON THE AUTHORSHIP OF THE DIVORCE POLICY

All history, like all judgment of contemporary things, turns upon a general knowledge of character. To no one should it occur that Henry could have started that hare himself.

In the whole of his twisted violent life you can point to nothing which Henry began, of his own accord; he acts always under the suggestion of another. Here and there a detail is interfered with by him. Here and there a small personal point is insisted upon against his advisers, but in no large matter of policy, from the Spanish War at the beginning of the reign, to the Writ for the execution of Norfolk, on the eve of his death, is he out of the hands of others.

Who suggested to Henry getting rid of a wife to whom he had been strongly bound for ten full years of his youth, whose family was at the very summit of European rank and power, who was, alone of the court, really and vividly popular with his subjects? Who was the model of virtue, as demanded of her, and whom moreover it would be impolitic, foolish and dangerous to supplant?

There are three theories upon the matter.

These three theories are—

First: that Wolsey was at the origin of the whole affair. Second: that the idea of a divorce was first put into Henry's mind inadvertently by the French Ambassador, the Bishop of Tarbes, when he came over in April 1527 to negotiate for the French Alliance. Third, that Anne Boleyn, in her carefully planned plot for the seizing of the Crown, first put the idea into Henry's mind. Of these three hypotheses, the third is not only the most probable, but almost certainly true. The second is demonstrably false, the first an error, but an error more arguable than the second. Why this is so, I shall now put before the reader.

That the Bishop of Tarbes, when he came on Embassy in 1527 first suggested the idea of a divorce to Henry's mind, I think quite demonstrably false. There is manifold proof of this. The divorce had been talked of two years before Tarbes came and appears in an official letter in the interval. Further, Wolsey, writing to Henry a letter for his eye alone in the first week of July 1527, tells him how he had gone to talk about the divorce to the Bishop of Rochester, Fisher, and in this letter alludes, as a thing which both he and the King were familiar with, to their having a put up plan to say the Bishop of Tarbes had started the idea.

The theory that Wolsey was the author of the whole thing must be taken much more seriously. Queen Catherine herself was persuaded of it; the mass of England believed it: indeed the idea was so widely spread that Wolsey had to ask the King to deny it publicly, which the King very warmly did. Now the King's denial is worth nothing, nor would Wolsey's play-acting in the matter be worth anything of itself. What is much more to the point is that Langland, the King's confessor through whose agency Wolsey was said to have acted, and whose word must be taken as something of much greater worth than either the Cardinal's or the King's, denied it, and was backed up in his denial by Henry. He had not, he said, put in the King's mind any scruple against his living with his brother's wife. The relation between a confessor and his penitent—even a Royal confessor and his penitent—is not something to be treated as indifferently as common political intrigue. Moreover, Henry said in this connection that Langland had, if anything, dissuaded him from going forward. This is much the most probable statement of them all. Only those who know something of the sacrament of penance can fully understand what I mean, but the common sense of the matter must appeal to all. A man in the privacy of that most important relation mentions scruples with regard to this marriage of many years' standing. His confessor dissuades him from such scruples in the name of common morals. That is what any confessor would do, and needs not to be a saint to do it. And, moreover, it seems clear that the man who first started the accusation against Wolsey was Tyndale, and Tyndale's fanaticism is a commonplace.

The third theory has to support it two converging effects, first, it is exactly consonant with Anne's character, her long and careful intrigue, and her triumph: secondly, it is the direct testimony of Reginald Pole.

Of these two converging facts, the first is of considerable strength, the second is convincing.

Henry had considered Anne as a possible *mistress* long before there was any talk of divorce at all. It was Anne who proposed to be not concubine but queen. Anne's whole character and procedure for seven years are directed by the one policy of forcing the divorce through. Anne alone could benefit by it. Anne not only became Queen by it, but did not become Queen accidently. She became Queen at the end of a whole series of steps, in each one of which her own will and action are apparent.

It may be asked as a supplemental question whether she was moved in the matter by her relatives, notably by the Duke of Norfolk? It is improbable, because such a character as hers needed no moving. She knew her own mind extremely well. Next, because, at the origin of the affair, no one who had not an intimate and private control over Henry could have thought its conclusion possible. It would have seemed quite inconceivable to anyone save to the woman who possessed full knowledge of the man she had subdued. Even so, all the first months and even years of the advance were ponderous and slow.

But, as I have said, it is the testimony of Reginald Pole that really settles the business.

There are two qualities in Pole as a witness which give him a peculiar value. The first is that he alone of all those whom we can put into the box was really competent to give evidence. He lived in the very heart of the Royal circle: he was part of it. Everyone knows what a difference it makes to a man's appreciation of some social matter, whether he is a member of the clique concerned or an outsider. Pole was a Royalty; and a Royalty close to the Royalties of whom he spoke. Secondly, though Pole may be condemned or praised for his strong Catholic enthusiasm, according to the temperament of those who praise or blame him, no one can deny the sincerity of his emotion. It might lead him to exaggerate, or to denounce unduly. It would not lead him to lie about a fact which had passed within the knowledge of his own immediate circle. Thirdly, Pole's testimony is addressed directly to Henry, not to third parties or to the public. The appeal in which it is written is an appeal put to Henry personally, following upon another equally passionate appeal in which he had almost dissuaded his cousin, the King, to leave the fatal path he had taken up. Now Pole's statement is quite unambiguous. It is a Latin sentence of which this is the translation:—

"She herself (Anne Boleyn) sent her priests, theologians of weight, who not only affirmed that you had the right to put away your wife, but even said that you were in grievous sin (by living with her)."

Pole had no doubt that Anne had acted thus, he took it for granted as a thing known to Henry as well as to himself.

How much he was in the very heart of the small group to which Henry and Anne belonged can be appreciated sufficiently even upon a general knowledge of his life. His mother was the daughter of Clarence, the Plantagenet brother of Edward IV. He was in direct Royal descent. Henry VII had married that mother to his own first cousin, the nephew of his mother, and Reginald Pole and Henry VII were first cousins.[1] Reginald was born eleven years after Henry, in 1500, growing up with the century; he was the same age as Charles V. He was a child nine years old, when Henry VIII came to the throne. The new King paid for his education at the rate of £300 a year, and generally acted as his guardian. He was bred for the Church, though he was so long in taking Orders, graduating from Magdalen at Oxford at 15, and increased in reputation as a scholar. Not only was he thus of the blood Royal and closely related to the centre of the Court, but his sister had married a son of the Duke of Buckingham. He, being amply provided with revenues, prebends, and deanery, lived thus in the midst of Henry's own surroundings, almost as a son or younger brother, until he was twenty-one, when he was sent off to travel in Italy, with ample provision of money from Henry's own purse. It is true that he was not in England during the critical years between 1522 and 1527, when the capture of Henry by Anne was effected, but he was in constant correspondence. He heard all that could be heard at first hand, and when he came back in 1527 he heard everything that anyone had privately to say in the Royal circle. He stayed on in England till 1529, a critical year, in which the attempt to get a Papal sentence in favour of Henry broke down. He then went to Paris to collect evidence reluctantly in favour of Henry's thesis from the University, came home the Summer of the next year, in 1530, and after Wolsey's death at the end of that year, was put forward to be Archbishop of York.

He loved Henry; he did not want to quarrel with his benefactor. He tried to compromise, but his conscience would not let him. There was a scene in that same York House which Henry had seized from the Church; Pole harangued violently like a prophet, against Henry's fatal infatuation. He spoke so eloquently that Cranmer, writing to the Boleyns, emphasized the danger of letting such words go abroad. Pole begged his Royal cousin to accept the Papal decision. He put forward that very strong argument in policy which the modern historian has forgotten—that to divorce Catherine was to endanger the succession. Usually the thing is put the other way.

Henry nearly gave way. He parted with his younger relative as a friend, and yet stood in some fear of him. However, he allowed Pole to go abroad in December, 1534. Cromwell was urged by the King to write to Pole that a man so eminent throughout Europe, and known to be a just and honest witness of all that had passed, should give an answer, yes or no, on the two main questions, whether marriage with a

[1] The mother of Reginald Pole was half sister to Margaret Beaufort, through whom Henry VII claimed Royal descent.

brother's widow were forbidden by Divine Law, whether the Papacy were of human or of Divine institution.

Seventeen months later, in May, 1536, his reply, painfully and laboriously put together, appeared—the famous "Defence of the Unity of the Church." And no one, I think, who reads the words he wrote can doubt the substantial truth of his accusation. The suggesting of the Divorce was Anne's work, and the man who knew most of what had passed testified to that truth.

NOTE H

ON THE SUPPOSED MOVE FOR A DIVORCE IN 1514

I have said in the text that the proposal for a divorce was novel and shocking in the year 1527. But it is necessary to examine a recent attempt to excuse Henry by suggesting that the idea had long been familiar. It stands on the very high authority of Professor Pollard.

It has lately been affirmed as an admitted historical fact, hitherto overlooked, that the divorce had been suggested as early as 1514. Let us see upon what evidence this is based.

Six references are given in the footnote to the affirmation made. These references are to the second volume of the Venetian Calendar, documents 479, 482, 483, 487, 492, 500.

This at first sight looks like a formidable array of evidence and as not one reader in a thousand will look up the originals, an impression is given that no less than six contemporary documents tell us that divorce had been decided upon in that year, 1514. But anyone who will take the trouble to turn to the actual texts, will, I think be surprised at the edifice built upon them. I will take these texts in their order.

The first, document 479, is a letter written by a banker in Rome referring to certain gossip which he had heard in that city. It is dated August 28, 1514. His name is Vetor Lippomano, and his words, as translated into English from the Venetian Calendar are "It is also said that the King of England intends to repudiate his present wife, the daughter of the King of Spain and his brother's widow, because he is unable to have children by her, and intends to marry a daughter of the French Duke of Bourbon." While later in the letter is a repetition that he means to annul the marriage.

There is no authority given; even the man who writes this phrase admits that it is only a "*Se dice,*" an "*on dit,*" a "so folks say." There is no mention of any informant, and no reason to believe that the talk this man had heard hundreds of miles away from England and with no special qualifications for making it had any basis worth regarding. Everybody knew that the King of England was very angry with his father-in-law and people who did not know what the Court of England was like, who did not know the strong affection between the couple, of how Catherine had been for years the chief influence over her husband might spin some stuff like this out of their heads. Clearly the writer, or rather those whose tittle-tattle in Rome he sends out for what it is worth, had not the elements of the situation, otherwise they would not have talked nonsense about Catherine having no children or about the idea of a marriage with the daughter of Bourbon!

So much for the first document. But the reader may say "It is backed up by five others."

Well, let the reader judge for himself. The second document, number 482, is a letter from the Venetian Ambassador in London at the time to the State of Venice. It is written on August 14, 1514, and there is not a word in it about any suggested divorce. It only talks about the strain between England and Spain which was notorious.

The third document, number 483, is from Alviano the Captain General of the Venetian forces. It is written from St. Germain-en-Laye, near Paris, also to the State of Venice, enclosing a letter from Rome dated the 30th of August 1514. There is not a word in it about any suggested divorce, only the particular that the English government has not included Spain in the proposals for peace, which again was part of what everyone knew to be the strained relations between the two governments.

The fourth document, number 487, is a Latin letter from Henry VIII to the Pope, written by the King's secretary on August 12, 1514. There is not a word in it about any suggested divorce, but only a statement equivalent to that which Alviano got hold of later that as the King of Aragon proposed to act by himself he had not been included in Henry's peace terms.

The fifth document, number 492, is a dispatch from the council of Ten in Venice to the Venetian Ambassador in France. There is not a word in it about any suggested divorce, only a commendation of the advice which the old King of France was giving to his proposed brother-in-law Henry, to attack Castile.

The sixth document, number 500, dated October 5, 1514, is from a Venetian merchant in London to his two brothers. There is not a word about any suggested divorce, only the remark that the Spanish Ambassador stays at home and that people comment on it.

The reader will I think agree with me that these last five documents 2 to 6 are quite irrelevant. All Europe was acquainted with the annoyance felt in England at the separate peace Ferdinand had made behind England's back and these five documents refer only to this commonplace of the time. There is not so much as an allusion to the proposed policy of divorce save in the first document, and the valuelessness of that we have already seen.

I have gone at such length into the statement of a supposed divorce policy at 1514 because it has such high authority behind it. But I cannot agree. No other allusion so far as I know has been discovered to any such intention on the part of Henry to repudiate a wife to whom he was at that moment deeply attached, and to whom he remained deeply attached for years to come. No one in England said it or thought it, I know of no phrase which can be twisted into the most remote allusion to such a policy. In the huge mass of evidence relating to the Court of England in those years the mere abstracts of which fill hundreds of closely printed pages, I know of no one who has found a syllable about anything of the kind.

Of the six documents only two are written on the spot in England and neither knows anything of a divorce. Four of the six are official and know nothing about it. One is from a merchant who has no access to the Court. One only has a reference. It is the most distant, the least informed, and even so talks of it as mere gossip.

NOTE I

ON THE AUTHENTICITY OF THE BRIEF

The Brief has been examined by experts in the archives at Vienna whither it was brought from Brussels. It had lain at Brussels ever since Ruiz de Puebla, the son of the Spanish Minister Puebla, had found it in his father's papers and handed it to Charles V. The experts who so examined it have no doubt of its authenticity, which may today be called an accepted historical fact. But it has naturally been attacked because religious passion enters into the question.

Of the arguments brought against the authenticity most are of little value, and some are based upon lack of information; but one is considerable and another really grave.

We may neglect the remark that it appeared "opportunely" for that would be true of any document produced only when it was required.

Nor is it true that the brief is not mentioned in the complete list of Puebla's papers. Those who speak thus are ignorant of the fact that what they take for the complete list is a list drawn up *after* the brief had been taken out from among them and handed over to Vienna, it is only a list of the *remaining* papers.

The silence of Accolti "who drew up the dispensation" is accounted for by the fact that Accolti did not draw up the dispensation.

The argument that the brief is misdated is also due to ignorance. It is said that we have record of its being sent in 1509, while *this* document is dated 1503. But we have no record of its being sent in 1509 and every presumption of its having been sent in 1504 (not 1503). The idea that it was sent in 1509 is based on a chance phrase in one of the attacks upon Queen Catherine. It is not even put in as part of the attack but casually and with no particular support.

What is really a considerable argument is that when a record of the brief was searched for in the registers at Rome on the demand of Charles the record was not found there. The point is remarkable but it must be remembered that an ambiguity of date may have led to the failure. It was presumably looked for under 1503, being so dated because the Papal year was reckoned sometimes from one date and sometimes from another. It should have been looked for under the year 1504.

Lastly there is the grave argument that Charles V when he asked Pope Clement to remedy the defects in that Bull—which he did on July 31, 1527, could not have known of the existence of the brief which would have made such amendments unnecessary. To this it can only be answered that at the time he *was* ignorant of the brief; it was only found later in the year by Ruiz de Puebla among his father's papers.

What seems to make the authenticity of the brief certain, however, apart from general arguments and the opinion of experts, is Ferdinand's message to Rojas, his Ambassador at Rome at the time when the dispensations were being issued. He says that a brief may not be necessary, but that the English are raising so many difficulties that he may as well obtain it. He goes on to give instructions as to what shall be in the brief, and they correspond to what we actually find there. This is surely conclusive.

ON THE DATE OF ANNE BOLEYN'S ACCEPTATION OF HENRY

In the absence of positive evidence, which in its nature is undiscoverable I think we can establish within comparatively narrow limits the critical date: the dates within which Anne brought her plot to its completion, the dates within which there were no further restrictions but straightforward relations between them and the full chance of her bearing him a child. It certainly cannot be later than December 1532, it cannot, on our reading of her character and Henry's, be placed earlier than the beginning of September.

What was the prime condition making her queenship certain? The obtaining of *what*, would, in most men's eyes, appear to be a valid and canonical declaration of annulment of Henry's former marriage? Failing the Pope (and that they could no longer count on, the Pope had long been hostile) one authority alone could fulfil the conditions and that was the authority of the Primate of England. Now Warham would not have acted as Henry's servant in the matter. To replace Warham, Cranmer, the creature of the Boleyns, had been designated, even though he himself did not know it. But they could not replace Warham until Warham died. Warham was ailing (he was also a very old man) during all that summer of 1532, but for Anne there was no discounting events. Had she been one who discounted events she would have yielded long before anything could make her certain. Warham died on the 23rd of August 1532. Anne was given a *royal* title within 10 days— on the 1st of September following. It is very important to note that title, she was not made Marchioness of Pembroke, she was made *Marquis* of Pembroke and was henceforward treated virtually as Queen. Henry took her with him to France, publicly and in full state, as destined for the crown, in the following month of October. It was known a little before Christmas that she was with child. I think that if all these dates be compared one with the other and be read in connection with the obvious and clear-cut plan which Anne had nourished for so many years the conclusion is obvious. Anne gave Henry his will between September 1 and say November 15, 1532.

ON THE CONSUMMATION OF PRINCE ARTHUR'S
MARRIAGE

The evidence as to whether the first marriage of Catherine of Aragon to Prince Arthur of England were consummated or not is as follows:

First, a body of testimony (not very large) brought before the Legatine Court in 1529. This body of evidence may be read in the Letters and Papers of the reign of Henry VIII, volume 4, part 2.

Second, the declaration made by Catherine herself.

Third, a certain statement made some years later by Campeggio, Legate and judge in the Legatine Court, and therefore a direct witness to the living impression produced by the evidence therein given.

Fourth, certain indirect pieces of evidence drawn from the attitude and actions of third parties.

Of these pieces of evidence the first is quite indecisive, the second strongly against the consummation of the marriage, the third doubtfully in favour of such consummation; the fourth wholly, strongly, and as I think conclusively against the consummation of the marriage.

I will now examine these four categories in their order.

(1) As for the first category, it consists of statements made by those who were contemporary with the marriage and present in the household. Some of them confess themselves incompetent to give an opinion, others merely give the conventional facts that the young people retired together on the night of the wedding and that during the few weeks of Arthur's life they lived ostensibly as man and wife. It may have been necessary to take such evidence but it was of common knowledge. In the whole body of evidence there is very little definitely relating to the physical point at issue; such as there is does not lend itself to public repetition, but those who consult it in the original will see that none of it is at all convincing.

For example, one of the strongest pieces of evidence in this group is a jest which the young Prince is said to have made one morning after leaving his bride and such as any boy might be led to make by way of a boast. We must remember that he was only 15 at the time. This does not make the thing impossible; there were cases (in those days of early royal marriages) of children born to a prince and conceived in their father's 16th year; but they were rare. It is of course admitted that nothing of the kind happened in Prince Arthur's case. There was no promise of a child. We must further remember that the boy was sickly, he was but 15 years and 55 days old when the marriage between him and Catherine was performed at St. Paul's on November 15, 1501, and he died but twenty weeks later on April 2nd of the next year, less than 15 and a half years old. We must also remember before we leave this category that there was very strong reason for the witnesses to incline in Henry's favour, and to make all they could in favour of the consummation of the marriage. For they were Henry's subjects, most of them humble and some of them in his employ, and Henry was not so well balanced that they rely on his temper.

(2) The second category consists in the declaration of Catherine. In public, before the Court of 1529, Catherine solemnly asserted that on her second marriage with Henry VIII she was a virgin. She had very strong interest in making the statement, and if one knew nothing of her character to the contrary that would afford a presumption against this declaration being true. But we do know her character, and it was, by the admission of all, singularly downright, straightforward and deeply impressed with a sense of duty. She frequented the sacraments regularly; she habitually confessed and communicated; and we have to decide whether it is credible that such a character living such a life could have told a falsehood of such magnitude on such an occasion. We may note for what it is worth (which is not much) that general opinion not only upon the continent but more especially in England supported her contention.

(3) The third category, Campeggio's declaration, has often been over-looked and deserves careful scrutiny. In July, 1533, the College of Cardinals sat in Consistory to discuss whether Julius II were entitled to grant the dispensation contained in the Brief to which allusion has so frequently been made in the text. Campeggio was present. Not in the Consistory itself, but soon after leaving it, he said to the Spanish agents that if Catherine's case had depended upon the proofs of her virginity at the moment of her marriage with Henry, he, Campeggio, would have had grave doubts about the justice of it. But as the case did not depend upon that point but upon whether the Pope had the right to give a dispensation—with which right he fully agreed—he never doubted of the result.

Now this is a strong point against Catherine's contention and in favour of the consummation of the first marriage. Campeggio also was of high character. His interest, if any, would rather have leant toward supporting Catherine at the moment when the Papal Court and Catherine's nephew the Emperor were friendly, and when Henry had shocked opinion by openly marrying Anne Boleyn. He spoke to Spaniards, to whom his words must have been unwelcome. Moreover Campeggio was a witness giving his impressions of events he had heard with his own ears, and of witnesses whose demeanour as they gave evidence he had been able to judge. We have to remember that there are certain countervailing considerations. He was a southerner, called to judge upon the probabilities of such an event in the case of the northern climate and character. Whatever his impression, it had not the value of Catherine's full and explicit declaration upon a matter in which Catherine and Henry alone could, in the nature of things, have real knowledge. Further, he does not record a conviction, he only records a doubt. Lastly his remark was made in connection with his emphasizing the indubitable Papal power of dispensation, and in order to emphasize that power he would naturally lean to admitting the reality of the impediment which a Papal dispensation alone could remove. However, Campeggio's declaration is a grave one, and must be given its full weight.

(4) It is rather in the fourth category that we find the most conclusive evidence against the consummation of the first marriage. In this fourth category the principal points are:—

(a) That Henry, upon being challenged publicly by his wife did not deny the truth of what she said:

(b) That there had been no assertion of the validity of the original marriage with Arthur during a space of twenty years.

(c) That Catherine was married as a virgin, clothed in white and with her hair loose.

(d) That Henry VII, Prince Arthur's father, after his son's death, proposed that he himself should marry Catherine; a proposal happily quashed by the indignant protests of Catherine's mother.

Of these four points the first (a) is very important. It was of the first moment to Henry to have stopped a false impression, if it *was* false, at the moment when it was given in the public court. He had already given ample proof, and was to give still further proof, that he was unscrupulous in such matters, and it is difficult not to conclude that if he remained silent on hearing his wife's passionate protest and in the face of her direct appeal to his own conscience and knowledge of what happened when he and Catherine first came together, it was because he found it impossible to deny what she said: he who alone, except herself, could give full evidence in the matter. It is further remarkable that in his treatise called the "Glass of Truth," probably written by him after the divorce was first publicly mentioned and certainly shown to the Pope before the commission for a Legatine Court was signed, he was careful, though he was putting forward all the evidence available in his own favour, *not* to affirm that the original marriage with his brother was other than a form. He says that for more than a month after his brother's death he was not given the title of Prince, because Catherine might prove to be with child. Such a delay would have been natural in face of the fact that a public marriage had taken place and there could be no open declaration of its futility. It is true that such a delay might have been based on some declaration made by Catherine herself; but he mentions no such declaration, and there is no mention of it at the time.

As to (b), it is a point of no great value either way. During all the undisturbed years of Henry's cohabitation with Catherine there would naturally be no insistence on the reality of the first marriage had it indeed been real, for that would have been an argument in the hands of enemies against the succession. On the other hand it is remarkable that over such a long space of time—the 21 years between the marriage with Arthur (1504) and the first hint of Henry's divorce (1525)—sixteen years between that first hint and Henry's own marriage (1509) no contemporary should have laid stress upon the probability of the first marriage having been consummated. This may of course have been taken for granted, but one might imagine the enemies to the Tudor succession (and they were numerous) would not have left the thing unmentioned had it been generally believed.

There were indeed objections made, before Henry's marriage, to its taking place with the widow whether nominal or real of his brother. Notably did Archbishop Warham express dissent. But this would be provoked as much by the public ceremony of marriage as by any private evidence upon its consummation.

As to (c), it is of greater weight though far from conclusive. It proves that when Henry married Catherine she was to be publicly regarded as a virgin. It amounts to a public declaration that the first marriage was officially regarded as not having been consummated. On the other hand it would have been to the interest of Henry and the succession that everything should be done at that time to make his marriage with Catherine appear to be the first real marriage.

Point (d) is the really conclusive point in all the evidence before us. Even if we had not such a point to go upon, Catherine's public declaration and Henry's silence in the face of it would I think decide us; but the proposal of her nominal father-in-law to marry her himself after his son's death cannot but convince us that he and she both knew that there had been no true marriage with Prince Arthur. One can believe many things in the way of wickedness, one can accept as possible *almost* anything on the part of the first Tudor, but hardly a thing

INDEX

WOLSEY

BY

HILAIRE BELLOC

WITH 12 ILLUSTRATIONS
AND A MAP

PHILADELPHIA & LONDON
J. B. LIPPINCOTT COMPANY
MCMXXX

ST. BONAVENTURE LIBRARY

334
W8
B4
1930a

COPYRIGHT 1930
BY HILAIRE BELLOC

MADE IN THE
UNITED STATES
OF AMERICA

Fourth Printing

20391

TO
CHARLES COWAN GOODWIN